Endorsements

"**River Never Smooth:** ***Reclaiming Power After Abuse*** is a compelling, insightful look into the world of relationship failure and eventual revival and survival. The author's writing compels you to continue reading just to reveal the next turn and sequence of each character. This book is a must read for those in need of abusive relationship realizations as well as those who might be in a position to assist others that are experiencing the perils of relationship troubles. I encourage all to take this ride along with Angelique as she takes you through every step and thought leading up to her final landing place of power and perfection. This is a must read for all audiences!"

—Reverend Francis S. Cole

"**River Never Smooth:** ***Reclaiming Power After Abuse*** is a captivating, compelling, powerful, riveting account of the experiences of one woman navigating the impact of abuse. Undeniably, it is an eye-opener. It is a must read for those who experience abuse and those who provide support for the abused."

—Karen McKinnie, Educator, Human Rights Advocate

"I met Angelique yesterday morning, and I could not part from her until I was assured she was in a good place. The time I spent with her took me on an emotional rollercoaster; I was terrified for her, devastated by her heartbreaks, and angered by her constant victimization. Thirty-two hours later, I was filled with joy to see Angelique come into awareness. She could now take in what the universe knew all along, that self-love is the way out. Angelique compelled my soul to forever embrace hope. Thank you for the pleasure of meeting her."

—Theresa Alvarez-Diaz, 4RWI Facilitator, Public Speaker

"Both a cautionary tale and a story of hope and perseverance, ***River Never Smooth*** is a compelling personal journey spanning twenty years of heartbreak, physical and emotional pain, and resilience. As she shares her story, the author's spirit shines through the often-bleak circumstances she recounts. Leaving behind the confines of destructive relationships, the author gradually finds independence, works towards a career, and discovers personal happiness. The cruelties of domestic violence are on full display; but this is ultimately a story of hope and courage. Anyone who has ever felt unworthy or without a voice for any reason will find inspiration within these pages."

—Kimberly Engel, Esquire

"***River Never Smooth*** takes the reader on a thoughtful, terrifying, tearful, and ultimately beautiful journey of self-discovery, set in a tropical paradise against a backdrop of unimaginable incidents of domestic violence. Fiona Harewood pulls you into her story with such ease it is easy to imagine her sitting beside you telling her story directly to you. This heartbreaking memoir is a must read for anyone who has loved someone under the most difficult circumstances before eventually learning that love of self must come before you can ever love anyone else."

—Theresa Brunson, Esquire

"**River Never Smooth**: ***Reclaiming Power After Abuse*** shows how even under severe stages of trauma, Angelique's determination made her a survivor. She reminds us that most abusive relationships don't start out with bruises. This book skillfully laid out varying forms of abuse during each relationship, showing how manipulation evolves from subtle blame to full blown verbal and/or physical exploitation. She also uncovered truth, although surreal, in how *so-called* love can progress to victimization. ***River Never Smooth*** uncovers Angelique's inescapable humiliation and pain and suffering at the hands of her abusers, but she shows that *prayer changes things.* This story is one that every woman should read."

—Myrna Campbell-Claxton, Master's Social Work (MSW).

"I encourage the young, middle age, and seniors to read this book, especially if seeking healing from abusive relationships or want to find out how to steer clear of making bad decisions regarding relationships. ***River Never Smooth*** brings to mind the commandment, *Children obey your parents in the Lord...* and reminds us that even parents need guidance in decision making. The abuse Angelique suffers during her two marriages and the pain she endured was unthinkable and cruel. I am glad she survived because of the Living God she served and trusted."

—Shane O'Dean, CNA

"***River Never Smooth: Reclaiming Power After Abuse*** is a fitting title for this book. Reading books is not one of my hobbies, but after being encouraged to read this book, I must say it was time well spent. As I started to read, the very first page was shocking and interesting. I was intrigued, I wanted to know more. WOW! WOW! WOW! flooded my thoughts as I continued reading. I could not put my kindle down and even though my eyes would be half opened, I still wanted to know what happened next. A beautiful love story, turned into a worst nightmare for

Angie and her kids. I cried at times. This book is perfect for young women and men who are looking for that perfect person to love and with whom to share the rest of their lives, and especially for women with kids who are in abusive relationships."

—Carlotta Lord, Business and Public Management

"In ***River Never Smooth: Reclaiming Power After Abuse***, we meet Angelique, a woman whose failed encounters with love place her on a quest for validation. While the demons of violence, abuse, neglect and betrayal are recurring in this story, Harewood's precision in detailing Angelique's journey compels the reader to feel admiration and compassion for this woman. Sadly, Angelique is a representation of too many women in the world today. Throughout the book, we fear, we cry, and we pray for Angelique, and in the end we cheer as the author skillfully weaves-in surrender as the healing balm for Angelique's severely wounded heart."

—Norka Blackman-Richards, Founder and CEO
4 Real Women International

"This is a powerful story of a young woman's pursuit for love and acceptance. During her search she faces adversities, exercises poor judgements, and lands in the arms of multiple abusers. The author takes her readers along the meandering paths of her riveting life's experience in search of *better* only to realize she had left God behind. It is inspiring to watch the metamorphosis that takes place after she gives up trying on her own and allows God to take charge. This book should be read by anyone who have ever reached their crossroads and felt like giving up."

—Ann Marie Clue-Melville, Registered Nurse

RIVER NEVER SMOOTH

RECLAIMING POWER AFTER ABUSE

FIONA HAREWOOD

AUTHOR ACADEMY elite

Printed in the United States of America

Published by Author Academy Elite
PO Box 43, Powell, OH 43035
www.AuthorAcademyElite.com

Identifiers:
Library of Congress Control Number: 2019919190
ISBN: 978-1-64746-052-5 (paperback)
ISBN: 978-1-64746-053-2 (hardback)
ISBN: 978-1-64746-054-9 (ebook)

Available in paperback, hardback, e-book, and audiobook

Book design by Jetlaunch.
Cover design by Raman Bhardwaj.

Also by Fiona Harewood

I DID IT…YOU CAN TOO!

Coming Soon

24 DAYS: Prayer To The Rescue Series

Dedication

For my husband, Grantley O. Harewood.

Thank you for allowing the Lord into your life, resulting in a marriage in which Christ is center. There is nothing I desire more. Thank you for your unending support. Just saying *thank you* cannot compensate for everything you did around the house while I spent endless hours in front of the computer.

For my three children, Donissa, Delon, and De-Ann, especially Donissa.

For the most part, you all walked this road with me. You suffered due to my bad decisions, but through Christ, you have matured into wonderful adults. If I were allowed to start over, I would definitely strive to offer you all a pain-free childhood. Donissa, thank you for forgiving me and agreeing to share our story so that someone else can either find healing, or steer clear of this path.

To my mother, Doreen Lord, and my dad,
the late James Reginald Lord, Senior.
In spite of my defiance, you always supported me.
Thank you. I miss you Daddy.

To my host of in-laws, nieces, nephews and cousins.

To those who have experienced domestic violence or any form of abuse, whether physical, emotional, financial, spiritual, sexual, or other, and have triumphed.

To those of you who are still in that situation, seek empowerment, believing that there is hope and strive toward that time when you will look back at these days and smile.

Contents

Part 2: A Fresh Start

Part 3: Penchant For Bad Choices

Part 4: The Decision & Getting It Right

Foreword

I met Fiona Harewood when she was a student at Drexel University, working on her Master's degree in Public Policy. My Program, Women in Transition, collaborated with Drexel on an Outcomes Measurement Project, and Fiona was one of the Drexel students assigned to that project.

Fiona stood out from the other students on the team. She was focused on the project goal and was willing to do the work and take necessary risks and sacrifices towards achieving that goal, despite working a full-time job and completing the requirements for her Master's degree.

My experience working with Fiona was the reason I agreed to read the manuscript for her new book about domestic violence. Even though I knew that Fiona was an accomplished author, I initially thought the manuscript would be like one of the many stories that I have read in my 23 years of experience working with survivors of domestic violence.

But I could not put the manuscript down. Fiona has a way of telling a story that documents what happened, while making the reader feel the emotions of the characters. She takes you on a journey where you are in the river with the main character, Angelique. You feel the river—smooth, rough, unpredictable, yet constantly flowing.

I provided feedback for the manuscript and was honored when Fiona asked me to write the foreword for this book. *River Never Smooth: Reclaiming Power After Abuse* comes out of Fiona's belief that we should dare to dream, then have the confidence to make that dream a reality. Her passion is to *lift up* those whose *rivers of life* have been muddied and blocked by the domestic violence in their lives. In the book, we learn that those ripples and waves contribute to life as a survivor.

Even though Fiona has a passion and gift for storytelling, in this book she went beyond the story. Along with formulating *discussion questions*, she created a *call to action* with online links within certain sections of the book so that survivors, family members, and professionals will learn how to move forward to reclaiming their power. If one of us is not safe, none of us are safe.

I am confident that the reader will be enlightened and empowered by Angelique's journey through life – from victim to survivor. No matter where you are in life, you will be uplifted by *River Never Smooth: Reclaiming Power After Abuse,* and your faith will be renewed. As Fiona says, "Treat yourself as if you are what you are hoping to become."

—Irene L. Brantley
Program Director, Women in Transition

Introduction

Grace, my friend, showed up at my house one day while the children were at school.

"Why were you crying?" she asked.

"Nothing. I'm fine."

"No, you're not. I hope you're not crying over that loser!"

"Girl, it is easy for you to say, but it is hard," I responded, tears blinding my eyes again.

"Angie, you got your children. If you don't stop, you will die and leave them. Do you want someone else to take care of them? You have a darn good job. You don't need him. Do I need to remind you of some of the crap you suffered at this man's hand, and he claims he love' you? How many months pass' by and he has not even contacted you? You need to move on…"

She sat on the sofa closest to the door.

"When will you get some sense, girl? You should be glad he gone his way. When you not cooking and cleaning for him, you giving him free airline tickets, satisfying his thirst to see the world. The sick part is that you had to pay your own expense on those trips; when it is not that, you trying to please him, saving what you don't have in the name of contributing to a relationship. What kind of relationship is that? It takes two, girl!

This man wouldn't help you buy food for your kids when you are broke; instead, he would rent limo service for his daughter; wouldn't do anything decent for you and you claim you love him! What is there to love about him? Girl, you're a trip! Stop being so stupid! Get over that loser! He is a liability! You can do without him, Angie! Do I have to remind you some more of what and who he is?"

Reflecting on some of the things Grace said made me question myself.

If I didn't let go of this man and this relationship and move on with my life, I could go crazy and come crashing down on three innocent children. Why would I give my love to someone so selfish, undeserving, and mean? I had no answer.

I sat staring into nothingness a few days later. The radio was playing but I wasn't listening to it. Suddenly, as if out of nowhere, the host on the show asked, "Are you in denial about your situation?"

Hmmm...denial about my situation. What situation? I wondered. *Am I in denial about my situation?*

"...Denial gets you nowhere. You have to face reality, accept how you have contributed to the situation in which you find yourself, and take steps to make it better."

What? Something within me became alert. *What is he talking about?* I wasn't sure, but I bounded from the sofa and grabbed a pen and a book. I drew closer to the radio. By the end of the program that question kept re-surfacing in my mind: *are you in denial about your situation?* Then realization hit me. I became aware that I needed to address the root of my problem – denial. I needed to take action to get my life together. It was that realization which changed everything!

Now looking back, although it had taken some time, with God's help I had not only moved on, but I started focusing on my children and me, our future, and I was doing things differently. With time, I even began feeling whole again and began encouraging friends who were in abusive relationships. And it is this realization that forms the basis of this book.

That day when I heard the radio program, I was struggling and was at the lowest point of my life. I felt like giving up. Used, abused and broken—two shattered marriages and a wrecked relationship. Falling head over heels in love with William, it was the first of many bad choices. Waltzing into the arms of a child molester didn't stop me, but then I hit rock bottom after being caught in a deadly love triangle with a man who swore his marriage was over. Facing a jail term, he walked right back into my life, but he was only looking for shelter during his storm until his river started flowing smoothly.

That's a place where many people find themselves. Used. Abused. Broken. The common denominator of this problem is that it knows no boundaries. Young, middle-aged, old, rich, poor, men, women, within our homes, churches, schools, on our jobs—people battle with this ugly situation every day of their lives. The problem with abuse is that some people don't know how to recognize it, while others sweep it under the carpet. Some live in the hope that their partner will change, others leave the relationship but keep going back. Some are embarrassed, afraid, and lack self-esteem, while many either allow others to define them, or they become paralyzed, thinking, *what will people say about me?*

But the fact that many people live for years in abusive relationships is only proof of how hard it is to solve this problem. In this day and age, family members are afraid to intervene, and if cops decide this is a domestic dispute, they will not get involved. What makes the problem even harder to unravel is when a spouse or girlfriend shows up at the courthouse, begging for her abuser, stating she will no longer pursue the case. Sometimes, families and communities are left reeling after gunshots ring out. By the time the police show up, an entire family is already dead. Or, a woman goes missing for weeks only for her body to be discovered in a dumpster. This is the tragic consequence of domestic violence and abuse that plague our societies even today.

According to Domestic Abuse and Domestic Violence statistics, 1 in 4 women fall victim to domestic violence at some point during her life. A current or former partner kills 1 in 3 female homicide victims, and women in their early 20's are at the highest risk of suffering domestic abuse. The National Coalition Against Domestic Violence (NCADV) reports that 1 in 4 men have experienced some form of physical violence by an intimate partner. An intimate partner has injured 1 in 7 women and 1 in 25 men. Additionally, it reports that on average, nearly 20 people per minute are physically abused by an intimate partner in the United States. This equates to more than 10 million women and men in a single year. According to the article, "11 Facts About Teen Dating Violence," 1.5 million high school boys and girls in the United States admit to being abused by someone with whom they are romantically involved over the past year. This list is by no means all-inclusive.

That night after listening to the radio program I cried out to God, realizing that I needed help but couldn't help myself. I pondered all that went wrong and the mistakes I made—from being disobedient to my parents and choosing a husband against whom they warned me, to getting into a second marriage, knowing I didn't love him. After emptying my mind of all the years of baggage, then getting on my knees before God, I literally felt better. A peace engulfed me and stayed with me, providing me with strength day by day to press on. And like I mentioned earlier, I began focusing on my children, loving myself, planning our future, and was doing things differently. I felt whole again and even became support for friends who were in abusive relationships.

This book will explain alarmingly simple, yet overlooked steps that will empower you to find healing and aid you in transforming from a victim to an overcomer. If you're in an abusive situation, whether in a romantic relationship or otherwise, or if you have walked away but have not found healing, this book will also help you to toss your past, live a life free of regrets, and rise above your circumstances. And if you have not experienced abuse in any way, it will help you to steer clear of it. Many victims of abusive relationships try to find solutions for their problems, but for the most part, they deal with the issue inaccurately. For instance, people holding on to abusive relationships do so, hoping their partner will change; they blame themselves and accept their abuser's excuses. If they eventually find the courage to leave, when the opportunity presents itself, they walk right back into the relationship. Victims may decide to move on, but they keep looking back, hindering their path to healing. Or they may become embarrassed and afraid. Victims aiming to live without regrets may find it hard giving up their past, resulting in them being unable to forgive or wondering what others may say about them. In their search for healing, victims might also be afraid to launch out; they doubt themselves, think they cannot change, and they listen to that person who willfully and erroneously defines them.

A saying goes that *only he who wears the shoe knows where it pinches,* meaning, you have to experience a situation to be able to offer the appropriate solution. However, sometimes we find ourselves offering solutions to other people's problems when we have had no experience. But these typical solutions fall short for many reasons, including human behavior and cultural trends. According to the article, "11 Reasons Why People in Abusive Relationships Can't 'Just Leave,'" it is said that people normalize unhealthy behavior, so it becomes hard for them to understand that their relationship is abusive. Additionally, the article states that society perpetuates a "ride-or-die mindset" which causes victims to feel they are in the wrong for leaving their abusers. Further, there is social pressure to be in a perfect relationship. With that being said, the truth is, people for the most part don't go through life thinking about other people's solutions.

You may remember it was the question the radio host asked, "Are you in denial about your situation?" that grabbed my attention and then led me to a completely different way of thinking, regarding taking steps to handle my situation. That question and the moment tremendously impacted my shift in thinking and propelled me to accept where I was and take action. And what was the radio host's solution? He said, "Denial gets you nowhere. You have to face reality, accept how you have contributed to the situation in which you find yourself, and take steps to make it better," right? But did the host initially tell his audience about a solution? No. He asked, "Are you in denial about your situation?" And in asking that question, he focused not on the solution he had, but on the problem that was causing me pain in that moment.

As I established, people don't care about other people's solutions. They care about their own problems and how to eradicate them. And in that moment, the radio host grabbed my attention, causing me to think of the root of my problem. After that realization, I faced the demons in my life head-on, but not alone. I knew I had made a plethora of mistakes and I had been trying to get my life together for a long time, but all I did was make one bad decision after another. Some chronic situations in our lives can only be helped by divine intervention. Divine intervention is what propelled me forward toward finding healing.

We falsely think that people's problems are solved when we craft their solutions. Still, the simple truth is that for people to find healing from abuse, they must identify the source of the problem, accept empowerment, believe in themselves, and rise above their circumstances by thinking positively and taking actions. This means that instead of being in denial of the presence of abuse in a relationship, a victim must accept the situation for what it is and take steps to change it. They must not be embarrassed of their past or find it hard to toss it. A victim must accept empowerment by seeking for, and finding help and moving on. Life is fragile. There is no time to live with regrets. Victims must be willing to let go of their pasts by forgiving themselves and taking steps to move on. A victim must cease holding on to a relationship, hoping their partner will change, and set boundaries. They must empower themselves to move on if those boundaries are crossed.

For instance, in my second relationship I told my then-husband, "I will not be hit again by another man." He probably forgot what I said or didn't care. One night he proceeded to hit me because I refused to have sex for the second time in one night. I had warned him, so the next day I went to the police station, showed up at the house with eight police officers, collected my clothes, and moved to a friend's house for about a week. He never hit me again.

Remember, people in abusive relationships are not unhappy and depressed by the absence of solutions. They are unhappy and depressed by problems of abuse they face every day of their lives. When I admitted I was in denial of abuse in my relationship and took steps to change it, my emotional state changed and I did things differently. There were some immediate advantages, but although it took a number of years, I began experiencing healing. My healing was so profound I forgot some of the actions and hurts my abusers inflicted. Then I was able to point others in this same direction when they shared their stories with me. After reading this book, it will equip you for the same results. Focusing on your pain and finding healing will completely transform your life.

Over the next 40 chapters, I will roll back the curtains to my deepest failures, hurts and secrets, revealing how I overcame abuse. In doing so, I have integrated solutions from experience, research, education, and faith. I have unfurled a workable model for finding healing, aiding anyone hurtling down the road of abuse, or those suffering, to reclaim their power after abuse and emerge overcomers. Remember, it is not about conventional wisdom, it is about ministering to your pain. Your problem. There is a lot of noise to conquer as you move forward, but if you follow the notion of loving yourself enough not to tolerate abuse, then you will be on your way to becoming an overcomer.

Prologue

Anniversary gifts come wrapped in many packages from the miniature box, containing a precious diamond necklace; to the medium-sized package, enclosing a sexy negligee. Or, it may come in the form of a husband, placing his hands over his wife's eyes, leading her to their front lawn, then, tadaaaaa! There, draped in broad, red ribbons with the largest gift bow ever, may be a brand-new, black Lexus or a BMW convertible.

But if anyone would've said my third wedding anniversary present would be wrapped in the finest beating ever, delivered with a 2x4 plank, by the man around whom my entire world revolved, I would've said it was a lie from the pit of hell.

It was a Sunday morning on June 26 during the early 1980s on the East Bank of the Demerara River, in the Republic of Guyana, South America. I was awakened to slender sunrays peeking through the peach-colored lace curtains of our ground-floor apartment which my husband,

William, and I rented from my parents. I lay in bed inhaling the fresh scent of dew, mixed with the fragrances from the yellow daffodils, red roses, and tiny white forget-me-nots. My parents lived on the floor above us, and the scent from my mother's garden was always a welcomed awakening. I smiled, looking across at William, sleeping beside me. He lay on his stomach, slight snores intermittently escaping his nostrils.

Slipping out of bed, I tiptoed to the small room adjoining ours. Our two-year-old daughter, Kianna, slept peacefully in her crib. Opening the wardrobe, I grabbed the *Happy Anniversary* gift bag, then tried to crawl back into bed quietly.

"Ummm . . . morning, hon. Why you up so early?"

"Happy anniversary, Will. Together for many more." I held out the colorful gift bag, smiled broadly, then bent over, and kissed his full lips.

William heaved his sturdy 5-foot 5-inch chocolate frame to a sitting position, bracing his back against the wooden headboard. He cocked his head to one side, knitted his brows, and looked up at the calendar on the cream concrete wall.

"Shoot! Forgot," he said, holding his head with both hands. "Sorry, Angie, but thanks."

Some of the joy with which I awoke dwindled away.

I watched William remove the package from the gift bag and unfold the wrapping paper, revealing a fawn silk shirt with a matching tie.

"You know you didn't have to do this. Was so tied up I forgot, but that'll be the first thing on my agenda tomorrow morning."

"Oh, no prob," I replied, "but let me name my gift since you didn't get it as yet."

"Sure, but don't be unreasonable now," he said, smiling.

"You know I have no unreasonable bone in my body," I replied, stroking his head, returning his smile.

"Still waiting to hear what you want?"

"Come to church with me today."

"Angie, please! Please!" William adamantly shook his head. "Now *that* is unreasonable. You know I worked hard all week, and today's my rest day."

"But Will, it's only 7:30. You can rest until around 10:00, and we can leave home about 10:45 for 11:00 a.m. church," I pleaded.

"Angie, naaah. I'm tired, and I'm spending this day in my bed." He started going through some cassettes on the nightstand. I got up and looked out the bedroom window.

"Then I will not go," I said, stifling a sigh. "I'll spend the day home with you."

William slid my favorite gospel tape into the stereo, and I quickly forgot about my denied request. Nothing lifts my spirit more than gospel music, and he knew it. My sister, Gloria, took Kianna to church, so we had a part of the day to ourselves. Among other things, we cooked together, and when our daughter returned, we had our lunch. After the meal, we relaxed in bed while listening to the cricket game.

Kianna eventually wanted to go to her grandparents. Scooping her up and collecting some of her toys, I noticed William got up from the bed, grabbed his towel, and headed for the shower.

No, he's just freshening up. He can't be going out.

By the time I got back, William was dressing. I was hurt. Maybe I shouldn't have been because he spent most of the day with me, but I was.

Can't he stay home for a day without going out? It's only 4:30; he ain't even spent a full day home and is on his way out again.

I said nothing. Grabbing a novel from my nightstand I tried reading but kept seeing the same line over and over.

"Angie, press this pants fo' me?" he asked.

I lay on my stomach, staring at the book and didn't respond.

"You're so easily angry when I got to go anywhere. You should know a woman's place is in the home. Why you think I gave you a daughter? She will keep your company," he said, pulling at my toes. My anger boiled, but still, I said nothing. I later heard and ignored every thud of the heavy iron against the creaky wooden iron board. Then he was ready to leave. He pulled at my toes again.

"Miserable, I'll be back in a while."

I didn't answer. And yes, I was angry. It was our wedding anniversary. Not only did he not get me anything, but he had also forgotten our important date. Then, he refused to go to church with me—the only thing I asked of him that day.

It was our wedding anniversary. Not only did he not get me anything, but he had also forgotten our important date. Then, he refused to go to church with me-the only thing I asked of him that day.

If this is your constant experience, it is not okay! Have a discussion. Don't wait for a next time.

William pulled at my toes yet again and gave me a playful slap on my butt. I glared at him.

"If you know what's best for you, you will leave me alone," I said through clenched teeth.

He then poked me with his fingers, sending a sharp pain through my side. Suddenly, I sprang from the bed like a leopard with one last chance at catching its prey, charging after him. He dashed out of the bedroom with me in pursuit. Reaching the living room, he struggled to unlock the front door. Realizing he would be through it before I got to him, I instinctively picked up the first thing I saw-a crystal vase, a wedding present from my employer. I hurled it at him. The vase struck the door a fraction of a second after he ducked. *Oh, shoot! I could have hurt him seriously had the vase hit him. Hell! I told him to stop provoking me.* The flowers fell to the vinyl floor, and some sand got into William's soft black hair, but most of it fell to the floor. Miraculously, the vase didn't break.

William rushed at me and started slapping me in the face and head repeatedly with both hands. Wildly and angrily I lashed out at him, kicking and punching. My retaliation angered him even more, and he struck me about my body, face, and head. Tasting blood and feeling it run down my chin, I cried out. William came at me again. I couldn't get away. I looked around; a glass picture frame stood on the china cabinet. It housed one of our wedding photos. Snatching it, I hurled it at his face. He dodged; the picture frame crashed into the concrete wall, shattering into many pieces. Stunned, William held his head, looked around to where the remnants of the picture frame lay, and then back at me.

"What! Oh, you playin' bad! Then you goin' take what bad girls get," he shouted.

Our apartment's back door carried a 2x4 plank measuring about six feet in length, used to secure the door firmly. William raced across the room to the kitchen door and yanked the plank from its iron holders. I tried getting out the front door, but I wasn't quick enough. My husband began beating me with the plank. I couldn't get away from him. One blow landed across my stomach. My feet gave way, and I collapsed to the floor, unable to fight back. I screamed for my parents and siblings, but no one came to my rescue.

I lay there in a crumpled heap, groaning. That was when the beating stopped. William then simply leaned the bar in a corner and went into the bedroom. He emerged shortly afterward with his hair neatly combed and his clothes straightened. Looking at him, one would never believe what had happened.

William stepped over me on his way to the door. Shaking his left index finger and with a pleased-with-performance smile, he said, "Don't you ever play you fighting with me again. When you play bad, you take what bad girls get."

He left, slamming the door shut behind him.

I either passed out or fell asleep because the next thing I knew the house was completely dark.

For a moment, I was startled, but then the horrific scenes from the afternoon came rushing back.

I held on to a chair and like an old woman, painfully pulled myself up and struggled to get my balance. My head throbbed, I was dizzy, and my throat was parched. Licking my lips to moisten them, they felt heavy and painfully dry. The musical clock on the wall chimed seven times, alerting me I had been out for roughly two hours. I fumbled in the dark to find the light switch, then limped to the bedroom. Glancing at the wardrobe mirror I saw my horrifying reflection. Both eyes were swollen with a black and blue mark under the right one. The front of my shirt was stained with dried blood, probably from my now puffed lips and lacerated forehead.

> Both eyes were swollen with a black and blue mark under the right one. The front of my shirt was stained with dried blood, probably from my now puffed lips and lacerated forehead—William could have killed me and no one would have known.
>
> **Abusive situations should never be allowed to get this far. Seek help before it is too late.**

I sank onto my bed, crying, trying to figure out my next move. I was ashamed to go to my parents' home, looking like this. Then again, I shouted for them, and no one came to my rescue, so why should I go to them anyway? William could've killed me, and no one would have known.

In Guyana, family members seldom involve themselves in domestic disputes. They lived by the motto, "You make your bed hard, you lie on it hard." Although I knew that, I couldn't believe my family would hear me scream for them and not come to my rescue.

Kianna's bedtime approached quickly, and I knew someone would soon either call me to get her or bring her home. I had to get out before anyone saw me. With much effort, I took a shower which made me feel slightly better. Unable to bear the thought of anything close-fitting on my sore body, I wore a loose dress. Placing a broad-brimmed hat on my head and pulling it down right above my eyes, I left the apartment without even going upstairs to say goodbye to my daughter.

On my way out, I was sure of one thing—William would no longer be in my life. Hailing a taxi, I went to my friend, Miriam's. She had married three months earlier and lived in the city. Rawle, her husband, standing nearly seven-feet tall, dark, handsome, and sporting a beer belly, answered the door.

On entering the living room, Miriam took one look at me.

"Angie, no! Don't tell me is William hit you! Tell me no!" Miriam said angrily, lifting my hat, holding my chin, and gently turning my face from side to side, examining my wounds. Before I had finished explaining to Miriam and Rawle what happened, Miriam excused herself. Five minutes later, she returned in jeans and a t-shirt with her hair pulled back in a pony tail. She meant to find William.

"Miriam, I know you annoyed, but where you think you goin' find William this night?" her husband asked.

"Even if I got to sit at he door till he come home, I goin' do it," Miriam responded, shoes in hand.

"Come on, sit down and cool yo' head. You can go to his work place first thing tomorrow mornin'. You might get more satisfaction from that," Rawle said, smiling. Taking her shoes, he gently led her to the sofa.

"Now you parents will say is the same thing they warn you about. If I could only catch he now, I would strangle he," she said, clenching her fists.

"I can't understand why he got to be like that. Is only a coward beat up a woman," Rawle added.

"Angelique, if I had me way, I woulda never let you go back, but that is a decision fo' you to make, not me," Miriam said. She headed to her bedroom, returning with a jar of iodine. Swiftly brushing a tear from her eye, she applied the medication to my wounds.

The following day, I felt as if I had been run over by an iron-wheeled donkey cart.

"You should go see the doctor," Miriam started.

"I was thinkin' so too." Rawle chimed in.

"No, I'm good, and I will be even better by tomorrow, I'm sure," I responded, at the same time getting up and excusing myself from the table. I knew if I went to the doctor, the police would be after William. I couldn't have my daughter's father locked up.

I knew if I went to the doctor, the police would be after William. I couldn't have my daughter's father locked up.

Most victims think this way. Wouldn't it be better to get help for the abuser than to die and leave your children?

It was Monday, a workday. Telephoning my job, I said I felt sick and requested two days off. While Miriam and Rawle went to work, I rested at their home took painkillers, and placed ice packs on the swollen parts of my body. I missed my daughter terribly but didn't want to explain anything to my family. After a while, I reluctantly picked up the phone.

My mother answered after the first ring, as if she were sitting there expecting my call.

"Angie? Where you? Wha' happen? Since when you does go out and spend all night? I asked William fo' you this morning, and he say you must be sleep at a friend. Since when you does do things like that?"

"Mom, I cannot explain right now. Is Kianna all right?"

"Yes, she okay, but she asking fo' you all the time. Angie, what happen? You and William had a fight?"

"Yeah, Mom, but I called to let you know I'm okay and to find out how Kianna doing. Kiss her for me. See you in a couple of days. Bye, Mom," I said, replacing the receiver before she had a chance to respond.

Two days later, still with some visible bruises, I made it back to my job at the lawyers' office. I was thankful nobody asked me anything, except Mr. Crumwell, my boss.

"Angelique," he started when I entered his office. "Your mother called here twice looking for you. I told her you called out. Is something wrong?"

"William and I had a fight, and I stayed with friends."

"I suspected something of the sort. Boy, that is disrespectful—your parents live right there. Why would he do such a thing? What are you doing about it?"

"I suspected something of the sort. Boy, that is disrespectful—your parents live right there. Why would he do such a thing?"

Outsiders looking on at situations like these may be able to help save lives if action is taken.

https://www.fionaharewood.com/resources

"Not sure, but I'd like an extended lunch hour to go see my daughter," I replied, hoping to dismiss his inquiry.

"Sure, go right ahead. I'll be here for most of the afternoon anyway."

I thanked him and walked away from his desk.

"Angie," he called after me. "Let me know if there is anything I can do to help."

Maybe file my divorce.

"Sure, thank you."

Gosh, all the others probably know too. And imagine, instead of William, it's my mother searching for me. I'm not surprised.

Lunch time couldn't come quickly enough. I took a cab to my parents' home. Kianna was looking out the window. She saw me and shouted excitedly.

"Mommy! Mommy!" Then she disappeared. The door was unlocked. I pushed it open to find her eagerly running down the stairs. Two steps away, I extended my arms, and she jumped into them clinging to me. Fighting back tears, I squeezed her to my chest.

"Mommy, Mommy, I cry for you. Why you didn't tell me you going out?" she asked, releasing her tight grip and pulling her upper body away, as if examining me. She touched the wound on my forehead.

"You fall down and hit yo' head? Wha' happen to yo' eye?" she asked.

My mother appeared at the top of the stairs.

"How you doing?" she asked quietly, worry in her voice. Then she stared at me. Hard.

"Look at you face with a lot of marks-o-violence. William lookin' for me to get trouble fo' he," she remarked, irritably.

"I'm okay, Mom, I'll be fine. How you been?" I said, forcing a smile.

"I was worried," she said, sitting and signaling me to sit across from her.

"I ask William for you, and he said he ain't know; that you probably at a friend house. I ask he why you would be at a friend house, and he said you and he had a little noise, and you left when he went out. I even call your workplace. If I didn't hear you that day you call, I would've find Miriam 'cause I know you had to be there. Wha' really happen?" she asked.

I explained about that Sunday evening, adding that I left without saying anything because when I screamed for help, nobody came to my rescue.

"Well, we all right here and ain't know or hear a thing," Mom said, shaking her head from side to side. "And you very wrong; I not goin' get in y'all story, but I wouldn't hear you calling and not answer. But you know something, the Good Lord does work in mysterious ways, 'cause if I did only hear, it woulda been a different ball game altogether. He think he bad, but the longest rope got an end."

"Y'all want to fight my daddy?" Kianna's voice interrupted us. She sat so still on my lap, I forgot she was there.

"No, Ki, no one wants to fight your daddy." I laughed.

"Oh," she said, sliding off my lap and running to the window at the sound of an approaching siren.

"That child is something else. You can't say or do nothing for her to hear or see. Don't worry, she gettin' big. She goin' deal with her father," my mother said.

"So true," I responded.

We entered the kitchen and Mom fixed a plate for her and one for me.

"So Angie, wha' you plan doin' and when you comin' back home?"

"Mom, I really don't know," I said, taking up a spoon of white rice with stir-fried eggplant. Mom separated her fried snapper into bite-sized pieces, then she looked up at me.

"Anyway, don't make no rash decisions and I advising you, whatever you do, think 'bout yo' daughter. She is a sweet child. For them couple days you away, she talk 'bout you all the time. Soon as she hear a knock on the door or the phone ring, she askin' if is her mother."

Kianna loved fish. She climbed into my lap and kept asking only for fish. After lunch, it was hard to leave her.

"You comin' back soon after work, Mommy?" she asked.

"I will be back as soon as I can, hon."

"What is soon as you can?"

"Don't worry, and I'm gonna bring you some juicy star apples when I come back."

"Good. You know I like star apples."

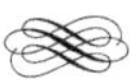

Around 8:15 that night, we heard a knock on the door while Rawle, Miriam, and I watched *The Golden Girls*. Rawle answered the door, letting William in.

"I can't believe you got the gall to show up here," Miriam shouted, rolling her eyes and sucking her teeth.

"Miriam, Miriam, please, you can talk to him better 'n that," Rawle said, walking over to her chair, patting her shoulders.

"Better 'n what? He ain't even deserve talking to. He lucky Angie ain't got an older brother."

"What would an older brother do, Miriam?" William asked, smirking.

Miriam sprang from her seat and headed toward William, but Rawle was quick. He grabbed Miriam and led her back to the sofa.

"Miriam, it ain't call fo' all that. I will talk with William," Rawle said, placing an arm around William's shoulder and leading him outside.

"Angie, if I was you, I would not go back with William."

"But where will I go, Miriam?"

"How you mean where you will go? I got my own apartment now—is not like when I used to live at Aunt Brenda. You could bring your daughter and stay right here."

"I can't impose on you, Miriam. You and Rawle only just married."

"Then go back at your mother house. I sure Miss Evelyn and Mr. Castor ain't goin' care."

Before I could respond, Rawle and William re-entered the living room.

"Miriam," William started, "I sorry to upset you, but Angelique is the one who caused it on herself. Look her right there, ask her who started it. She first threw the vase at me. I was only playin' with her, and she got real mad."

"Even if so, you got any marks from her? Look at you, clean like a whistle and look at her, from her face right down is marks-o-violence! You should be locked up!"

"... but Angelique is the one who caused it on herself...."

Abusers always point the blame back to the victim.... Don't accept it. Seek help!

"Anyway, I here to take Angelique home. Angelique, get your things," William said, dismissing Miriam.

I was ready within a few minutes.

"Thanks for everything, Rawle and Miriam. I will be in touch." Without looking over at William, I headed out the door.

On our way home, William acted as if nothing happened. He never admitted he was wrong; neither did he say he was sorry. *Was it male ego? How could he be so cruel and refuse to admit his faults?*

"I will go for Kianna," I said, getting out of the taxi.

"No, she all right. We have plenty making up to do, you'll see her in the morning," William said, placing his hand on my shoulder, trying to guide me in the direction of the entrance to our place.

"William, I miss her. Lemme go check on her. If she's sleeping, I'll leave her until tomorrow; if not, I'll bring her home."

On our way home, William acted as if nothing happened. He never admitted he was wrong; neither did he say he was sorry.

Some abusers never apologize, while others always apologize but never take steps to change. Be alert!

"Fine, go ahead," he said, irritation etched in his voice. He made his way to our apartment while I rang the doorbell to my parents' home. Mom appeared at the doorway—sleepy, but not surprised.

"Kianna sleepin'. Why you don't le' her stay the night? I know you miss…"

"Mom, may I sleep here too?"

"Hmmm, sure. You know we got lots of space. You tell William you staying here tonight? He tell me he did goin' to bring you home."

"No, let him wait down there like the dragon. I suppose he knows better than to come knocking. If he had killed me on Sunday, he would be doing without me now."

That was the beginning of my five weeks as a single woman again. Only this time around, I had a child. Most times it happens that way—you may leave as one, but return as two. I wouldn't trade my daughter for the world, though.

PART ONE

Bad Choices & The Abuse

ONE

The Silent Treatment

Miriam was happy and applauded how I dealt with William. Three days later, I answered the telephone at work and William was on the line.

"How are you?" he asked. I didn't respond.

"Angie, are you there?" I still didn't respond.

"Angelique, I know you are there. I can hear you breathin'." Nothing.

"Why aren't you answering me?" Still, I didn't respond.

"Angie, you overdoing it now—Don't think because you get away so far you can keep doing stuff like this. You are wearing my patience." I had yet to say a word.

"Angelique, are you hearing me? Is something wrong with your line?" I sighed.

Almost ten minutes later William hung up the telephone. Giving him the silent treatment felt good. That would get to him much more than screaming ever could.

After a week, I noticed that William had developed a new routine. He was home early, as usual, but instead of going out again, he would collect Kianna and keep her until her bedtime. Sometimes we met at the bus terminal and even took the same bus home, but I said nothing to him regardless of what he said to me. I still had my keys, so when I needed something, I would go to the apartment when he wasn't there.

Sometime during the fifth week of this act, my mother and father spoke with me.

"Angie, you ain't think William learn his lesson now?" Mom asked, joining me on the floral sofa in the sitting area of their home. Dad and I were watching *MacGyver*.

"I don't believe he would ever learn," I replied.

"Me ain't think so, neither," Dad agreed. "But the two y'all is husband and wife and y'all got to learn to settle y'all differences. In the first place, you cause that on yourself. All we try to talk you outta that relationship, you still go ahead."

"Alright, Eric, it ain't call fo' all o' that. No sense crying over spilt milk," Mom said. "He did very wrong to treat you how he did, but at least you can notice some change. He don't go out so often now. He always tellin' you that he sorry and always begging you to go back home. I think you should go back," my mother said.

"Me think so too," Dad said.

"I'll think about it," I promised.

Two days later Kianna and I went back home. William grinned from ear to ear, hugging and kissing me.

But this could've been avoided, had I only been obedient to my parents. My world could've been a better place.

There is always a blessing in obeying our parents when they give us the right advice

https://www.fionaharewood.com/resources

"Angie, glad you home, girl. I promise that wouldn't happen again. It was really lonely in this house by myself."

I was tired of hearing those lines and I wanted to believe him, but I couldn't.

They say making up is the best part, but can it ever erase the pain, or heal the hurt that caused the break-up in the first place? But this could've been avoided, had I only been obedient to my parents. My world could've been a better place.

TWO

Love Changes Everything

I was the first of eight siblings; loved the Lord and gave my heart to Him at age 12. By 14, I dreamed big, intended to graduate high school, and planned to do something more than become a housewife. Society started changing from the early seventies, and I admired the women who worked. I wanted to be an author. I loved writing. I believe I inherited that skill from my mother whom I noticed was always writing lengthy letters to far-away family and friends. I also loved reading and many times would read entire series of books over a short period of time. Often while in school, I would place whatever book I was reading in my textbook and read while the teacher taught—of course I got caught and was punished a few times.

My father was a building overseer with the government. He never allowed my mother to work outside of the home, but Mom always encouraged all of us, especially my two sisters and me, to equip ourselves with a good education and be independent.

During the late 1970s, mainly children of affluent families attended the only university we had in Guyana. My family wasn't in that category, but I still considered a higher education. By 15, I stood just over five feet, was honey-brown in complexion, and skinny. I didn't lack friends even though I was reserved and shy. I wasn't what would be considered pretty, but I had a smile which lit up my face.

My parents were strict and didn't allow me to go out often, so even my irregular church attendance was a treat. Mom had me when she was 16 and didn't want her children sharing the same tragic experiences she had. She often lamented the fact she had to drop out of school to take care of me.

I was a member of the Assembly of God Church, and at 15, I was assistant leader of our young people's program called Christ Ambassadors. Our church often held concerts and around my birthday in February 1977, there was a gospel concert featuring Calvary Assembly Choir at Houston Government School. Music was my passion, and a concert was one of the few places my parents allowed me to go. I was excited to attend the concert with my friends, Miriam, Carol, and Jennifer.

Miriam, with her round, flawless features, stood nearly six feet tall. She was sturdily built and was a few years older than us. Jennifer and Carol were sisters; Jennifer was the older.

At last it was Saturday, the evening of the concert. I quickly did some half turns in front of the wardrobe mirror, admiring my shiny jet-black hair, parted at the side of my head and hung in drop curls to my shoulders. *Aunt Joy did a great job with the hot comb.* Turning sideways, ignoring my skinny legs, I quickly tied the sash around my blue cotton dress. Grabbing my bag, I did a few more turns before joining my friends. We were on our way to the concert.

The auditorium had no air conditioning, and it became warmer by the minute, being packed to its capacity and buzzing with the chatter of the anxious audience. Carol and I sat together while Miriam and Jennifer found seats in the row behind us.

"Why would he wear a bow tie when his neck is so short?" Carol piped up.

I followed her eyes, and we giggled at an elderly man with a beer belly who pulled at his neckwear as if it were choking him. About ten minutes after being seated, the band struck up the national anthem, "Dear Land of Guyana," and we all stood at attention. The Agape Sisters set the mood with their powerful rendition of "Are You in the Ark?" Two more artists followed, then screams and cheers broke out when the moderator welcomed Calvary Assembly Choir to the stage.

The leader was a brown-skinned, young man who wore a well-groomed moustache and a neat afro. He introduced himself as William Larrier, the band's leader. Their first selection was "Two Open Doors," one of my favorite songs. I became totally mesmerized as William sang and played the rhythm guitar. Carol must have said something funny because she started laughing, but whatever it was, I didn't hear. My eyes were glued to William, the bandleader. Gazing at him sent a thrill through my body.

William sang four more songs. His voice was a distinct alto and every song was better than the previous one. I wondered if I could meet this guy, but I dared not mention that absurd thought to any of my friends. Carol would never stop teasing. Jennifer probably would give me her sideways, up and down glance which said, 'beware,' and Miriam would likely say, in her deep Berbician accent, "Angelique, none o' that. You ain't goin' cause me to answer to you' parents."

Around 10:00 p.m. after two more entertaining bands, the curtains were drawn, and the noisy, but satisfied audience, made their way out of the school hall. The young man I admired was still on my mind. I was taken aback when he emerged from the crowd with one of his band members.

Just then Miriam shouted, "William!" she waved wildly. I couldn't believe she was calling the same person, but surveying the crowd, I saw William waving back at her. By then he was surrounded by four ladies who appeared to be talking to him all at once.

"Hi Miriam," he shouted above the babble.

"You know him?" I asked.

Before Miriam could reply, he caught up with us and the two were locked in a tight embrace, both grinning. The rest of us watched, mouths hanging open.

"Guys, y'all meet me friend, William," Miriam finally said.

William jokingly attempted to kiss Jenny and Carol's hands then bowed slightly. It was then my turn. He made one step towards me. I stepped back. I felt far away. I couldn't even hold William's gaze. My heart pounded wildly.

"Wha' happen to you, Angie? William don' bite," Miriam said, chuckling.

Forcing a smile, I returned his handshake.

"Nice meeting you. I'm Angelique."

"William Larrier," he said, our eyes locked for a moment.

"Let's go to the canteen for something to drink," William offered.

We squeezed our way into the school's packed canteen. Approaching a table with four chairs, he noisily dragged over a stool from the counter so he could join us.

"Be back in a minute," William said, over his shoulder before disappearing into the throng at the counter.

My friends were busy chatting, but I was quiet. William's handsome face and broad smile crowded my mind. Soon, he reappeared, balancing a large plastic tray on the palm of one hand. He sat the tray down on the table. We helped ourselves to glasses of fruit juice. I couldn't believe my good fortune. I would've never thought within an hour after the concert, I'd be sitting at a table across from the person I was admiring all evening. Up to a few short hours before, I always wondered why girls act crazy over boys they claim to like. Now, here I was, my heart thumping wildly and as if butterflies were fluttering in my chest. I tried avoiding eye contact with William, but every time I glanced in his direction, our eyes met. Shyness caused words to evade me, but my thoughts were roaming. *Will I have an opportunity to be alone with him? If so, what would I say? What would I do?*

"Guys, I hear the sorrel drink is real good. Y'all want try some?"

"Sure," Miriam replied.

"What about you—aaaah—Angelique it is, right?" William asked.

"Yes, th-thank you," I stammered.

"Okay, then I'll get for everybody," William said, rising to his feet. He returned with another tray. I sipped on the wine-colored herbal drink, savoring its delicious acid taste, which was mixed with clove and ginger. The conversation continued and I paid close attention to everything William said about himself, including he worked as a clerk for the government.

"Time to go," Miriam said eventually.

On my way out, I enjoyed the gentle wind drifting off the Demerara River, rippling through my hair.

"Miriam said you ladies live about a mile down the road. Prefer a cool walk or should we wait on a bus?" William asked, looking up at the sky.

"We can walk," we replied in unison.

I pinched myself. Yes, it was real. I walked along with Jenny while William trailed behind, with Miriam and Carol. *I have to find a way to walk and talk with him.* I didn't have to wait long.

"Angelique, always this quiet?" William asked, catching up with us.

"Ha, ha, ha, sometimes, but don't judge the book by its cover. You observe a lot in less than an hour," I replied.

"Quite a few more things I noticed too. Wanna hear?" William asked, leaning his head forward, looking past Jenny, smiling at me. Jenny slowed down, joining Carol and Miriam.

Walking along, William and I chatted on. Conversation flowed as if we knew each other for a lifetime. I found out we had some similar interests, like our love for God, music, church, and concerts. He was 18 and the youngest of five children, while I was the oldest of eight siblings. William planned to further his studies as an accountant.

My house was the first on the route and William and I got there before the others.

"When will I see you again?" he asked.

"Not sure."

"Why?"

"I hardly go anywhere besides school and church."

"Why? Your parents scared you get stolen?" he chuckled.

"They're strict."

"Then what about calling? Y'all have a phone?"

"No."

"Okay, then I'll become a regular visitor to your church."

I felt uncomfortable. Up until then, I had had no real problems with my parents' rules but hearing me lay them out to William made me feel rather foolish. Before I could respond, a smiling Miriam approached us, shaking a finger at William:

"Don' even think 'bout it!"

"Think about what?" William asked, sheepishly.

"Angie, go 'long, le' we see you get in. Goodnight." Miriam said.

"Byeeee!" they chorused. Unlocking the door, I slipped inside.

My mother was waiting up. "Angie, ah glad you come. I can now sleep better," she said, getting up and heading to her room.

I was anxious to get to bed too. There were so many things I wanted to go over in my mind. Closing my eyes, I saw William's face and wondered if my friends felt this way when they claimed to be in love. I drifted off into sweet sleep.

Two weeks later Miriam stopped at my home on her way from church.

"Angie, I got something fo' you, and a message too."

I beamed, knowing it had to do with William. Miriam rolled her eyes and smiled, revealing perfect white teeth. "Somebody sen' this and say tell you a special hello," she said, handing me two cassette tapes. "He say they are B. J. Thomas gospels."

"Wow!" I responded, pulling my green plastic outdoor chair closer to hers.

"You saw William! How's he?"

"He say something 'bout missing you and can't get you outta he mind," she smiled.

"I feel the same way," I said, sighing, turning the cassette tapes over and over in my hands.

Another couple of weeks went by before I saw William again. It was Easter of 1977 and my parents allowed me to go to a Sunday night service because there was a special speaker. Miriam, Carol, Jennifer, and I were on our way home from church when we ran into William and his friend. He had just left his church and was on his way home, which was about three miles from his church. His friend, Steve, and he turned around and walked with us. At first, William and I were shy and said nothing much, but once we started talking, we were old friends again who hadn't seen each other in years. We talked until we got to my house.

Even though I didn't see William often, I didn't go a day without thinking about him. Miriam went to church regularly, so she ran into William often. He sent me more cassettes with his gospel music recordings, and I felt special.

Another three weeks went by before I was allowed to attend church again. It was a breezy night and a full moon hung over the village. Leaving church, we found William and two of his friends waiting.

"Now, now, now William Larrier, wha' you doin' here?" Miriam asked, faking sternness. She walked up to him and playfully grabbed the front of his shirt.

"We just left church. Thought we'll pass by and see how you ladies doing."

Carol, Jennifer, and I looked on, laughing.

"How *we* ladies doin'?" Miriam mimicked. "Or you mean how *one* lady doin'?"

William freed himself from Miriam's grip, blushing. Then he started walking beside me. We walked and chatted for a while, then William slowed his steps.

"Angelique, wait a minute," he said.

We were approaching the lonely and dimly lit industrial area which was laid out with several factories, including a garment and a paint factory. It amazed me how quiet this vicinity was during the nights in contrast to its noisy and busy days.

We trailed behind the others and William took my hand.

"First time in my life, everything is just right, Angelique," he said, his voice in a deep, soft whisper. "You light up my world. Since the night I saw you at the concert, I can't get you out of my mind. I miss you a lot too." My heartbeat quickened; I didn't know what to say.

"Same here. You're always on my mind too," I managed.

William drew me to himself and kissed my lips. For a moment it were as if time stopped and my heart started somersaulting. He then released me, and we looked at each other sheepishly.

"We should be catching up with the others," I said, feeling I had to say something. Anything.

Later that night I lay in bed, thinking about William. I was sad because I didn't even know when I'd be able to see him again. I decided to talk with Miriam, asking her what I should do. Miriam told me I should let my mother know about William before I continue speaking with him. I took her advice, figuring I wouldn't have to play hide-and-seek with my parents. Maybe they would allow me to see William more regularly.

Wednesday night I sent a note to William with Miriam, telling him I plan to talk with my mother about him because I didn't want to continue talking to him without my parents' knowledge. In his response, he said he was scared, but he also thought it was the right thing to do.

My mother and I had a good relationship, but I cannot say I felt free to approach her about everything. Like most West Indian and South American parents at that time, she didn't discuss boys and sex with me. Two weeks went by before I mustered enough courage to talk about William with her.

Two weeks went by before I mustered enough courage to talk about William with her.

Parents must cultivate relationships with their children so they can approach them with anything.

https://www.fionaharewood.com/resources

"Mom," I began one night while washing dinner dishes. She busied herself putting away leftovers from our meal. "I have something to tell you, but please don't get upset."

"Wha' now?" she asked, already sounding displeased.

I contemplated changing my mind, but since I had already started, I decided to get it over with.

"I met a boy and I think he likes me. I like him too, but I thought I'll tell you before I really start talking much with him. His name is William Larrier and he lives in Lodge. He goes to Calvary Assembly Church in McDoom."

Whew! It were as if a heavy weight was lifted from my shoulders. I noticed my mother continued what she was doing as if I never spoke. She was just over five feet tall, stout with a headful of wavy black hair. Her thick dark eyebrows almost joined together, and she had a habit of pouting the moment she didn't like what was said to her.

"Mom, did you hear me?" I asked, noticing her pout was present.

"Yes, Angelique, I hear yo', but whatcha want me to say? I tell you a'ready, this is the time fo' you to concentrate on yo' studies and nothing else. You also know wha' yo' father stand for and I know he goin' be mad when he hear this."

Blam! It was the sound of the cupboard door, and then she left the kitchen.

My heart sank and I wondered if I did the right thing. I didn't like my mother's response. I reached out to her, but she acted as if it was better not to tell her anything.

Two days later, I was washing dishes when Mom brought up the subject again. She made it clear that neither she nor my father was pleased with my actions. They thought I should be concentrating on school instead, and not even entertain the thought of a boyfriend, even more, a serious relationship.

"Don't you ever see that boy again. From now on, you ain't going no place besides school. Church is out too!" she yelled.

I felt as limp as the dish rag I held. Before I could protest, my mother was out of the kitchen. I knew better than to argue with her. I stumbled to the dining table and sat down heavily. *Is she really telling me I cannot see William again? What will I do now*?

"And furthermore," Mom's sharp voice intruded my thoughts. I looked up.

"I tell you a'ready, the men out there ain't no good and instead you concentrate on going to university and making yourself somebody, you thinking 'bout man at this age? This is wha' I sendin' you to school for?" She stormed out of the kitchen. I was only too glad to finish cleaning. Afterwards, I hurried to the haven of my bedroom, crying. It was the beginning of my long walk down misery's lane.

THREE

Special Delivery

The familiar sound of "Three Blind Mice" from the musical clock in the living room woke me at 5 AM the following morning. I rolled over and opened my eyes. Then I remembered my predicament. I prayed that once I told William about what my parents said he wouldn't tell me to forget about our relationship. I didn't know if this was real love, but I knew I felt different, somehow, for this man, than I had for any other person. I wanted to find him and let him know what happened when I told my parents about him. I also needed to let him know that I would always love him, despite what happened.

I couldn't study my schoolwork that morning. I laid there and thought about William. It was after 6 AM when I dragged myself out of bed and crept, unseen through the spacious sitting and dining rooms, on my way to the bathroom. The last thing I wanted was for my family to see how distraught I was. While showering, an idea came to mind.

Miriam saw William more often than I did, so I decided to ask her to take a letter to him. I had to let him know what happened. My plan gave me a glimmer of hope and I left for school feeling a tad better. During break I wrote to William, telling him my parents said I should not see him again. I told him I will always love him and looked forward to the day when I would be free enough to do what I want, without having to worry about my parents. The day felt like one of the longest because I had to wait to get the letter to William. I attended all my classes, but my mind wasn't there. I longed for 3 PM dismissal.

After arriving home, I hid William's letter in a novel and told my mother I was going to visit Miriam.

"Like yo' had a hard day, pal?" Miriam remarked, looking at me. She sat at her sewing machine.

"At least the day was better than my night," I responded, taking a deep breath and flopping down on the soft brown sofa, facing an open window in the dining room.

"Lemme guess – you talk with yo' mother and it ain't went good," Miriam stated flatly.

"You always hit the nail on its head," I said.

"I know Ms. Evelyn—that ain't surprise me one bit. So sorry, Angie. So wha' y'all goin' do now?"

"That's why I came," I said, retrieving the letter from the novel. "Would you take this letter to William?"

"Yes, sure. I could deliver it. I know how you must be feel."

"Thanks," I replied with a teary smile.

"But Angie," Miriam said, "How you know this ain't puppy love? A passing something. Most young girls go through that phase. It may only be a crush, Angie."

"Miriam, even if that is so, all I know is the thought of living without him is not good."

"Well, ah hope is the right thing. If not, ah wish yo' get ove' that feeling quickly. Yo' not much fun to be aroun' as is."

We smiled.

On returning home, I reminded myself to keep a lookout for Miriam after church that night.

Once at home, I tried to appear normal and even took part in conversation around the dinner table. A little later, I welcomed the opportunity to retire to my room to do my homework, and it took all the effort I could muster to keep from thinking about William. It was Tuesday night and if William went to church, Miriam would certainly find him. Complaining about the heat in the house around 8:30 that evening, I sat outside on the porch, waiting for Miriam. About an hour later, I saw her coming. Running down the stairs, I shouted to my mother that I was chatting with Miriam.

Miriam said she saw William and was late getting home because after William read my letter, he asked her to wait until he quickly scribbled a response.

"Gosh, Miriam! Sorry, but thanks." I said, flashing her a smile. "I hope I can repay you some day."

"Anything fo' you, Angie, you know I love you a whole lot—not only William love you," she teased.

I thanked Miriam and started for the doorway.

"Angie," Miriam said with a note of seriousness in her voice.

I looked over my shoulder.

"Pleaseee! Make sure that letter ain't fall in the wrong hands, okay? Be careful," she warned, shaking an index finger. "And, I hope it neve' happen, but if Mr. Castor and Miss Evelyn find out, please, ah begging yo' Angie, don't call me name. Yo' know if Miss Evelyn find this out, she would crucify you and hang me."

We both laughed.

"Don't worry Miriam, I'll be careful. And if anything happens, I will take the blame. Promise."

In the privacy of my bedroom, I read William's hurried handwriting:

"Hi babe," he wrote.

> *"I had no idea mentioning me to your parents could turn out like this or I would have asked you to wait a little longer. I feel bad you're so sad. Sorry. I know that I am the one who caused it. But I want you to know, nothing anybody do or say can ever separate us. You're not alone. I am with you through this and remember I will always love you. Try not to take it on so much and I'm sure things will work out. After a while, we may even be able to see each other without them knowing. Write me often and send the letters with Miriam. Love you baby.*
>
> *Will."*

The words from the letter gave me strength to go on. I still felt bad, but I slept better that night and took the letter with me everywhere. During spare times, I read it over and over.

Life again became a routine of school, home chores, and studies. William and I continued writing each other on a regular basis and good old Miriam remained the faithful postwoman. I missed William and longed to see him and be with him. Occasionally, I found him waiting a block away from my school to walk me to the bus terminal. Those walks were like treats, and every day I found myself wishing he would meet me, but the days when he was able to leave work were few and far between.

FOUR

The Impossible Dream

It was about six months later when my mother told me I can start going back to church. It was a privilege to be able to attend church again, but at the back of my mind I also knew opportunities would present itself to see William. I reported the good news to Miriam.

"Angie," she said somberly, "Ah glad fo' you, but you better be careful because if Mr. Castor and Miss Evelyn only find out that you still seeing William, it will be trouble."

"I will be careful, Miriam. I promise." I said.

For more than a year, our relationship remained a secret from my parents. William and I mainly saw each other some Sundays on our way home from church. We still wrote letters but not as often. On Tuesday nights, I would do my homework while waiting on Miriam to get home from church, but on this particular Tuesday night, when I glanced through the window, I could see Miriam was not alone—William was with her. I waved to him wildly; he stood under the street light, blowing kisses at me.

Miriam crossed the road to my house, leaving William. I hastily ran down the stairs, tripping on a half pair of shoes. I gave Miriam a big hug.

"Eh Eh! You very happy tonight, but is not me you gotta hug, look he across the road," Miriam said, laughing, pointing to William.

"Mom and Dad have turned in for the night. Think I should let him come over?" I asked.

"Now that is risky, and I very 'fraid fo' you, girl," Miriam replied, looking up at an open window. "William insisted that he walk me home," Miriam said. "You sure Mr. Castor and Miss Evelyn sleeping?"

"Well they went in a while now and hardly likely they'll be up again."

"Alright. If you want call he over, do it quickly, but Angie be careful. Ah begging yo'."

"Right, I'll be careful," I replied, breathless from anticipation.

With a quick gesture of my hand, I signaled William to cross the road. The traffic was heavy, which indicated the Demerara Harbour Bridge, the largest floating bridge in the world, had probably just opened, giving way to backed-up traffic.

William finally crossed the road and we ran to each other. For a few moments, we were locked in a tight embrace, William covering my face with kisses.

"Miss you so much, babe," William kept saying while stroking my hair which hung loosely at my shoulders.

"I miss you too, Will," I responded.

"Ehmm."

Looking around, Miriam stood there, a smile of approval on her face.

"Oh, so sorry—," William began.

"No, don't be," Miriam interrupted, looking up again at the only opened window at the front of the house. "But I scared that somebody goin' appear at that window," she said, pointing.

"Okay, lemme leave now. I don't want Angie gettin' in trouble," William said, giving me a quick peck on the cheek.

That night, I lay for hours going over those moments, bit by bit in my mind, before drifting off into sweet sleep. I knew it was the beginning of many more Tuesday nights to come and I couldn't wait for those special nights.

June 1979 was quickly approaching—the scheduled time when I would take my General Certificate of Examinations (G.C.E.). These examinations, now replaced by the Caribbean Examination Council (C.X.C.), are crucial in the lives of high school students, preparing them for the world of work or for further studies.

I spent hours studying for those exams, hoping to be successful and live my dream of becoming an author. William was also busy at work. Time was limited, but we still made it a point to drop each other a note and, although not every Tuesday night, we spent some time together—still secretly.

Before I knew it, it was the morning of my first examination. The tests lasted nine days and I was relieved to see the end. I did five subjects but wasn't comfortable with any. English Language, English Literature, Office Practice, and Typewriting weren't too bad, but I hated Mathematics and found the problems very complicated.

By July 1979, I was 17, had completed high school, and awaited my examination results. Those were boring days, and I missed school. Around that time, the six churches in our district, which included mine and William's, planned a two-week crusade and I asked my parents if I could attend. I figured it shouldn't be a problem since I was older now and had no school or exams on which to focus. My parents consented and I became actively involved in the meetings, distributing tracts, and leading out in the worship team. William attended night after night too.

Meanwhile, my friend Carol hooked up with Steve, William's friend, and they were madly in love. Unlike my parents, Carol's parents allowed Steve to visit her at home. When the meetings were finished, we walked home in a group of about nine, but for most of the one-mile walk, the majority of the group was ahead of us while Carol and Steve walked together and William and I followed.

One morning during the last week of the crusade, I was preparing breakfast when my mother entered the kitchen.

"Lemme tell you something, she said crossly, slamming cupboard doors and noisily dropping utensils in the white enameled sink. As of this mornin', when you finish breakfast, put on some clothes and go find yo'self a job," my mother stated, emphatically.

I couldn't believe what I heard. I stopped slicing the bread and looked up at her.

"But I'm waiting for my results, Mom. How will I find a job without certificates? The plan was for me to go to university, not to work at this time."

"Well, I believe that finding a job is the best thing fo' you right now because when you wan' go and look fo' man, yo' should be able to maintain yo'self."

What in the world is she talking about? Did someone tell her something?

"Mom, what're you talking about?"

"Moon does run till day catch it." That was another of her sayings that meant when someone does wrong, he or she will be eventually found out. "You leave here to go to church every night, but you also got other plans. Last night I pass in a car and see you and some man walking down the road. Who was that fella?"

"That was William, Mom."

"I thought we stop' you from seein' he. So, you mean that you neve' stop talking to he?" she asked, taking a step towards me.

"We hardly see each other." I started backing away towards the kitchen exit.

"Look, before I start hitting you head to all them post in this house, leave here and go find a job. I ain't caring fo' no woman. And two women can't live in one house."

I knew my mother wouldn't listen to me, so it made no sense defending myself. I felt I was old enough to have a boyfriend and didn't think I did anything wrong.

Two hours later found me downtown, walking from office to office asking various receptionists if there were any vacancies within their companies. Everybody gave me the same negative answer. After a while, I became tired and frustrated. The mid-day sun overhead was hot, beating down on my already sweaty body. I felt the tears welling in my eyes and I wished I could talk with William, but he was at work.

Please God, help me find a job so I can take care of myself and be out of their house soon. I am tired of my parents' rules.

By this time, I was on Brickdam, walking past many government businesses, including the Ministry of Education, Ministry of Health, and Guyana Telecommunication Corporation. It was senseless, inquiring verbally of vacancies within those offices because they had a formal method of hiring via applications. The fresh scent of bougainvillea lit up Brickdam; the trees, some with yellow flowers, others red, lined the road on both sides, their fallen petals, sprinkling the sidewalk.

I walked a few blocks, then turned left on to a short cross street, then left again on to Croal Street, the street of lawyers. I decided to only go into those offices where there was no one, besides the receptionist, in earshot. I was embarrassed at everyone hearing me ask if there were any job vacancies. I came upon a two-storied shingled building, badly in need of painting. Wild vines ran up the side, facing me and parts of the front. *These lawyers make a lot of money. Why can't they maintain their buildings*?

There was a black and white sign outside which read 'Ashmead Chambers.' Glancing through the open push-out windows, I saw a woman who appeared to be in her early forties, standing at the counter. Her head was bowed as if she were reading something. I walked into the office. She looked up.

"Good afternoon, and how may I help you?"

"My name is Angelique Castor, and I'm looking for a job," I said, forcing a smile. "Do you have any vacancies?" I asked, seemingly for the fiftieth time that morning.

"What kind of job are you looking for?"

"Clerical, secretarial, typist," I replied, realizing this woman was the first person who didn't answer my question with a flat 'no' or 'not at the moment.' My spirit lifted. She looked directly at me, as if assessing me.

"You are pretty young; do you have any experience? Have you worked before?"

"No, but I learn quickly, and everybody has to start somewhere in order to gain experience," I replied, flashing my willful half smile.

Just then, a short, dark, brawny gentleman, wearing a low haircut, a pair of thick spectacles, and dressed exquisitely in a white shirt, black tie and black jacket, emerged from the office on the right and approached the counter. He paid no attention to the woman or me but seemed to be observing the passing pedestrian and vehicular traffic on the road.

He has to be one of the lawyers.

"Mr. Crumwell, the young lady's looking for a job," the woman said, turning her attention away from me, to the lawyer. Before responding, Mr. Crumwell picked me apart from head to toe, causing an uncomfortable feeling to well up within my stomach, but I looked pointedly back at him without flinching.

"Okay, ask her to have a seat and I will speak with her in a minute," Mr. Crumwell finally said, making his way back to his office.

The woman introduced herself as Miss Foster and invited me to sit. She said she was secretary to the Senior Counsel. Although I disliked the building because of its appearance, while I waited, I prayed this would be my final stop.

Meanwhile, I observed my surroundings. The building appeared older on the outside than it was on its inside. The inner walls were varnished and there hung some framed certificates and a photograph of an older lawyer, dressed in wig and gown. A counter separated the outer office from the waiting area. There were two work stations, one being utilized by Miss Foster, while the other was vacant.

Eventually, Miss Foster's intercom buzzed.

"Proceed to the office on the right, Ms. Castor," she said.

A short corridor separated the two inner offices. Upon my entering the office, Mr. Crumwell rose to his feet from behind his large, polished mahogany desk, outstretched his arm and introduced himself. I was about to sit when I remembered being taught in my office procedures class, one shouldn't sit before being invited to do so, especially at a job interview. Mr. Crumwell offered me a seat then began telling me about the firm. It consisted of three lawyers. He shared that building with the senior counsel while the third, a junior lawyer, occupied the Federation Building next door. They were looking for a third secretary to assist

Mr. Crumwell, who started private practice three weeks ago; prior to that he held the position of Director of Public Prosecutions. Mr. Crumwell also told me that the candidate they choose would be trained in the legal aspects of the job so they were not specifically looking for someone with experience, although that would be a plus.

The interview went better than I expected, and I knew the lawyer was pleased with my performance. At the end, Mr. Crumwell told me he was unable to make a decision right now because he had to consult with his senior partner, who would also want to interview me. He asked me to wait for the Senior Counsel who was still at court. While waiting, Mr. Crumwell instructed Miss Foster to give me a typewriting test.

Although typewriting was one of my favorite subjects, I was nervous. My fingers trembled when I first started, causing me to pause a while to regain my composure. Beginning again, I was confident.

Then, I heard a voice.

"I am not satisfied with the outcome of this alimony suit; neither is my client. As a matter of fact, I am taking this case back to Chambers next Tuesday!" the loud authoritative baritone remarked. I knew it was the senior counsel even before I saw him.

Glancing towards the entrance, I saw a tall, stout, chestnut complexioned, bald, but fine-looking gentleman, wearing a black silk gown, flying behind him in the wind. He said good-bye to someone, then entered the office, folders in his hand and a male clerk hurrying behind, carrying his briefcase. I knew the latter interview would be challenging.

After an hour, Miss Foster ushered me into the senior counsel's chambers. Mr. Crumwell was already there. The senior counsel remained seated behind his cluttered desk, took a quick look at me, and introduced himself.

"Sampson," he said. Without allowing me a chance to introduce myself, he began examining my typewriting test, asking at the same time,

"So, what school did you attend, Miss Castor?"

Still standing, I replied, "South Georgetown Secondary, Sir."

"May I see your certificates?"

"Sir, I do not have my certificates as yet," I said, feeling rather foolish, shifting from one foot to the other. "I'm waiting on my results. I did exams June, last."

"Miss Castor, you may sit," Mr. Crumwell said, before turning his attention to Mr. Sampson.

"Yes, S. C., I mentioned to you, she is waiting for her results."

"You did? I apologize," replied Mr. Sampson, looking very pleased with himself, a smirk plastered on his face. He quickly scribbled something at the bottom of the test paper. "Then I am sorry, madam, I suggest you return when you are in receipt of your results, then we will go from there. In the meantime, we will hold your application on file."

I was never more disappointed. Mr. Crumwell instructed me to give my name, address, and telephone number to Miss Foster on my way out. Leaving the office, tears blinded my eyes. I couldn't deal with another negative situation that day. I wanted to be alone. I didn't even want to face people on public transportation, so even though I had bus fare, I slowly walked the three plus miles home, hardly wanting the journey to end. Reaching home, I grimly reported the day's happenings to my mother.

"You goin' go again tomorrow and try other places," Mom said, without sympathy.

I dreaded the thought of job hunting again mainly because of my sore and aching feet.

It was almost dark that same evening, when there was a knock on the door.

"Angie, somebody here to you," my sister said.

I was surprised seeing Ralph, the clerk from Ashmead Chambers, standing in the doorway.

"Hello, Miss Castor," he greeted me even before I reached the door. "I have something for you," he said diving into his briefcase, pulling out a white envelope.

"What is it?" I asked, excitement overcoming me. *Don't get too excited in case it's not what you think.*

"Open it," Ralph urged, looking at me, a smile spreading across his face. I quickly tore open the envelope and unfolded the letter. Its contents read:

"Dear Miss Castor,

Ashmead Chambers is pleased to hire you—" I jumped into the air after reading the first few words. Then hardly even realizing what I did, I hugged Ralph tightly, screaming,

"They hire' me! They hire' me!"

Hearing the commotion, most of my family gathered around to see what happened.

"Continue reading," Ralph prompted.

"Okay, okay." I said, "Let me finish."

> *".... as Assistant Secretary to our Firm. Should you accept our offer you are required to commence work at 8:00 a.m. on Monday August 28th. Your starting wages for the first three months will be $65.00 per week, and your job description will be discussed in detail at a later date. May we be the first to extend our congratulations.*
>
> *Yours truly,*
> *Rickford Sampson, S.C.*
> *Attorney-at-Law*

"Angie, I want a chicken and milkshake from Demico from yo' first pay," my sister, Gloria butted in.

"Only chicken? Girl, you'll get more than chicken."

"Miss Castor," Ralph started. "I'm happy for you. Congratulations. I'm glad I am the bearer of good news."

"Thank you, Ralph."

"And Miss Foster was glad when they came to the decision late this afternoon. Le' me tell you this," he said, asking to be excused, holding my arm and walking me outside. "It appears that after you left the office, Mr. Crumwell and Mr. Sampson had heated words. Mr. Crumwell was mad because the senior counsel turned you away. You were the fourth person to be interviewed and Mr. Sampson didn't like any of the applicants."

Ralph cupped his hand to his mouth, leaned slightly toward my ear and whispered. "Possibly personal reasons." He looked at his Timex watch, then hastily continued, "But eventually Mr. Crumwell was able to convince him. Anyway, I have another stop to make before I go home, but give the job your best shot, work hard and be honest—they will like you. Congratulations again, see you on Monday."

I stood lost in thought for a while after Ralph left.

"Angie," Mom's voice interrupted, "At least ah glad you get the job and you ain't got to go looking again tomorrow. It ain't had to be this way, but when parents try to show y'all what is right y'all don't listen. Y'all prefer to learn the hard way. Anyway, I still wish you the best."

That letter made my day and there began a new era in my life.

FIVE

Caught!

Placing my dreams of becoming an author on hold, I started working. Earning my own money made me feel grown-up even though the amount I kept for myself after contributing at home wasn't substantial. A sense of freedom engulfed me. I was expected to return home after work in the evenings, so I spent most of my lunch time with William. Also, my job gave me the opportunity to be away from home which, to me, became more and more unbearable.

On the other hand, the horizon seemed dimmer because even if I had passed all five subjects, I couldn't afford to put myself through University, and as far as my parents were concerned, I was off their financial list.

My examination results eventually came, and I failed miserably. Mom and Dad, though upset, weren't hard on me, and I believe it was because they knew I studied hard. Mr. Crumwell encouraged me to retake the subjects.

Miss Foster, the secretary at Ashmead Chambers, possessed a pleasant personality, but her eyes portrayed loneliness or hurt. From what she said to me I learned why, and I took it with me wherever I went. "Never sleep with the same man who has to be your boss the next morning."

Within six months, I worked with minimum supervision. I became efficient in the preparation of deed polls, affidavits, drafting divorce petitions, and mastering many aspects of the legal work, which earned me increased wages after my probation assessment.

One Tuesday night, about four months after I started working, I sat on the porch of our home, waiting on Miriam to return from church. I expected William to be with her. A while later, they came strolling down the road. I became comfortable seeing William at my home on Tuesday nights without my parents' knowledge. I ran downstairs to meet him, certain my parents had already turned in for the night. Miriam spoke with us briefly, then left.

Our house was a massive two storied wooden and concrete building. There were two apartments on the ground floor while we lived only on the top floor. An inner polished mahogany staircase led upstairs, while the entrance to the apartments downstairs was at the side of the house. That night, William and I sat on the bottom row of steps. From there we observed a lot without anyone from outside seeing us because a thick hibiscus hedge fenced us in. From upstairs, one had to either bend down or descend the stairs to get a good view of below. It was cozy.

William and I were kissing when suddenly, slow, purposeful footsteps started descending the stairs. I froze. Before we could even move, we were face to face with my dad.

Surprise, then anger covered his face at the scene that met his eyes. Sucking his teeth, he shouted, "Angelique, what the hell you doin' down here this time o' night with this man?"

Fear overcame me, but I managed to stand up. My knees buckled and my heart began beating uncontrollably. William started backing away and left before I had a chance to look around, leaving me to face the music alone. My tongue became hot, and my body felt as if a thousand needles were lightly pricking away at it.

"Ah talking to you! Answer me!" Dad screamed, advancing toward me. By this time, my mother appeared at the top of the stairs, wrapping her pink night robe around her, looking confused.

"D-D-Da-----aa-dy," I stammered, "I came downstairs to talk with William."

"Wait, after all this time you mean you not goin' listen when we say stop talkin' to that boy?"

"Ah really can't believe what ah seeing and hearing tonight," my mother chimed in. "When we think you in bed, this is what you doing? How long this been goin' on?"

I stood there, within the enclosed stairway, wishing the concreted ground on which I stood would open and swallow me up. My dad, who always carried a cane, put it to work. I screamed from the blows my dad dealt all over my body. When he possibly felt he might have killed me and gotten himself into trouble, he pushed me outside, then slammed the door shut.

A few moments later the lights upstairs were turned off and I found myself alone in the night barefoot, wearing only a pair of shorts and a T-shirt. I looked across the road and wondered about William. Embarrassed and not knowing what to do, I leaned against the concreted wall of the house and the tears rolled down my cheeks. About twenty minutes later, William returned.

"They put you out? Shucks!" he whispered.

"What do I do now?" I asked, my shoulders wracking with sobs.

"I will work something out, babe…have to work something out. I am so sorry. I didn't want to leave you, but I was scared too," he whispered, drawing me close to him and wiping my face with his handkerchief.

Good old Miriam was the first person I thought of.

"Could you go find Miriam? Ask her to bring me a dress and a pair of slippers. I will stay here in case my parents let me back in the house."

"Good. I'll be real quick," William said, hurrying on his way.

There was no one in sight and only a few cars were passing on the busy two-lane East Bank public road, so, I figured it was after 11 PM.

About twenty minutes later, William returned with Miriam. She brought me a dress and a pair of slippers and I hurriedly slid into them. The expression on her face was nothing short of worry.

"Just as ah thought, me worse nightmare come true," Miriam said, shaking her head. "Angie, ah had a feelin' this would happen, and ah know ah got to prepare meself to take the blame, cause Miss Evelyn know you does be out here wit' me. Don't worry though, she can't be mad all the time."

"Gosh, why this had to happen?" William asked more to himself, pacing the concreted yard.

"William," Miriam said turning to him, "ah sugges' you go down the road outta sight. I goin' knock' this door 'till Miss Evelyn or Mr. Castor open. I ain't care how mad they get."

"Sounds good to me 'cause I prefer not be here when they open. I'll be about a block away," William replied, leaving hurriedly as if glad for the opportunity to escape.

*Knock, knock, knoc*k—we began gently with our hands at first. Then, after about five minutes, Miriam pulled off one of her black leather slippers and hit the door continuously.

*Creeeeakk*k—that was the sound of our next-door neighbor's window opening. Embarrassed, I looked around and up. Mr. and Mrs. Payne and their seventeen-year-old daughter huddled together at one window of their white two-storied wooden house.

They're so fast. Now, I'll be the talk of the town because Mrs. Payne talks about everybody else's children and never see the faults of hers.

Another ten minutes elapsed, then lights flooded the overhead porch and my mother appeared at the doorway. Some of her large curlers were hanging out of place about her head as she crossed one arm about her waist, holding the wrap of her pink night robe in place. By then, another two sets of neighbors were looking out of their windows.

"Listen to me, you two," she shouted angrily. "Don't knock on that bloody door no more or I goin' call the police. And as fo' you, Miriam, you can take her in now because you is the one encouraging her to get man."

"Miss Evelyn," Miriam said calmly. "Please don't get angry and act without thinkin'. This is yo' daughter, and it ain't make no sense putting her out in the night like this. Whatever happen' I sorry, and I sure Angie sorry too. You can find another way of punishment, Miss Evelyn—please, not this way."

"Oh, you want tell me how to run me house now? You can continue running Angelique life, not me own. And you, Angelique, as long as I live, I ain't wan' nothing to do with you." She slammed the door and the house plunged into darkness again.

"This is bad," Miriam said, frowning, shaking her head from side to side. "This is really bad. But Angie yo' can't stay out here; come wit' me."

William was not too far away observing the proceedings from behind a parked van; he caught up with us while we were walking to Miriam's house.

"Shucks man! Thought they woulda open'," he said.

"Don't worry, William, Miss Evelyn bark worse than her bite. She may be different by morning. Angie is her child, and she only actin' this way 'cause she upset. I will talk with her tomorrow," Miriam said.

"I'm really sorry, Miriam, we both should've known better, and I pray things work out. I hope by tomorrow morning Angie's parents will have a change of heart," William said.

We arrived at Miriam's home and found Aunt Brenda, Miriam's aunt, sitting alone in the semi-darkness on the front steps. Aunt Brenda's apartment was on the first floor of a two-story wooden house with two apartments on the ground and two at the top floor.

Unaware of my predicament, Aunt Brenda seemed to be enjoying the night's cool air. "Something ain't look right," she said, looking at me searchingly, through narrowed eyes. "What Angie doin' here so late? And Miriam ah wonder' where you get up and disappear so quick without saying anything."

Miriam explained my dilemma but before she was finished, Aunt Brenda got up from her sitting position and started pacing the hard clay ground.

"Lard 'ave us mercy! What this y'all tellin' me tonight?" she said in her sing-song voice, both hands flew to her head, and she grabbed at her already scattered hair.

"Angelique, you know how you mother and father stay and you goin' risk something like this? Ain't that dumb? And to crown it all," she continued her flow of words, "all two y'all should know better. Ah disappointed in you, Angie."

Aunt Brenda appeared deep in thought. We were all looking at her, as if expecting her to solve my problem. She then headed towards William, walking, dropping heavily from one foot to the other.

"Now you see what does happen when you like play man?" she said, shaking her index finger at William. "You ready to get marry? If me know Miss Evelyn good, she goin' be talking 'bout wedding," Aunt Brenda said in a lighter tone, laughing and grabbing William by his shirt collar. "You better prepare yo'self to meet the Castors, you playing man, huh," she said before letting William go. Then she became serious once more. "Angie, the best I can do is wait 'till mornin' and take you back. By then they mind should cool. William, it getting late, go home in peace. Y'all don't know when y'all got it good, till it bad."

"Thanks very much for allowing Angie to stay," William said before leaving.

Restlessly, I tossed and turned, sharing Miriam's bed that night. Early the following morning, I put on another of her dresses which was nearly three sizes bigger. It fit better after I placed a belt around my slim waist. Aunt Brenda took me home, hoping to ask my parents to be more lenient with me.

Mom opened the door after we knocked a few times, and a smile brightened her face when she saw Miss Brenda, who was a good friend of hers. Then she saw me, and the smile vanished. Without a word, she slammed the door.

Miss Brenda's eyes widened with disbelief, and she started pounding on the door, but my mother didn't open. I couldn't go to work that day because I had no suitable clothing.

Later that afternoon, Miriam and her Aunt Brenda took me to my grandmother's home in Craig, on the East Bank.

"Angie, you know William shoulda be with us," Miriam said, making her way ahead of me down the sandy, winding lane to my grandmother's house.

"He probably went to work," I said.

Now that she mentioned it, I could really do with some support from him.

"I ain't know, but from last night I get this feeling like William ain't actin' responsible enough," Miriam commented.

"Then is not me only thinking like that," Aunt Brenda added.

Of her nine grandchildren, I was Grandma Stella's favorite and she enjoyed boasting about her first grandchild. She was the sweetest old lady I'd ever known. Sometimes I wondered about her because a few times I heard her remark that she never had good breaks with the men in her life. Love radiated from her, but she was stern with us when needed. She was now my only hope.

"I ain't know, but from last night I get this feeling like William ain't actin' responsible enough," Miriam commented.

Look for signs in your relationship. Does your partner act responsible? If not, deal with it now, don't wait until after your marriage.

"Eh eh! what happen Ang?" Grandma Stella asked after opening her side door.

She hugged me, greeted my friends, then led us through the tiny kitchen to the cluttered living room.

"Something wrong. How come you not at work? Yo' mother sick or something? Where's yo' father?"

"Gran, it's nothing like that. Mom and everybody's okay."

"So then what is it?" she questioned, impatience rising in her voice.

"They put me out," I said matter-of-factly.

"Why? What you do?" she asked, sitting down as if suddenly tired.

I told my grandmother everything.

"Ang, now you know that wasn't right. Why you didn't take he home to them and introduce he before now?" Grandma asked.

"I tried when we first met, Gran, but they wanted to hear nothing of me having a boyfriend."

"Then you should've listen to yo' parents. They ain't goin' put you wrong. You young yet; you think the world running away and leave you'? It ain't goin' nowhere."

"Miss Stella, you goin' have to go and talk to them 'cause Miss Evelyn real upset," Miriam said.

"It hard to get through to Miss Evelyn when she like that," Aunt Brenda added.

"But they can't put her out. Evelyn like she goin' crazy or something. I know Angie wrong, but she don't give them problems. Evelyn could've find another means o' punishment," Grandma said.

"Then you should've listen to yo' parents. They ain't goin' put you wrong. You young yet; you think the world running away and leave you'? It ain't goin' nowhere."

Too often young women find themselves in this predicament because they ignore parents' advice.

"Exactly. Is the same thing I tell her," Miriam said.

After having some cold lemonade, Miriam and Aunt Brenda left. Grandma Stella let me stay with her until the following evening, hoping by then, my parents would be in better moods.

Early Thursday morning my grandmother went to the store and bought me a complete outfit. It was a brown crepe, semi flair skirt with a beige short sleeves blouse which stopped at the waist and buttoned down the back. She and I wore the same sized shoes, so she had no problem finding me flat brown strap shoes. And she didn't forget underwear. She had me looking good—who said grandmothers couldn't shop?

Around 6:30 PM, hoping my father was home from work, we started our forty-five minute journey to my home.

Gloria answered the door.

"Hi, Gran, how you doing?" she asked, hugging Grandma Stella. Then she saw me.

"Gosh, Angie, glad to see you," she said, pulling at my hair, "I wonder' if you still at Miriam and I wanted to go across by her but ah couldn't get away. Nice outfit though; where you get that?"

"Miss you, girl. Where's Mom and Dad?" I asked.

"They upstairs—still mad—was talking about you only just now."

In the meantime, three of my other siblings showed up and warmly greeted Grandma and me.

"Gran," I said, "I think I should stay downstairs until you're finished talking with them."

"Oh no, you coming with me. They can't do you a thing while I here," she said taking hold of my arm, pulling me behind her and starting up the stairs.

"Evelyn and Eric how y'all doing?" she called out to my parents loudly while making her way towards the sound of their voices, coming from the kitchen of our two-family home.

"Eh eh! How you doing? I ain't had nobody like you in thoughts—you visiting?" my mother addressed Grandma Stella.

My heart began racing uncontrollably and embarrassment of Tuesday night's happenings washed over me. I wanted nothing more than to get out of there. Relieving my grandmother's grip, I stepped behind the door that separated the kitchen from the dining area, not wanting them to see me.

"Mrs.," my father started, "How you? Yo' look nice, man. Is why yo' dress up so?" My dad always teased Grandma Stella and that was his usual way of addressing her—'Mrs.'

"Eric, you could never leave me alone, what you want with me outfit, huh?"

"Come le' me get you a chair. The kitchen cooler than in front," he said, and I heard him drag a chair across the hardwood floor.

"Ah hope y'all not still mad from the other night," Grandma Stella began.

"What? Angelique went at you?" Mom asked. I heard the smile fade from her voice.

"So what? Y'all ain't expect her to live on the road—Ang, look, come here," Grandma Stella called. Head bent, I walked slowly into the kitchen.

"Good evening, Mom and Dad."

"Good evening," Mom answered after a short pause, but Dad didn't respond. There followed a long uncomfortable silence.

"Si' down, Ang," Grandma Stella said, pointing to the seat next to her.

"She don't listen. You know how long we talkin' to her 'bout this Larrier boy? When we think she in bed, she with he. Heaven knows how long that been goin' on. She don't deserve to come back in this house. She is a woman. She free now to go with he," my mother said.

Dad rose from his seat, preparing to leave the kitchen.

"With all due respect, Mrs.," my father began. "Evelyn can take Angelique back home if she want, but if she do that, I leaving."

"And too bad, I ain't goin' allow that to happen 'cause Angelique can't take care o' me and seven young children. When yo' don't hear, yo' does feel," my mother said, shaking her right index finger at me.

"But, wait," Grandma Stella said, standing up, placing her left hand on her hip, and waiving her right index finger a couple of inches away from my mother's face. "You don't get me annoyed now, Evelyn. You think I had it easy with you after you meet Eric? And lemme remind you, in case y'all forget—In spite of all the problems you give me, I never even think about puttin' you out. And if y'all don't know it, y'all got a good daughter. Angie ain't no problem."

The argument went on for another five minutes before my father who was pacing the floor spoke up again.

"Alright, alright. Angelique going return home under one condition."

"And what is that?" my grandmother interrupted, pulling the chair away from the table and sitting down again.

"Can you give me a minute to speak, please?" Dad asked, holding up his right hand.

"We want to meet with this William, whoever he is, tomorrow evening at 6:30."

"Why? Hope you not thinking 'bout planning wedding 'cause Angie young yet," my grandmother said, tilting her head and squinting her eyes as if studying my father.

"End of this discussion. This is me house and whoever live here, play by me rules, and," turning to face me before exiting the kitchen he said, "you not sleeping here tonight neither, come back tomorrow when William comin'."

My mother then told me to pack a few of my clothes before leaving. Some of my siblings followed me to my room. For a few moments, nobody spoke. They all looked sad.

"Angie, you coming back?" Eric, my second of five brothers asked.

"Yes, Eric, I'll be back." I sat next to him and kissed his forehead.

"Don't worry Angie, don't worry, I goin' tell Daddy I will go live at Grandma Stella with you if he ain't let you come back, and he goin' tell you come back home," Gloria said. She sat on the pillows at the head of my bed, one hand folded across her waist, the other propped her right jaw. On another occasion, I would have screamed at her for sitting on my pillows, but in response to what she said, I forced a smile.

"But wait, you didn't tell me where you get the skirt and top? Ah never seen you with it before," she said.

"Tell you another time," I replied. I hugged my siblings, then said goodbye to my parents. Mom answered with a short "Okay." Dad didn't respond. I walked down the steps behind my grandmother, grateful she was there for me.

The following day, I called William from work and told him of the developments and of my father's request.

"You mean I have to go to a meeting with your mother and father?"

"That's what my dad said."

"Shucks!" he exclaimed, "My goose is cooked!"

"I cannot even tell you what it is about, but I am scared," I said.

"All right, come 6:30 we will handle them the best way we can, only sorry it had to be this way."

"Okay. Will, I have to go now, so see you this evening."

"Bye now, and remember I love you, Angie."

"Love you too. Bye."

SIX

The Ultimatum

William arrived on time, but we all, including my grandmother, were already waiting in the sitting room. William was still in his work clothes, perspiration beading his forehead. He introduced himself for the first time to my parents and grandmother. My father offered him a seat on the burgundy and cream floral sofa and started the conversation, telling him he was sorry they had to meet under such circumstances. The discussion, although casual at first, was strained. Mainly, Dad and William spoke while Mom eyed him at every opportunity. They talked about how they spent their day, and then about current events. The conversation slowly progressed to William's job and his family. He volunteered information that his parents were separated and that he lived with his mother and sisters. Then without further hesitation, my father got to the meat of the matter.

"Well young man, it is my understanding that you are interested in Angelique," he eyed William over his spectacles.

William shifted uneasily in his chair; he focused on some ceramic ornaments which lined the stump wall that separated the study from the sitting room. Both my parents always amazed me how they spoke broken English among the home circle but showed off a good command of the English language when in formal company.

"I want you both to know, this situation is causing problems within my household," my father continued. "I have to work hard for my family as it is, and I think it will be unfair to me, to have to maintain a grandchild too, so, I want to know your intentions."

William sat forward in his chair, grasping one of his hands with the other, then sat back, looked at me, and then awkwardly at my father.

"Angelique and I…I…li…like…each other and if we are given some time, I am hoping we could be engaged," he said.

"And how much time are you looking for?" My mother sternly butted in, robbing Dad of the chance to respond.

"Well, Angelique is young, and we hardly see each other. We need some time to get more acquainted. That way, we would be able to decide if we want to continue with this relationship, or not. I don't think it makes sense to rush into anything," William calmly responded, but the perspiration which he had previously wiped away appeared on his nose and forehead again.

"To me, you sound as if you want to have fun, and

I want you both to know, as soon as young people think it is time to get boyfriend or girlfriend, they should also consider marriage, not even engagement.

Although parents may not be as harsh today, it should be noted that sometimes parents too, need to seek counsel prior to advising their children.

---

right now fun is the last thing in my book," Dad said, removing his spectacles.

"We told Angelique to end this relationship, but she disobeyed us and continued seeing you. I want you both to know, as soon as young people think it is time to get boyfriend or girlfriend, they should also consider marriage, not even engagement. If you want to continue seeing Angelique, then you have to fix a wedding date," my mother added, with hostility.

My grandmother sat upright at the edge of the sofa. "You don't think it too quick to consider marriage, Evelyn?" she asked.

"No," Mom responded, stomping her foot on the lacquered hardwood floor. "She playing a woman and he is a man, so is time they start working towards their own apartment."

Both William and I were stunned. Resigned, I sat back in my seat, my hands grasping each other and my knuckles bloodless. We never expected to hear we should be considering marriage at this stage of our relationship. It was true we met a while ago, but we couldn't remember spending as much as an hour at one time, alone. I stared at the floor, tears stinging my eyes, unable to think. I looked across at William. He was motionless, staring out the window, a faraway look in his eyes.

"In the meantime, while you are both making up your minds," Dad said, interrupting the silence, "Angelique can remain at home and you both can let me know your decision one week from today. And the next time we meet, I prefer to see you with one of your parents, or both."

Dad then excused himself. Mom followed, leaving William, Grandma Stella, and me. Grandma Stella sighed heavily, then sat back in her seat.

SEVEN

Revelations

Both William and I were gloomy.

"What will we do?" I asked him the following day. We were sitting across from each other at a table for two, in a little café, two blocks from my job.

"Angelique, I don't wanna lose you, but I never thought about getting married so young. My plans were to study so I can be promoted in my job and get a house of my own."

"I know what you mean. Neither did I consider the thought of being married at eighteen. Yet, I cannot bear the thought of walking away from our relationship. Also, it is becoming unbearable living at home."

"Your parents seem only to want to hear one thing, so, I suppose the best we can do is get married. Both of us are working so we should manage."

"I never expected things to happen like this. I'm sorry, William."

"We're in this together. We'll get through it," William said, a worried look in his eyes.

One week later, William and I were in a similar meeting with my parents. My grandmother wasn't there, neither was William's parents.

"I'm not sure how my parents will cope with this, so I prefer to leave them out for the time being. Anyway, Angelique and I have decided to get married," William informed my parents.

"When will that be?" my father inquired.

"Well," William started, looking directly at my father. "We will have a great deal of planning to do and money to save, so possibly about one year from today."

"One year!" My mother echoed him in an aggravated tone, "That is too long. We give y'all six months."

"Yes, six months is good enough, and y'all decide on a date tonight," my father added.

Unable to withstand my parents any longer, William finally consented, and a wedding date was fixed for March 30th of the next year.

After that, William was able to visit me at home, but only twice a week. Later I met William's family. His mother spoke softly and appeared not to be in a hurry to do anything, judging from her leisurely movements. I also met Joan, William's older sister.

We had dinner with them and throughout the meal, conversation flowed, mainly between William and Joan, and they included me occasionally. Joan was the younger version of her mother, only twice her size. Prior to meeting Joan, William told me she was 32 and had a five-year-old daughter. Theresa, Joan's daughter, clung to me soon after I arrived at their home, until the end of my visit.

Soon it was time to leave, and it bothered me that William said nothing of our pending wedding. On our way back to my home, I considered asking him why, but opted against it, not wanting to upset him.

Our dating continued and we enjoyed picnics, concerts, and went shopping, but the times we spent together were mainly taken up with plans for our wedding and our future. We intended to have a simple morning wedding followed by breakfast. My parents offered us one of their apartments, rent-free for one year, as well as to provide my gown and some of the food for the reception.

This should've been a happy time for us, and we did enjoy each other's company, but we were sad. It was already January, two months prior to our wedding day, and William hadn't mentioned whether he had informed his family about the wedding. And when I paid visits to his home no one ever mentioned anything about our wedding.

"Will, have you spoken to your family yet about our plans?" I finally asked.

We were standing at the massive manatees' pond in the Botanical Gardens, in Georgetown, feeding grass to the huge mossy-back sea mammals. They were diving to and fro, then surfacing near the shore as if glad for visitors.

"Not yet," he replied, bending down, pulling a handful of green grass and tossing it at the manatee nearest to the shore. Quickly, the manatee ate up the grass and swam away, re-joining the others.

"I cannot understand. It's two months before our wedding day and you're acting as if it's no big deal," I said.

"Angelique, you worrying unnecessarily. I got everything under control."

Six weeks before our planned wedding date, William and I went to my pastor to make arrangements for marriage counseling and our wedding ceremony. The first appointment was set for the following Saturday at 2:00 PM. While at the meeting with the pastor, I noticed William was unlike his usual jovial self and he was abrupt when I tried making conversation with him. After the meeting ended, he appeared only too glad to say goodbye, and didn't even offer to walk me home. William boarded the first bus that came along and promised to see me soon. I was frustrated and felt as if I were pressuring him to do what he didn't want to do.

I saw William only once during that week—the Friday night before our Saturday appointment, but he had called my office a couple of times during the week and complained of how busy he was at work. When he eventually showed up at my home, he still didn't seem his usual self. He did little talking and declined Eric's request for a game of dominoes.

"Something's bothering you, William. What happen?" I asked after Eric left.

"Everything's fine," he responded abruptly.

Even communication between us was strained. Before he left for home that evening, I reminded him of the counseling session scheduled for the following afternoon, and we arranged to meet at the pastor's office.

I awoke Saturday with a strange feeling. It felt as if all wasn't well. During my quiet time, I prayed that everything would work out for William and me. Since we planned to meet at the church, I didn't want to get there long before him, so I left home in time to arrive about five minutes ahead of the scheduled 2:00 PM appointment.

The change of weather surprised me. During the morning, it was bright and sunny, but only five hours later, the sun seemed to have taken a vacation. Making my way to the church, dark clouds raced swiftly overhead and black birds chirped noisily, as if telling me something. I looked up and smiled ruefully. *It's approaching my wedding day and*

I used to think this would make me the happiest woman in the world, but I'm sad…so sad.

"Come in please," came his deep voice when I knocked on the pastor's door.

I entered and found him typing on his typewriter. He flashed me his usual warm smile and invited me to sit.

"You're right on time, young lady," he said, glancing up at the oval shaped wall clock. "And where's that fiancé of yours?"

"He should be here shortly."

"Then make yourself comfortable. You can grab a book while I finish this report," Pastor Johnson said.

I wasn't in a reading mood, but I haphazardly chose a book and started thumbing through it.

"You think William has forgotten this appointment?" Pastor Johnson asked after a while.

"Aaah, I don't think so—I reminded him only last night."

"Then probably something delayed him. He may be here soon," Pastor Johnson said absentmindedly, continuing his typing.

An hour passed, then another thirty minutes. I used the church's phone to dial William's home number, but it rang out. I excused myself and went to look up the street to see if he was anywhere in sight. Besides a few children playing cricket on the narrow street, there was no one. I started feeling miserable and wondered if William was backing out of the relationship and marriage without informing me. Reentering the office, Pastor Johnson stopped working on his typewriter and our eyes connected.

"Any sight of him?" he asked, concern etched in his voice.

"No, I haven't seen him," I replied, fighting back the tears that stung my eyelids.

"Angelique, I'm not saying this to discourage you, but I do get the feeling that neither you nor William is ready for this marriage commitment. Is someone forcing you to do this?"

Suddenly I felt as if I needed to talk with someone. Instead, I stared at the floor without saying a word.

"Angelique, you can talk to me," my pastor encouraged.

Eventually, I told Pastor Johnson everything that led to my present situation. He listened, and from time to time asked a few questions.

"Angelique," he began when I was through, "Marriage is a serious commitment, and no couple should marry against their wishes or be forced to do so because, more than likely, they may encounter a lifetime of hell or a life of regrets. I'm sure you'll not want your life to be like that."

"I believe that once William and I are married, things will work out. I'm tired of my parents pressuring me, and furthermore, it's too late now to change our minds. We have already sent out our wedding invitations."

"I believe that once William and I are married, things will work out . . . "

Many people think similarly, but it never works. If certain issues are not addressed and remedied prior to marriage, there is no likelihood it will work out during the marriage.

I couldn't hold his gaze, knowing there were loads of truth in what he said. The fresh air entering through the open window was as smooth as new linen across my face. I inhaled deeply. *How embarrassing it would be to have to cancel our wedding now. Pastor Johnson had to be kidding.*

"Marriage changes no one, Angelique, and pressure from your parents shouldn't be a contributing factor for marriage." He paused, then began filing documents in a folder. "Neither is it ever too late for anything. I think you should reconsider this situation and get back to me, whatever your decision. In the meantime, we've waited two and a half hours for William, and he hasn't shown up. Angelique, I think you should go home and think this matter through," Pastor Johnson advised. Swinging away from his desk while still sitting in his swivel chair, he lightly got up, stretched himself, and walked over to my seat on the opposite side of his desk.

"The best place to be is in the perfect will of the Lord. Angelique, let's pray His will be done," he said, resting his hand on my shoulder.

I slowly walked home, wishing the journey would never end. On my way, I wondered why William hadn't shown up and what I would tell my parents. My mother was on the porch when I reached home. She took one look at me and knew instantly something was wrong.

"How did it go?" she asked, looking down at me from the top of the stairs.

"William wasn't able to make it."

"How yo' mean he wasn't able to make it? Why didn't he go? He send a message? He call'?"

"Mom, until I hear from William, I cannot answer any of your questions. I have the same questions too," I said, heading towards my room.

"Yo' see? The same thing we trying to tell yo'. If he was any good you think he would allow you to show up fo' marriage counsel and he stay home? You' make yo' bed hard, you goin' lie in it hard!" This was another of my mother's sayings which meant I made bad choices and would have to live with the consequences.

"Mom, how do you know he remained at home? Something may have happened."

"Alright," my mother said, shaking her right index finger, "yo' goin' to learn, me child. Yo' goin' to learn."

William showed up at my home after 8 PM that evening and instead of coming upstairs as customary, he asked my sister to get me.

Descending the stairs, I decided not to fuss with William or ask him anything; I would let him tell me what happened. He appeared much calmer than the last time I saw him. We talked a while and then William said he had gone home from work around 12:30 PM that day, done his laundry, and had a long nap.

He can't be fo' real. I'm not hearing right.

"Did you forget about our appointment with Pastor Johnson?"

"No, I ain't forget, but I wasn't in the mood," William said matter-of-factly.

It felt as if someone had dumped a bucket of ice-cold water down my spine. A deafening silence fell between us. I started getting up but sat down again. One part of me told me to get this man out of my house while another part restrained me. I sat there on the steps, not knowing what else to say or do. I took a deep breath.

"Aaah soo--- are we still getting married?"

"Angelique, I love you, but at this time, I really don't know," William replied, extending open palms and heaving his shoulders. We sat in an uncomfortable silence, each with our own thoughts. Finally, he got up.

"Have to leave. See you another time."

I couldn't help noticing his care-free countenance: he joined some friends who were playing cards across the street.

I lingered downstairs a while longer, my heart heavy. I wished my life was different, and I was able to enjoy it like a normal 18-year-old. My mother confronted me when I went upstairs.

"So, what is the story now?" she asked as if already knowing William had no logical excuse.

"Mom, I don't want to talk about it now," I replied, sidestepping her and attempting to make my way to my bedroom.

"Now, you listen to me, Angelique," Mom said, grabbing my shoulder and spinning me around, facing her. "Is now six weeks before yo' wedding day, and if *you* want William to make *you* an idiot, he ain't goin' make me one. What he say?" she demanded.

"He had no excuse," I said, tears running down my cheeks.

"Oh, he had no excuse? And *you* didn't ask he?"

"Ye--yes, I asked him -- but he said he was not in the mood this afternoon," I replied, almost choking on my words.

"Le' me tell *you* this tonight, he can try makin' you a fool, but he better don't test me. Did he tell he mother anything, yet?" she demanded, standing with her hands at her hips and eyes wild.

"I'm not sure," I replied, my shoulders wracking from sobs.

"Then we goin' know tomorrow, 'cause me and *you* goin' to see he mother!"

"What Mom? You can't do that!"

"Oh yeah! Then *you* watch me," she replied, storming away towards the kitchen.

As sure as dawn, Mom and I turned up at William's home the next afternoon, uninvited of course. Mrs. Larrier was alone. She offered us seats while she remained standing, braced against the wooden wall. After apologizing for the unexpected visit and making some small talk, my mother asked Mrs. Larrier if William told her anything about him and me.

"Well, he introduce Angelique to me as his girlfriend—is something wrong? Is Angelique pregnant?" Mrs. Larrier inquired, turning her attention towards me.

"No, I'm not pregnant, Mrs. Larrier," I answered, feeling rather insulted. *How dare you?* I wanted to scream at her.

"So, did he not tell you about the wedding?" Mom asked, squinting her eyes, looking at Mrs. Larrier a bit more closely.

"Wedding! What wedding?" Mrs. Larrier asked, glancing at my mother, then at me, then back at my mother. She took a few slow steps and sat down opposite us in an overstuffed sofa.

Mom quickly outlined some facts of the situation to Mrs. Larrier who silently listened, her chin propped against her hand. By the time Mom finished, Mrs. Larrier sighed audibly, a hurt expression in her tiny eyes.

"Well, I suppose he know his family poor and cannot help him, so he decided to keep we out of it," Mrs. Larrier replied.

Nothing more was said for a while, and an uncomfortable silence hung over us, causing me to blush from embarrassment. We left shortly after.

It was after 9:00 PM that evening when my sister shouted for me, saying William was there to see me. Skeptically, I descended the stairs.

"What the hell was that stunt you and yo' mother pull this afternoon? Y'all could've killed my mother. Did you know she is diabetic and suffers from high blood pressure?" William said without even greeting me.

He roughly wiped away perspiration from his face with a white handkerchief and slapped his hand against the outer wall of the house several times. I was dumbfounded. I stood there gazing at him. I had never seen him annoyed before.

"Okay. I know I'm not talking to myself, but if you gonna stand there and not answer me, listen, and listen good. Given all that is happening, I will not go ahead with this wedding," he said. "Angelique," he continued in a slightly softer tone, "I want you to know I will love to have you as my wife, but because of circumstances beyond my control, I have to disappoint you at this time. Anyway, if you care to, you can wait for me until I am able to sort things out." He then left.

I was at the mercy of my parents' rage. I was also left alone to deal with the embarrassment of having to let our invited guests know there will be no wedding. As if that wasn't enough, there was the agony of being without the man I loved—not knowing if he would ever return.

EIGHT

Strained Relationships

Home became a battle ground between my parents and me. Day after day they fussed at, ridiculed, and condemned me. My dad even stopped speaking to me after we had a talk one afternoon.

"So, Angelique, what you decide to do now? You see fo' yourself that fella had no good intention from the beginning." We had just finished dinner. My siblings had retired to another part of the house, while I did the dinner dishes. My parents were still sitting at the kitchen table.

"Dad, I'm not sure, I really don't even want to talk about it."

"What you mean yo' don't want talk about it?" Ah really can't believe you so stupid. You know how much money we spend on wedding gown and repairing that apartment? Then he act as if he ain't care—the money ain't come from he pocket so he could care less, and you just like he."

"Dad, if you really want to know—I intend to wait on William."

"This is crazy. All these years we send you to school fo' nothing? You that dumb? You can't see he is a playboy?"

"I sure all her brothers and sisters got more sense than she," my mother chimed in. Then she shouted for some of my siblings.

They cautiously entered the kitchen, eyeing our parents, then me.

"Gloria, if you was Angelique and somebody do you wha' William do, what would you do?"

"First of all," Gloria replied, "he couldn't do me that. I woulda finish with he for life."

Mom turned to Steve. "What would you do, Steve?"

"I don't know."

"Eric, boy, wha' you woulda do?"

He was poised in the doorway between the kitchen and the dining room.

"I don't know," he replied. "Only when somebody is in a situation and act, then they know."

I wasn't surprised at his answer because even though he was the third child he had a no-nonsense attitude. He seemed to have given our parents something to think about, at least for the time being because after that, I was left alone. She didn't even bother to involve my other siblings in asking what they would do. The topic of William hardly ever surfaced and whenever I was around, an uncomfortable silence ensued.

Meanwhile, I longed for William's company. He seldom contacted me at work anymore and whenever he did, he spoke nothing of our cancelled marriage. I remembered him telling me once, he felt my pain, and assured me, it will not always be that way. That was a thread of hope.

Through those difficult times Miriam was supportive, showing up with novels and spending time with me most nights paying no attention to my mother's displeased countenance.

"Hello Ms. Evelyn, how yo' doing tonight?" she would politely greet my mother.

"I alright," my mother would respond and either promptly leave the room or continue whatever she was doing without even looking up.

"Miriam, you're not scared she starts quarrelling with you?"

"Angie, I don't take on Ms. Evelyn. Ah know she can't stay mad all the time, she will come around sooner or later."

But whenever we spoke about William, Miriam became upset.

"You know what annoys me?" she asked, drawing her chair closer to mine. "He know how yo' parents are and still do something like this. Is embarrassing Angie, and you can't be mad at them."

Two weeks later, Miriam saw William. He told her he was really sorry how things turned out, but he had to do what he did for himself.

The church is one of the places most people find solace, especially during a crisis, but I was uncomfortable there. For once, I was thankful that my attendance was irregular. Eyes turned in my direction. I was already skinny and lost even more weight. My appetite dwindled and sleep became a stranger. I knew I couldn't continue like that; I had to do something to maintain my sanity. Finally, I enrolled at the Government Technical Institute and started a two-year diploma in Secretarial Science and I plunged into my job—answering telephones, making appointments, filing, drafting legal documents, interviewing clients, typing, and attending court sessions to request adjournments, hoping to dispel the pain William created.

Eventually, less heads turned in my direction and after about six weeks, it was almost normal. Thankfully, I spent less time at home due to my classes and work. By the time I reached home I was exhausted, and it was almost bedtime.

More than two months after our breakup, I answered the telephone while at work.

"We need to talk," came William's voice on the other end "A lot has happened, and I don't blame you for being mad at me, but we need to talk. When can I see you?"

I explained to William I really didn't have the time because I had started classes at the institute and get home close to 10:00 PM every night except Fridays.

Two days later, William showed up at the institute. He claimed he had to see me. I was glad to see him too. Our conversation was light and jovial but after a twenty-minute walk to the bus terminal, I still wasn't sure why he was there.

"I have a question?" I said.

"Sure."

"Are you still interested in our relationship?"

"Why would you ask such a question? Would I be here if I wasn't interested?"

"I'm not sure anymore."

"Listen, Angie, I've never stopped loving you, but I couldn't bear the pressure your parents put me through. All I need is some time."

"You could have done it differently . . ."

"At the time, there was no different way I could think of, Angie," he interrupted. "Believe me, I am really sorry, and I would be only too happy to make it up to you. Please, give me another chance."

> My head said no, but my heart said yes. I should've chased him away, but there he was begging for another chance.
>
> **For the most part, abusers beg for many chances. Many times, we know the right thing to do but we allow our judgment to be clouded.**
>
> https://www.fionaharewood.com/resources

The bus arrived and he held my arm, preventing me from entering.

"Angie, another chance is all I need, and you'll see the kind of person I really am," he pleaded.

My head said no, but my heart said yes. I should've chased him away, but there he was begging for another chance. And I still loved him.

While at the institute I had acquaintances, but Ellen and I became friends, possibly because we sat together in class. By that time, I was 20 and she was a few years older, tall, ebony in complexion, and had bright, lively eyes. We shared the same bus routes, and on our walks to the terminal, she always talked about her husband and their three children. Kevin was her high school boyfriend and after four years of marriage, they were still madly in love. At the time, he was in Georgia, in search of a better life for them. She said for the many years they knew each other, this was their first time apart, and she was miserable. She started the diploma program to keep her mind occupied and to ease the pain of separation.

Ellen's desire was to be reunited with her husband. She chattered on and on about Kevin. Anytime I listened to her, I longed for a relationship with William like Ellen had with Kevin.

In the meantime, William rarely attended church. He suddenly discovered an interest in the latest movies, the hottest discos, and happy hour. It was a bit disturbing, but being wrapped up in a hectic day-to-day schedule, I quickly forgot about his whereabouts. Then one evening, he met me after class with a friend's motorcycle and extra helmet and talked me into going to his home.

"Only for a little while," he coaxed "I wanna show you something."

When we got there, nobody was at home. He had hardly closed the door behind us, when he started kissing and caressing me. At first it felt good, but before I realized what was happening, William raised my dress and was removing my underclothes. I struggled to free myself, but he overpowered me.

"Let me go or I'll scream," I hissed between clenched teeth and unsteady breathing.

He continued struggling with me, but I didn't scream. Embarrassed and hurt, I started crying. Instantly he let me go.

"Gosh, Angie, I'm so sorry—I don't know what got over me—this will never happen again." He tried hugging me.

"Don't you touch me again or you'll regret it," I said, withdrawing. After a while, I composed myself, straightened my dress, fixed my hair, and left for home. Uninvited, William followed me to the bus stop. I never heard anyone beg as he did. He wanted me to forget the issue, but I never uttered a word in response to his pleas.

That evening was stamped on my mind. I wanted to share it with Miriam but was too embarrassed. The next day William called me at work, and it was as if nothing ever happened. He was his charming self again. Following that incident, whenever we spoke, he would tell me that I needed to realize he is a young man with needs. He shared that he couldn't be around me and not *want* me. Sex before marriage was one of the things Pastor Johnson condemned from his pulpit. My conscience wouldn't allow me to do what William wanted, and I tried explaining that to him.

Then the rumors started. One Friday evening, Miriam and I were playing a game of snakes and ladders.

"So, Angie, how things wit' you and William?"

I wasn't prepared for the question and from experience, I knew better than to lie to Miriam, but I still tried.

"Okay," I answered, avoiding her eyes, moving my dice down the longest snake on the board which relocated me from 87 to 6.

"You say that *okay* very quick," she said, smiling, eyeing me suspiciously. "You sure everything alright?"

"Well, not really because he keeps pressuring me for sex."

"What?" Miriam shouted, almost upsetting the game board. "Ah can't believe wha' ah hearing—look, Angie, I goin' tell you this now—le' he go he way, you hear? This shouldn't surprise me, though, it really shouldn't!" Miriam said, shaking her head.

"What you mean—It shouldn't surprise you?"

"Ah hear from reliable source that he usually visit this girl, Caroline, in Agricola at nights."

It was my turn to be surprised.

"Eh? No, Miriam, you kidding, right?" I said, looking around, ensuring my siblings and parents were out of earshot. My heart thumped wildly. "You mean Caroline Caesar who has those two children and lives by herself?"

"Same one. And the person who told me ain't goin' lie on William."

I knew Caroline only from seeing her and I admired her. She was a senior at South Georgetown Secondary, while I was a junior. Caroline was always neatly dressed in her uniform and was our head girl. She was an only child and lived alone with her mother. But after she left school, something went wrong. Instead of joining the corporate world, she quickly became pregnant with her first child. Her mother died shortly afterward, and before the first baby started walking, she was pregnant again.

"Who told you, Miriam?"

"Mother Cummings. She told' me don't tell you, but I think you should know."

Mother Cummings was Carol and Jennifer's mother.

"Gheeze man! Mother Cummings' sister lives in the same street as Caroline," I said.

"Exactly! She see he there more than once and tell Mother Cummings."

"Does Carol know?" I asked.

"Yes, Carol was there when Mother Cummings tell me."

I hardly wanted to believe it, but I had no reason to doubt Miriam or Mother Cummings. Suddenly I felt sick. I wanted to choke the life out of William. Instead, I sat still in my seat, feeling as if the world had stopped turning.

I searched my heart. I still loved William and felt a deep sense of loss—a loss which caused me to be distracted in class and start losing interest in my job. But I played along, not letting him know I was aware of his misdeeds.

Life for us continued as usual for a while and I wondered if I was waiting for William to tell me of Caroline. Then to my disappointment and hurt, his calls became less frequent and he often had an excuse for not being able to meet me after class. *Probably it was for the best we weren't married after all. Perhaps my parents were right--maybe he was never meant for me.*

Habitually, I got up early every morning. One particular Sunday morning, I didn't plan to study, but when I awoke it was just after 4 AM. I lay still in bed for a while, marveling at the deafening silence in the house, interrupted occasionally by light passing motor traffic on the road. I worshipped, then lazily reached over to the nightstand and grabbed my accounting textbook. Of all my subjects at the institute, accounting was most challenging. After about ten minutes, I tossed the book aside, got up, stretched, and headed towards the living room. Glancing at the grandfather clock standing tall in the corner, I noticed it was 5:20 AM. Flopping down on the sofa, and reaching for the remote, I started flipping channels. Nothing interested me. I opened the front window which gave a perfect view of the main road—something I would hardly do at that hour of the morning.

Then to my disappointment and hurt, his calls became less frequent and he often had an excuse for not being able to meet me after class.

Victims see the signs of abuse. They just hope things will get better. Angelique and William's wedding was postponed, which was probably better for them due to their inexperience.

But what about the couple who live together for years, add children to the relationship, and there is either no marriage proposal, or commitment is indefinitely postponed?

That behavior contributes emotional, mental, and physical abuse.

Pay attention to signs in your relationship.

I froze. There was William. Standing at the window, I stared until he was out of sight. After regaining my composure, I pinched myself, wanting to believe I was still asleep. But I wasn't. I slumped down on the sofa and that scene replayed vividly in my mind—William riding past my house at top speed, as if daring the bicycle to go faster than it was designed. Upon hearing the creaking window, he instinctively glanced in the direction of the sound and for a quick second, our eyes connected. Without a word or a wave, he sped on his way. *Only guilt would provoke such a reaction.* I concluded William slept at Caroline's that night and was then heading home. First instinct is normally right.

Hurt, then anger washed over me. How could he do this? How could he? I kept asking myself. I slowly got up, closed the window, and made my way back to bed, hardly realizing the tears were streaming down my cheeks—feelings of love, hurt, anguish—too many to name, overwhelmed me.

Eventually, I wrote a letter to William, telling him never to contact me again. *I am finished with this relationship! I've had enough!*

Although I told William not to contact me again, I found myself missing him. He was the first and only man I'd ever loved, and I would have done or given anything to be with him, but I couldn't bear the thought of him cheating on me. Yet, every time the phone rang, I wished it was William calling. Day one passed at work, and I was really sad. Day two—I felt lost, lonely, and helpless. By day three, it were as if I was going out of my mind. *It was I who told him not to contact me. Why am I feeling this way?* Finally, on day four, I answered the phone and there was his usual smooth, deep voice.

"Angie, please, listen to me - pleeeease!"

My heartbeat quickened and I hesitated for a moment.

"I don't care to listen to anything you have to say," I responded, hanging up the telephone. I stared at a document in front of me without seeing anything. *Did I really do that? I've got to be crazy!* Apparently, the phone rang immediately afterwards, but I didn't hear it.

"Angelique, it's William," Miss Foster interrupted my thoughts. I looked at the flashing red light then at Miss Foster. She had returned to her filing.

"Miss Foster, do me a favor, please—tell him I'm busy."

"Pardon me? You never refuse to speak with William. You two had a fight?"

"Yes, and I'm through with him."

"After one fight you're through? You gotta get tough, girl."

"Miss Foster, will you please tell him for me? I really don't want to speak with him."

"If you say so," Miss Foster replied.

She then released the hold button on the telephone.

"William? Thanks for holding. Not sure what has come over Angelique, but all of a sudden, she is too busy to get the phone."

Miss Foster replaced the receiver then turned to me.

"Over the past few days, I sensed something bothering you, but I didn't realize it was this. I'm sorry, but I hope you know what you're doing."

"Thanks, Miss Foster. And the truth? I'm not sure I know what I'm doing."

After that, William called my job twice every day—once in the morning and once in the afternoon. Most times he got me directly on the telephone, but I would hang up immediately. On a couple of occasions, Miss Foster answered him, and after a while, to my amusement, she didn't even consult with me before telling him I was busy. Then William started showing up again at the institute every evening to walk me to the bus terminal.

I asked Ellen not to leave when she saw him. Sometimes, she did go on her merry way, but a few times, she stayed. Whenever Ellen left and William was able to walk with me, I was forced to listen to his apologies, pleas and excuses. At those times, I chose to be silent. He bought cards and flowers. I refused them all. I listened to, and heard every statement he made, but uttered not a word in response. I was actually enjoying the game. I enjoyed seeing him suffer after what he did. One evening, he admitted he had an intimate relationship with Caroline, but swore it was over. I believed him because of all the attention he showered on me, but I paid him no mind. Instead, I continued with my oath of silence like a Catholic monk.

After three weeks, William realized he made no progress with me, so he went to Miriam.

"Angie," Miriam said one night while we were making our way home from church. "Guess who been at me and spend a long time last night? And to crown it all – shedding crocodile tears."

"Who? You don't mean William?"

"Who else yo' think? He got the gall. Man, ah blister he. Imagine he sayin' you hard on he, and how he beg 'till he can't beg no more, and you not giving in. Ah tell he you right 'cause he know fully well what you going through with yo' parents, and he act as if he ain't care." Miriam said she eventually felt sorry for him, but she asked him why she or I should trust him again. He told her it was only a mistake, and we

---

I felt sorry for him, but I agreed with her. I should hold out a little longer without speaking to him.

Giving the abuser too many chances allows him/her to underestimate the victim. Those hiccups should be used as tickets to freedom.

---

have to accept his word. He begged her to talk with me for him. Miriam counselled me to stay as long as I could without talking with him. While Miriam talked about William, I felt sorry for him, but I agreed with her. I should hold out a little longer without speaking to him.

It was a Thursday morning, more than nine months after our cancelled marriage. Everything seemed to be going in my favor. William wasn't even in my thoughts. *Great! I'm probably getting over him.*

The telephone rang and it was William. It were as if butterflies started fluttering in the pit of my stomach.

"Please have lunch with me today, Angie."

I paused. "Okay. What time?"

"Twelve-thirty—I will meet you at your job," William said. His voice seemed to have regained life within seconds. "And Angie?"

"Yes?"

"Thank you."

"You're welcome."

I put the phone down and stared blindly into space. I hoped he had learned his lesson.

We went to Arapaima, one of the best fast food and pastry joints—ten minutes away. We sat opposite each other, and William shifted uncomfortably in his seat, looking away every time our eyes met.

"Angie, thanks for having lunch with me," he said, taking a sip of his tamarind drink. I know I've done more than my share of talking over the past weeks, but I still need to let you know I am really sorry for hurting you. I know I mess' up big time, but I hope you can forgive me. I promise. It won't happen again."

I stared coldly at him, then looked away, hardly wanting to continue eating the white pudding and mango sour I so loved. He reached for my hand across the table and covered it with his, then continued: "Angie, look at me."

Our eyes locked.

"Will you accept my apologies?"

A long pause followed between us, and the disgusting scene of him riding past my house early that Sunday morning flashed across my mind. I removed my hand from under his, and it was my turn to shift uncomfortably in my seat.

"Do you realize how much you hurt…"

"I know, Angie, I know," he interrupted, "and you have all right to be mad at me, but please, can we start over?" he asked, his eyes searching mine. William left his seat and came around to mine. He bent down and hugged me. It were as if electricity rushed through my body at his embrace. At that moment, the ice began thawing.

NINE

You Still Wanna Marry Me?

Since we 'started over' as William called it, things couldn't have been better. William lavished me with attention, gifts, and it was one surprise after another. Then about three months later, he met me after class. It was an ordinary warm night. We were walking hand in hand along Camp Street in Georgetown.

"Do you still wanna marry me, Angie?" William asked. Not expecting the question, I looked at him and didn't answer. "Let's get married Angie," he said, stepping in front of me, facing me.

"When?" I asked.

"In about six months. Let's fix the date and then talk with our parents."

There was no engagement ring or nothing, just a verbal question and consent. After some discussion we decided on

June 26, 1982, six months later. William called my dad and requested a meeting with him and my mother. The meeting was set for the following day. They appeared somber, as if we had bad news to deliver.

William apologized for canceling our first wedding. While he spoke, I watched him shift in his seat, stammer, and nervously crack his fingers. William informed my parents of our plans to get married on June 26.

"Well, to tell the truth," my father said, "I will be lying if I say I'm happy after hearing what you both said. But, Angelique, if this is what you want, then it's fine with us. Also, we will have the apartment available when you're ready. It will be rent-free for one year and we will assist in whatever way we can with the wedding."

"Well, to tell the truth," my father said, "I will be lying if I say I'm happy after hearing what you both said."

For something as important as a wedding, parents' full blessing is essential. If they don't give it, be careful.

"Well, thank you, Mr. and Mrs. Castor," William said.

"Thank you, Mom and Dad," I said. Neither responded.

Gosh, I can't believe it. They're acting as if we're making funeral arrangements.

Unlike the first time when we were planning our wedding, William took me to his mother and informed her of our plans.

Then the big day came. The day most women dream of. Strange, it were as if a collision of emotions washed over me. Feelings of happiness, nervousness, and sadness, were all bottled into one jar in the pit of my stomach. I looked outside and thanked the Lord for a beautiful day. The weather forecast promised a sunny 85 degrees. I sat down with my family that morning for my last meal as a single woman. Conversation was light around the table.

After breakfast, Dad excused himself, telling my siblings to hurry up because the boys had to go to the barber while Gloria and my youngest sister had to be dropped off at the hairdresser's. Mom and I had our hair done the day before.

After they left, Mom said she was sorry I was leaving them. She also mentioned that since I met William, our relationship became strained, but she never stopped loving me. "You are one of my best children," she said. She then reiterated the fact that she loved me and didn't want to see me get hurt. "I hope William know he find a good wife, and I hope he treat you well. Teeth and tongue will bite, but remember yo' favorite saying—'A family that prays together stays together.' Don't eve' forget that," she said, hugging me. Releasing me, there were tears in her eyes.

"The good thing is, I wouldn't be far away, Mom, so, you can expect me to come knocking at any time."

"Sure, and remember, this is always home. You welcome here anytime."

"You are one of my best children," she said. She then reiterated the fact that it was because she loved me so much she did not want to see me get hurt.

Although parents are expected to guide their children, sometimes it is better for them to do their part, then step back. It is found that parents getting too involved in their children's relationships may eventually be detrimental.

https://www.fionaharewood.com/resources

"Thanks, Mom. Gotta leave here soon. Miss Mentore wants me to fit my dress again, around noon."

"Okay, me daughter, God bless you."

It was a 5 PM wedding at Calvary Assembly, William's church, and I began dressing at 3 PM. Unlike most brides, I didn't dress in front of the mirror, but what I saw when I did look at my reflection was spectacular.

In keeping with tradition, my white laced stockings were the something old, while my gown was the something new. The gown was graced with heavy embroidery and scattered diamanté. It had a dropped waistline and long balloon-top sleeves. The something borrowed was my three-tier head dress of tulle and embroidered edging. The veil, the shortest tier, when thrown back, exposed the cutest silver tiara. The second tier extended to a beautiful train with scattered appliqués, while the third tier, a replica of the second, stopped at the hips. Meticulously, I chose my underwear to complete the old tradition of something blue. Diamanté sparkled on the front of my white satin stilettos, and I carried a bouquet of fresh white roses sprinkled with tiny peach flowers.

My sisters were too young, so I chose Hannah a friend and co-worker as my matron-of-honor. She met me with a broad smile.

"Angie, you—look—beautiful!" she whispered, stressing her words slowly. "Just smile, Angie! Smile!"

Those words of encouragement lit up my face, and I was a smiling bride on my father's arm, stepping down the aisle to meet my waiting groom.

William wore a beige suit, plaid shirt, and brown shoes.

Our wedding was simple, but lovely. I enjoyed the ceremony, especially when we repeated our vows to each other. I meant every word I said. The organist played "Wedding March," and a sense of pride enveloped me, stepping down the petal-strewn aisle as Mr. and Mrs. William Larrier.

Driving to the Botanical Gardens for pictures, William and I talked about and giggled at some of the funny things that transpired in the church. After the minister pronounced us man and wife and William told he 'may now kiss the bride,' Senior Counsel Sampson's voice disrupted the silence after William gave me a light kiss on the lips.

"Hey! Hey! Hey! You're not stealing! She is yours now! Do that again properly, man!"

Shrieks of laughter erupted in the church, while others shouted their agreement with Mr. Sampson.

Not only was Miss Mentore my seamstress, she also lent her professional touch to both our cakes. William's, however, was the center of attraction. The cake, shaped like a guitar, was covered with peach and white icing. It was engraved with the words "Get Me to the Church on Time" and a miniature statue, dressed in a black suit, stood in walking position between the iced strings of the guitar. Mine was a three tier Guyanese black cake, a moist, rich cake, traditionally served at weddings. It was decorated with peach roses and mint green icing petals. A small church was placed at the top with a bride and groom making their exit.

After a long night, we retired to our apartment where we celebrated our love and reveled in the memories of our day.

TEN

Storm Clouds Roll In

The weeks and months flew by. Like most newlyweds, we did everything together. I still attended the technical institute, causing my evenings to be busy, but we had the weekends for ourselves. We shopped for some furniture and appliances and decorated our home. We attended church and did other fun things. I enjoyed it when we were home together and for the first time in years, I was happy and I thought William was too. Our families also became more involved in our lives.

Eight months after our wedding day, I became pregnant with our first child. William and I were elated at receiving the news from our family doctor and began preparing for the 'little Larrier,' as we called her. There was no technology back then to tell us our baby's sex.

Around this time, William began gradually changing. I was three months along in my pregnancy when he started staying out later than usual, and some nights, he didn't make it home at all. On weekends, he began attending meetings at work and whenever he didn't claim to have Sunday meetings, he was too tired to make it to church. His dwindling church attendance bothered me because I believe a spiritual foundation does well for a marriage.

I kept our marital issues to myself, putting on a cheerful front. Miriam and a few friends would sometimes ask for William, and I made excuses for him.

Miriam and a few friends would sometimes ask for William, and I made excuses for him.

Be careful when you find yourself making excuses for a spouse. You may be in denial of an abusive relationship.

I heard stories and also read in pregnancy books of husbands who didn't enjoy their wives' company while she was carrying their child, and I figured this was the case with William. Yes, I was difficult to get along with at times and occasionally, I felt depressed and started crying for no apparent reason, but the few times that happened, it passed quickly.

"Will," I began one Sunday afternoon while we were relaxing in bed. "Are you happy with the way things are going with us?"

"What you mean, 'the way things are going with us'? I ain't see no problem. Is something wrong?"

"We're not as happy as we used to be, and sometimes, I feel my pregnancy is having a bad effect on you."

"I don't know what you talking 'bout. If you have a problem, I don't have one," William replied, getting up and grabbing his towel. "Oh," he said, hitting me playfully with the towel. "It slipped me to mention, there is a tennis game in the park this afternoon—the guys at work playing another corporation."

"May I come along?" I asked.

"Now, now, babe, that's no place for you—you need to stay home and get some rest," he said, bending over and rubbing his hand in a circular motion over my bulging tummy. William left home shortly after, and I spent the evening in bed staring up at the ceiling. Daylight faded gradually and the room became darker, as did my world.

By the time I was six months pregnant, the situation grew worse. William continued staying away from home. In the beginning, he got home before me and started cooking dinner. Sometimes he would even collect me from class, but his schedule hardly included me anymore.

Clement, thirteen at that time, was a loving brother, and looked out for me. As soon as I reached home, he would show up.

"Big belly, how yo' doing?" he would ask, smiling, "what yo' want help with this evening?"

While helping me, he would chat from one thing to the other, but when he noticed I was quiet, he worked silently, leaving me to my thoughts.

Miriam also helped me whenever possible. Little by little, I started sharing issues about my marriage with her. By that time, Carol and Jennifer had migrated to Grenada, their mother's homeland. Miriam confirmed she knew of some of the issues, even before I told her, and mentioned that two people said they saw William

. . .although I had reasons to be concerned due to William's actions, I turned a deaf ear to anything negative I heard about him.

Marital issues should be addressed and not be ignored. If one party is unreceptive, seek counseling.

at different clubs with a woman. I knew there was truth in what Miriam said, but I tried to ignore it. I remembered during marriage counsel, Pastor Johnson told us not to listen to rumors about each other, and although I had reasons to be concerned due to William's actions, I turned a deaf ear to anything negative I heard about him.

ELEVEN

The Discovery

One of my mother's hobbies was going to the movies, so, at least once every two weeks she would treat herself to a good film. The movie, *Guess Who's Coming to Dinner,* was in its second week, and it was the *talk of the town*. That Thursday evening, I wasn't feeling well, so I skipped classes and went home.

"Good to see you trying to cook, Sis," I teased Gloria, "Where's Mom?"

"Gone to the cinema of course; don't know why she couldn't cook before she went along."

"Oh, she's gone to see *Guess Who's Coming to Dinner*, huh?"

"Yes, and leave me to face the stove."

"Hush, stop complaining, girl. How often you cook anyway? I'm hungry. Lemme get something to eat," I said, opening the refrigerator and taking out a bowl of diced pineapple and watermelon.

"Ah know you eating fo' two, but don't finish that, okay."

"There's more where this came from, ain't there?" I replied, pulling up a chair and sitting down at the table. "Come on, hand me a bowl and a fork, please."

"You know, you lucky you pregnant or you woulda get it yo'self. And furthermore, I not doing anything fo' you, is me niece or nephew, whatever yo' got in there, I doing it for. Ah hope is a boy 'cause little girls are babies fo' too long," she said, smiling and handing me a salad bowl and a fork.

I ate, rested a while, then went home to start dinner. *If it wasn't for William, I wouldn't cook this evening. I'm so tired, and my feet are swollen.*

About half an hour later, I was in the kitchen when I heard a knock on the door.

"Who's there?" I asked, grabbing the paper towel, and drying my hands before getting the door.

"Angie, is me," came my mother's voice.

"Thought you went to the cinema…you back early," I said, opening the door, letting her in. There was something peculiar about her facial expression—as if she was upset.

"What happen', Mom?"

She took a seat, shaking her head.

"Yo' preparin' dinner?"

"Yeah," I replied, returning to the sink, and starting to wash the rice. "But you didn't answer me. Why're you home so early? Tickets sold out?"

"You would neve' guess, girl."

"Guess what?" I stopped washing the rice and turned around to face her.

"Where is William?"

"He's not home yet. Whenever he's this late, it's most likely he has a meeting or something."

"That is what he tell you? Y'all are marri'd people now, and ah don't want get in y'all business but you is still me daughter and when you hurt, I hurt."

"What are you talking about, Mom?"

"The movie in the cinema started and ah sit down enjoyin' a bag o' popcorn. To my surprise, guess who I see walk in with a woman, and take a seat, two rows in front o' me?"

My feet felt as if they would give way beneath me. I turned off the stove, pulled up a chair, and sat down beside her.

"Mom, you don't mean William? Do you?"

"Who else yo' think?" she asked, getting up and pacing the dining room. "Anyway," she continued, sitting down again. "Ah calm down and talk to meself. Evelyn don't get too hasty, must be he friend." After that, ah ain't see a thing on the screen no more because I ain't take me eyes off them 'cause ah ain't want talk what I ain't know."

Every word my mother spoke, were as if the blood drained from my body.

"Angie, ah ain't had to wait long—next thing ah see, he and she kissing, and not lip kiss, tongue kiss. I sure, from the time them enter the cinema 'til they leave, them ain't see nothing on the screen. Child, ah get so mad ah had to resist the urge of getting up and going and grab he and she. Ah couldn't take it no more, so ah get up and come home. If ah did stay in there, ah woulda get charge fo' murder, and not fo' one person—two."

I sat, staring blindly ahead of me.

"Angie? You listening to me?"

"Yes, Mom, and I heard every word you said, but I really don't know what to say or do."

"Girl, I ain't know wha' to tell yo'—y'all marri'd. But ah can't believe he, not even two years in the marriage and he got woman. Look at you," she said, rising from her seat, holding out her hand, gesturing my large stomach. "Pregnant! He don't care fo' you or he unborn child. Ah wonder what more we got to expect? We did warn yo' but

I not goin' into that." Heading to the door, she looked over her shoulders, "Angie, I gone, and don't take he on and get sick."

I had no urge to continue dinner; I sat gazing into space with my mother's words turning over and over in my mind. My head throbbed and I began pacing the living room, trying to figure out how to deal with the situation. I couldn't think of a way to approach William without telling him it was my mother who saw him and told me. Eventually, I sat down again and was lost in my thoughts. My world was falling apart. *No wonder he was always out. Why did he get married if he wanted to continue seeing other women....?*

I must have drifted off to sleep. The next thing I knew, light flooded the living room; I heard William's voice and was startled.

"Hon, what's the matter? Why didn't you go to your bed?"

For a moment, my mind blurred, but then everything came rushing back. William immediately started going through the mail on the table. I stared at him without saying anything. Were we the same couple who were so much in love for nearly four years? It took much effort to remove my cramped feet from the top of the center table. I then stood up and limped my way to the bedroom. I couldn't confront William. I couldn't.

"You didn't answer me, Angie," William said, making his way to the kitchen.

"What is there to answer to?" I asked, more to myself than to him.

I had hardly reached the bedroom when I heard William scream from the kitchen—at the same time he slammed the cover down on the half full pot of water I had put on to cook the rice, but had never finished.

"Angelique, what the hell going on? Is now after 10 o'clock and you ain't finish dinner yet?"

By that time, he was in the bedroom screaming. I absolutely ignored him and was about to walk past him. Mistake. He pushed me violently. I hit my back against the edge of the wardrobe, lost my balance, and fell to the floor.

"Can't you hear I'm speaking to you? You suddenly gone deaf? Why haven't you prepare' dinner?" he asked, anger flaming in his eyes.

I was stunned. My back hurt intensely, but I was too upset to cry. I held on to the rail of the bed and slowly picked myself up. Anger welled within me, but calmly I replied, "I ate at my Mom and I thought the person you took to the movies would prepare your dinner."

For one moment, I thought I saw confusion in William's face. He quickly looked from side to side, then back at me.

"*What*?" he hissed, taking a step towards me. I tried backing away, but the wardrobe barred me. When he spoke again, venom spewed from his voice.

"What are you talking about? Who you been gossiping with?"

His words were slow, but they were etched with an anger I didn't know he possessed. His eyes seemed suddenly filled with a hatred I never thought possible.

"Oh?" I began calmly. "So are you saying you weren't in the Globe Cinema tonight making out with a wo—"

A hard slap from the back of William's hand penetrated my mouth and a part of my face. My head spun and I tasted blood instantly. Somehow, I ended up sprawled across the bed.

A hard slap from the back of William's hand penetrated my mouth and a part of my face. My head spun and I tasted blood instantly.

Physical abuse is wrong and should never be tolerated. Address the issue.

https://www.fionaharewood.com/resources

"Don't you ever accuse me again, or you wouldn't like the end result," he threatened, storming out of the house. He slammed the door behind him.

Dear God, please don't let me lose this baby, I prayed.

I placed ice on my mouth to ease the swelling. The following day, I stayed home from work and didn't visit my parents. William returned home early that morning, quickly dressed for work, and left again.

For more than a week after the incident, we lived in the same house, slept in the same bed, but said nothing to each other. William appeared happy that we had a fight, taking that opportunity to get home later, or not at all.

After eight days, I couldn't keep up the charade. *I'm either in this marriage or out.*

On Friday evening I went home, prepared dinner, and instead of eating and retiring to bed, I grabbed a book and started reading, waiting on William's return home. He eventually arrived after 11 PM. He greeted me, but never looked in my direction.

While he showered, I warmed food for both of us, laid it out on the table, and told him dinner was ready. Half of the meal went by in silence, but I didn't wait up that late for us to remain silent partners.

"Will," I began. With his fork halfway to his mouth, he looked across the table at me. "How long will we continue like this?" I inquired.

As if in relief, he emptied the forkful of peas and rice into his mouth and chewed on it

before replying.

"Like what?"

"Is this how we will spend the rest of our lives—not speaking to each other?"

"You're the one making life difficult," he said. "I hate it when people accuse me of things I know nothing of."

Is he really telling me I listened to a lie? The cinema is normally dark. I wonder if my mother saw someone else.

I never knew my mother to tell lies and although I knew William was the one lying, I heard myself say, "Will, I'm really sorry. This will never happen again."

That night, we made up and life was nearly normal.

I never knew my mother to tell lies and although I knew William was the one lying, I heard myself say, "Will, I'm really sorry. This will never happen again."

Victims blame themselves and may think everybody else is right.

Don't blame yourself.

https://www.fionaharewood.com/resources

TWELVE

$5.00?

Three weeks before the birth of our baby, I graduated from the institute with a Diploma in Secretarial Science. It was far from becoming the author I anticipated, but there's a saying that goes, *as long as there is life, there is hope*. My family attended the graduation, but William didn't—he said it was impossible for him to take time off from work.

It was good riddance to school and studies for the moment—a heavy workload, pregnancy, sometimes a stressful marriage, and my home chores—all were overwhelming at times. At last, I relaxed but not for long. Soon, I'd have a baby screaming in my ears. Still, I didn't think the baby's screams would be as stressful as my studies were. As if she heard me, I saw and felt my baby move from one side of my tummy to the other. It was a matchless feeling.

My pregnancy was uneventful, and I worked to the end, but my delivery didn't go as well. It was four nights and three days of painful, sporadic labor, before our bouncing baby girl made her way into this world. Weighing in at five pounds three ounces, she was the picture of perfect health. I loved my daughter. From the moment I saw her, all pink, slimy, wriggling and screaming at the top of her lungs, with a head full of straight black hair, I forgot all the pain which preceded her arrival. She looked like my brother Clement, with puffy eyes, a small mouth, straight nose and ears that pointed at the top like a little elf. Clement was the closest person to me during those months. I wondered if this had anything to do with the baby's resemblance—but then again, Clement looked like me.

When William saw the Little Larrier for the first time, during visiting hours, he swelled with pride with a wide grin plastering his face. Back then, it was uncommon for men to observe a child's birth. The nurse placed the tiny bundle into his arms, and he stood there looking from her to me, then back at her.

"Looks a whole lot like Clement, but we'll call her Kianna Wendy," he announced.

Three days later, I was discharged from the hospital and went home to a new set of responsibilities. For the first two months, William was around and was helpful. He assisted with the laundry, made me soups, and did chores around the house.

Although I enjoyed my daughter, I often felt lonely and depressed but was never sure why. My parents adored their granddaughter and after the first two months, when William wasn't around, Kianna and I spent most of our time with my mother while I was still on maternity leave.

Before Kianna was three months old, William was back to staying out late, but whenever he was around, he was pleasant, playing his role of dutiful husband and loving dad. I accepted the situation as it was, thinking it could've been worse. Working around the courts, I'd seen many women place their husbands before the judge for physically abusing them. We hardly ever argued anymore. Or, did I avoid issues that would result in quarrels? Whatever it was, I was determined not to let William's continuous absence from the home keep me down. Prayers became an integral part of my life. Those were times I drew nearer to God and that was my coping mechanism.

The next thing I knew, William hooked up with a partner in crime, Brett. He was tall, slim, brown as the Congo, and giggled at everything. There used to be a time when William condemned the wrong things Brett did, but suddenly wrong things turned right, and they became close friends. Brett married a gem of a woman, and like me, her parents were disappointed with the union. Even though they tried, they were unable to stop the marriage.

One Friday morning, I was preparing for work. Checking the refrigerator, there was nothing for lunch unless I cooked something. There was no time to cook, and I had no money either. It was pay day, but I was never paid before 4 PM. Also, William had stopped giving me money. He used to contribute to groceries, but after grocery shopping, I had to account in writing, how I spent every cent of his money. Eventually, I got tired of that arrangement and one day I blatantly

He used to contribute to groceries, but after grocery shopping, I had to account in writing, how I spent every cent of his money.

Look for signs of control in one of the least discussed forms of abuse – financial abuse -- address it.

https://www.fionaharewood.com/resources

told him to keep his money. Groceries were then added to my already lengthy budget.

That day, I swallowed my pride and asked William for five dollars to buy lunch.

"All I have is five dollars, and I hate to leave my pocket empty, so tough luck, Babe," he responded without even checking his wallet.

I could've done without asking him.

"Thanks. Do have a good day," I said, hurrying to catch the bus.

The Bible says—'when God is for you, no man can be against you.' I earned one hundred dollars that morning from preparing two Deed Polls—a document people used to change their names for legitimate reasons. I was able to buy myself more than a five-dollar lunch that day. The first idea that came to my mind was to call William and invite him to lunch, since he too had no money. Instead, I opted against that and invited Hannah who worked with the junior counsel in the Federation Building. She was matron-of-honor at my wedding. Miss Foster kept the office while Hannah and I went to The Pepperpot, a newly opened restaurant in the heart of Georgetown City.

Arriving at The Pepperpot, there was the usual long line. The food was laid out and there were servers. The tantalizing and mouth-watering aroma of pepper pot, their main dish, and many other delicious foods made me realize how hungry I was.

People talk of premonition and I'm not sure there is such a thing, but suddenly I felt as if something was wrong. I dismissed the feeling, then began scanning the line ahead to get an idea of how long we had to wait. My mouth fell open and I grabbed Hannah's arm.

"What happen, Angie? What's the matter?" she asked, her eyes following mine. "Oh no! Angie, let's get out of here," Hannah said, attempting to pull me out of the line. William was in the line too. He stood behind a young lady—she looked about 20 years old. His left hand rested on her hip and he whispered in her ear.

"You gotta be kidding, Hannah, I'm not leaving here, one way or other he's got to stop," I said coldly, as if Hannah was the target of my anger.

We continued looking on. Then it was William's and his partner's turn to be served. I watched William hand the young lady the plate and silverware, then took his, all the while smiling. Finally, the waiter served them. I became numb from anger, watched William approach the cashier, take a wad of notes from his wallet, and paid. Then they both headed to a table for two. He got her chair, then William sat facing us, while his partner faced him.

"I'm going over to that table," I said, digging into my purse and retrieving the money so Hannah could pay and get us take-away, instead.

"Angie, you can't. Please don't make a scene—wait until you get home, pleeeease!" Hannah begged, her eyes wide with fear.

"Who said I'm going to make a scene?" I asked, becoming more aggravated. "I want William to know I saw him because he will deny it. And you know what hurts most?" I continued, "Only this morning I asked him for five dollars to buy lunch, and he told me he only had five dollars. Now I am standing here, seeing him pay for lunch; not only for himself, but for his lady friend too."

I glanced back at William's table. William had vanished—only the young woman sat there eating. Surprise replaced aggravation. Hannah and I exchanged glances with the same puzzled expressions.

"Where'd he go?" Hannah asked. Her mouth opened and her eyes searched the crowded restaurant.

"Don't know," I said, glancing quickly around. "He probably saw me, didn't know I had already seen him and went into hiding."

"The gents' is over there," Hannah said, pointing ahead, "He may have gone there."

"I'm going to that woman."

"Angie, please, no! Let's go somewhere else and get our lunches," Hannah pleaded again, this time attempting to take hold of my arm.

"No, you stay in the line, order two take-aways, pay, and by the time you're finished, I'll be back."

I started making my way between tables in the packed restaurant, heading towards William's partner who was eating away at her meal.

"Hi," I said, slipping into William's vacant seat. "Where's the guy who was eating here with you?" I took in her appearance. She wasn't even anything to look at.

"In the gents'," she replied.

She stopped eating and stared from me to the gents' room. One instinct was to barge into the gents' room; another was to eat his lunch while I waited. Knowing William, he might have spotted me, chose not to venture back to the table, and have me wait like the dragon. I looked over at the line. Hannah wildly beckoned me. I ignored her.

"When he returns, tell him Mrs. Larrier was here," I said, rising from the chair and walking away. "Oh," I said, turning around, "next time, be sure to check before you accept lunch dates with someone else's husband."

I watched her eyes grow wide. Still sitting, she slid her chair slightly away from the table and started rising. "Oh no, don't do that," I said tapping her shoulder lightly. "He got the chair for you earlier, allow him to get it when you're ready to leave."

Hannah breathed a sigh of relief when I made it back to her, trouble-free. On our ten-minute walk back to the office, I said nothing, even though Hannah tried consoling me. At the office, I tried eating, but my stomach felt suddenly full. After moving the food around in the container for a while, I got up and threw it into the trash. What a waste! After lunch, I placed all my effort into concentrating on my work again.

The telephone rang for the first time that afternoon and Miss Foster answered it.

I couldn't believe it was William calling! I was stunned for a moment and at a loss for words, but eventually I furiously blurted out, "Hold a minute, you actually got the gall to call me and behave as if it were I who did something wrong? I was not the one who refused to give my wife lunch money this morning, and instead took a bad looking woman to lunch at one of the finest restaurants in town. Somebody's confused here."

"She was a co-worker and invited me to lunch, so you only made yourself look foolish," he exclaimed.

Suddenly, I felt tired. I had no more energy to fight.

"Look, I'm at work," I said, replacing the telephone receiver.

Lies and more lies. When will it ever end?

THIRTEEN

Messy Morals

Ellen, my friend whom I met at the institute, contacted me about three months after Kianna was born, sending me a letter and a package via her brother–in-law. Excitedly, I laid the package aside and burst open the letter. Ellen had finally joined her husband in Miami, but was unable to take her children with her. They were left with their grandmother, Mrs. Mackee, so she asked me to visit them when I had time. I discussed the letter with William and showed him the lovely things Ellen sent for Kianna. He encouraged me to visit the children and I started doing so frequently. On a few occasions, I had them spend a day or a weekend over at my home.

"I saw Mrs. Mackee downtown today, Angie," William said one night. "She said the children asking for you."

"Oh really? I've been very busy lately. I haven't seen them in nearly three months." I stopped folding the clothes and wiped the damp hair from my forehead, trying to figure out when would be a good time to have them over or go visit them. By then Kianna was two.

"When do you think you can go see them?" William asked.

"Not sure. I have so much to do and then there is church camp next week."

"Remember, Emancipation Day is next Monday—camp is not until weekend. You can make some arrangements with their grandmother, take Kianna, and you two have a nice day out," William encouraged. He sat down on the bed and helped me fold the clothes.

"Oh, that sounds good. Thanks for suggesting it. I'll do that."

As planned, on August 1st, Emancipation Day, I got up early, completed my chores and by 10:30 Kianna and I were ready to leave.

"Time you planning on getting back, Angie?" William asked, yawning and stretching. He was still in bed.

"We should be back by 5:30 or so. Why?" I asked. He turned over on his stomach.

"Thinking I can either meet you at the bus terminal this evening, or even at Mrs. Mackee's so I can help you with Kianna. You know you always complaining that once she on the road she doesn't like walking. Then we can stop at the new ice cream place by the bus terminal and get some ice cream."

"Wow! What's gotten into you? You probably slept on the right side of the pillow," I teased.

Beware when your spouse is suddenly being nice or going out of their way to please you.

"Wow! What's gotten into you? You probably slept on the right side of the pillow," I teased.

"Anyway, sounds good." I bent over, kissed him, and Kianna followed suit.

"Okay. See you at Mrs. Mackee—5:30 the latest," William said, snuggling deeper under the sheet. I left home in high spirits. *So glad Will thought about picking us up this evening.*

When Randy, Shonette, and Kevin Jr., saw us, they were thrilled and began jumping up and clapping. Immediately, Shonette, eight, wanted to show me the new steps she learned at her ballet dance class.

"Angie, how you doing, girl? And this little woman of yours getting so big," Mrs. Mackee said, hugging me, then taking Kianna.

"Gran, you knew they did coming?" Randy, ten, asked, suspiciously eyeing his grandmother.

"Yes, I knew....."

"So why you didn't tell us?" Shonette interrupted, stopping her newly learned steps and accusingly looking at her grandmother.

"'Cause I didn't want nobody asking me how long more we got to wait to see Auntie Angie and Kianna, what time they coming, and all the other questions," Mrs. Mackee said, beckoning me to follow her to the kitchen.

We spent the day playing games, watching movies, and pushing the children on the swing. The saying goes, 'Time flies when you're having fun.' It was soon time for us to leave and we were ready and waiting by 5 PM. While waiting on William, we enjoyed a Bill Cosby comedy on tape. The film was so good that I didn't realize it was already

6 PM and William wasn't there yet. I got up and looked down the street, but he was nowhere in sight. Impatiently, Kianna threw her feeding cup to the floor and started fussing. She didn't like having on her shoes while still in the house. Eventually, at 6:30, when William didn't show to pick us up and I didn't hear from him, we left. Night quickly approached, and I wanted to reach home before it was dark. *I should've never let William talk me into this. I should've known better. Maybe he was late with whatever he was doing and will meet us at the terminal, instead.*

He didn't.

By the time I got home it was almost 8 PM. Mom, Aunt Joy, and Gloria were on the porch. Gloria came and took Kianna.

I noticed a grim expression on Mom's face. I was too exhausted to worry. I proceeded to my apartment.

"Come upstairs a little, Angie," Gloria shouted.

"I'm tired. Kianna is not easy to carry anymore, you know. Keep her while I rest a little, then I'll come get her for her bath."

As expected, William wasn't there. Exhausted, I flopped down at the end of the burgundy half circle sofa. Sitting there, I got the feeling something was wrong. I slowly raised my eyes and looked at the opposite wall. My mouth dropped open. The framed wedding photo of William and me that usually hung there, wasn't. Without getting up, I began looking around the room. *Why would Will take down the picture? Or I wonder if it fell. But had it fallen, where would he put it?* Then I realized my large bridal shower book and wedding album, which had a permanent home on the magazine rack of the center table, weren't there either. *What on earth is going on?* Forgetting my exhaustion, I sprang to my feet and started looking around our home.

In Kianna's bedroom, I found her cradle bed rolled up and tied with a string as if not in use. There was no evidence of her—no clothes, no shoes, no toys—absolutely nothing! By this time, I felt faint and I placed my hand on my chest, trying to still my thumping heart. I dashed to our bedroom. The first thing I noticed, the bed well-made—something William never did, and I recalled leaving him in bed that morning. Normally, I would return and find the bed as slept in the night before. The rack where we kept our clothes, which were worn but not yet ready for laundry, was bare, except for William's clothes. Certainly, my night clothes, a pair of blue pants, and a pink plaid blouse were hanging there when I left. Only William's shoes were on the shoe rack! I pulled open the wardrobe. Not a piece of my clothing was in sight - only William's. *Now, this is crazy!*

Realizing the trend, I rushed to the bathroom. Only William's laundered underclothes were on the organizer. My undergarments had disappeared.

Tears of frustration and hurt blinded my eyes. *I cannot believe this.* The traces of a woman and child were completely wiped from our home—But why? *Did William bring a woman here today and didn't want her to know he was married?*

I went upstairs to my parents' home.

My mother, Gloria, and Aunt Joy had moved to the kitchen and sat at the dining table. Kianna slept in her playpen, not far away. At my entrance, their conversation ceased. Pulling a chair away from the table I sat down. My mother still carried that disturbed expression on her face and I figured they had to know something, but no one said anything. Their stares sent a chill through me.

"I gave Kianna her bath," Gloria said, smiling, "and Aunt Joy fed her."

"Good. Thanks."

"She growing too sweet, Angie. Care she, girl," Aunt Joy said in her soft sing-song voice. Silence fell over us again and it became unbearable. I shifted in my seat, wanting to bring the stillness to an end.

"I cannot find any personal things for Kianna or myself anywhere," I said to no one in particular.

"What yo' mean yo' can't find any personal things fo' you and Kianna?" Mom responded, sucking her teeth.

"That's what I mean, Mom. Kianna's crib bed is tied up; there are no toys, shoes, or clothes for her anywhere. Wedding photo gone from the wall. I don't see my clothes, or shoes, wedding shower book, album—even the organizer in the bathroom is cleared of my things. I really don't know what's happening," I finished, warm tears rolling down my cheeks. There was silence for another thirty seconds or so when suddenly Sean, my youngest brother said, "Angie, when you and Kianna wasn't home today, William had a girl in the house all the time and he left with her late this afternoon before you and Kianna come back. And she nice too. She tall and dark and she got Gheri curl."

"What!" I wanted to scream. Sean confirmed my worst fears, but the words were barely audible; multiple feelings of embarrassment, hurt, and anger simultaneously enveloped me.

"I will kill him," I said, between clenched teeth, more to myself than anyone else. Getting up and picking up my daughter, who suddenly seemed to weigh a ton, I felt the remaining energy drain from my body.

"Don't get yo' self in any trouble, Angie," Mom said. "And go and look carefully fo' yo' clothes. They got to be somewhere 'cause he ain't leave here with anything."

"And Angie, yo' cousin, Raymond say call he. He say he got something to tell you," Aunt Joy said.

Our things must be under the bed. Descending the fifteen stairs, halfway down, I turned back.

"On second thought, keep this child tonight for me," I said, placing Kianna gently back in her play pen. She began shifting from side to side. I bent over and patted her lightly back to sleep.

"Angie, you better stay here tonight too," Mom said.

"Mom, I cannot believe y'all right here, know this, and said nothing to William. It's as if y'all side with him to betray me. I can't believe this. My own family!"

"So, now you trying to blame us fo' what happening to you?" Mom responded, irritation evident in her voice. "Don't blame me. In the first place we tell you he ain't no use. You wouldn't listen, so don't expect me to clean up yo' mess now."

"I don't expect you to clean up my mess, but I'm your daughter. You should've said something to him."

I went on my way without looking over my shoulders, but made a mental note to call Raymond, Aunt Joy's son. *I wonder what he wants.*

"Angie, I can keep yo' company if you want," Gloria volunteered.

"No thanks," I shouted from halfway down the stairs.

At my apartment, I crawled to the side of the bed and peeked under. Everything missing was there, packed in a large suitcase and plastic shopping bags. *I can't believe this. I can't believe it.* I sighed, retraced my steps, and flung myself down on the sofa. Instantly, I sprang up. That part of the sofa was wet. *No, they couldn't be doing that on my bed and on my sofa too!* Anger, hurt, and scorn like I had never known before welled up within me. Had William been there then, I couldn't have been held accountable for what may have happened to him. I entered the kitchen, and with trembling hands, picked out the sharpest and largest kitchen knife I could find. I sat in another chair, placed it beside me, and waited on William's return home, hoping he would show up that night.

While waiting, the real Angie told me to take a shower, get something to eat, pray, and deal with the situation in a different manner. But the vengeful Angelique was plotting every move she'd make when William entered the door. Yielding to vengeful Angelique, I waited for about two hours. Then, as if it were a normal night, William unlocked the door and entered the apartment shortly after 11.

"Hi, Angie, sorry I couldn't make it to pick up you and Kianna. Had a good day?" he asked, glancing quickly in my direction, fidgeting with his keys on the ring, a malicious smile plastered his face. Jumping out of the chair I rushed at him, the knife raised high in my hand. William, taken by surprise, his eyes widened, and he dashed to one side of the dining table.

"Angelique, what's with you? Something came up and I couldn't pick up you and Kianna as we plan'. You ain't even give me a chance to explain."

"You liar! What something?" I screamed so hard, I felt the strain at the back of my throat. I dashed to his side of the table.

"What came up? You spend all your time wiping the trace of your wife and child out of the house to entertain your whore? That's what came up?" He dodged me around the table, I pulled chairs out, blocking his path, but he pushed them back and kept moving swiftly around the table.

"What're you talking about?" he asked, dropping his mouth open, knitting his brows. His question and pretended gesture triggered something within me. I grabbed a chair and threw it at him. It fell with a heavy thud halfway on the tabletop, then slid the rest of the way to the floor, carrying the basket of artificial fruits and table mats with it. I rushed from the dining to the sitting room. Everything

I could get my hands on, I hurled at him—a vase which I heard shatter to pieces as it hit the refrigerator and fell to the floor, ornaments galore—some did hit him. I then threw a barstool at him, before he charged across the room and held me firmly, while I kicked and screamed.

"How could you do this to me, William? How could you? My family live right upstairs, how could you?"

All this time he said nothing. When I calmed down, he let me go. I slumped to the floor sobbing. Finally, there were no more tears. I got up and faced him. He sat motionless on the sofa.

"I've had enough of your womanizing. Wasn't it enough you having her, whoever she is? Why did you have to bring her in our home and on our bed? Consider this marriage over. And furthermore, this is my parents' apartment. I want you out by the time I return from camp meeting—that's nine days away." I stormed into the bedroom; struggled to pull the mattress and its bedding off the bed, then dragged it through the house and threw it into the yard.

". . . Wasn't it enough you having her, whoever she is? Why did you have to bring her in our home and on our bed?"

There is no greater disrespect of a marriage than a spouse defiling the marriage bed.

Even if the victim leaves the marriage, forgiveness is necessary, despite it being hard. Get help.

https://www.fionaharewood.com/resources

Two days later, accompanied by my cousin, Raymond, I found myself knocking at a woman's door—Roxanne St. Hill. A gorgeous lady answered. She had a chocolate brown complexion and wore a white midriff top and red hot pants. Standing about 5 feet 11 inches, she looked like a model. She had a body some women would die for—firm breasts, an extra neat waistline, and striking hips which curved in the right places. Please don't let this woman be Roxanne, I prayed. *Probably she is, judging from Eric's and Raymond's descriptions.*

"Good afternoon," the woman said cheerily, pulling the door halfway in behind her, stepping onto the porch, "And how may I assist you?"

Raymond stepped aside, but remained within earshot.

"I'm here to see Roxanne St. Hill." Watching her closely, my heartbeat rapidly increased.

"I am. But do I know you?" the woman asked, tilting her head, looking at me from head to toes.

"I don't think so, but I believe you know my husband."

"Who is your husband?" Roxanne shifted from one foot to the other, then pulled the door shut as if to block out voices from traveling inside.

"You spent last Monday—the holiday—at our home with him."

"Oh, you mean William." Roxanne sighed audibly; her lips parted into a beautiful smile revealing perfect white teeth. She made me angry.

"What's there to smile about?" I asked, placing one hand on my hip, taking a step toward her. I felt Raymond draw closer.

"But why're you interested? You pick up his daughter and went along anyway. William said is only a matter of weeks before the divorce becomes final."

"Then I'm here to set the record straight," I said, advancing another step closer and pointing my right index finger at her. "William and I live together. Monday last, I spent the day at a friend's while William had plans for you to be at our home. He talked me into waiting on him until 5:30 when he knew he wasn't going to pick us up. He only needed to be sure I didn't return home prematurely. I suppose before you arrived, he managed to wipe all traces of his wife and child out of the apartment by hiding everything under the bed. He did all that only to give you the impression he lived alone. Lovely bachelor's apartment you thought, huh?"

All this time, Roxanne's face was expressionless. She stood with her arms folded across her naked waistline. I took a couple steps back and leaned against the rail of her porch, then continued.

"Look at you—young and strikingly beautiful. Is this the kind of person you want to be in a relationship with? If that is what you want, go right ahead, but I made that mistake and it will be great if you can learn from my experience. Anyway, thank you for your time," I finished, turning and starting down the stairs.

"Wait! Wait!" Roxanne called after me, "I have a question."

I stopped and looked over my shoulder.

"How you find me? How you know it was me?"

I turned 90 degrees, facing her squarely.

"My aunt lives three houses from here. She has four boys. This is the oldest of her sons," I said, pointing to 20-year-old Raymond. "They all know you very well and have been observing you and William for a long time." Turning around, I walked down the stairs.

"Thanks for the information and advice, but is far too late for that now."

Hearing the response, Raymond grabbed my arm. "Come on Angie, don't worry with her." He hurriedly led me away.

William and I were strangers under the same roof. I don't know if he went apartment hunting. Although I felt a serious sense of conviction that as a Christian I was being mean to my husband, I operated as if he were non-existent. I ate at my parents' and our pots were turned down—I stopped cooking for him. Many times, he tried talking to me, but I refused to listen to anything he said. Something within told me to pack William's belongings and throw him out or gather my things and leave. Either way, I couldn't find the courage to do it.

Something within told me to pack William's belongings and throw him out or pack my things and leave. Either way, I couldn't find the courage to do it.

When you cannot find the courage to take action, counseling should be the next resort. Counselors should be able to assist you in making the right decision.

I arrived home Friday evening and met Pastor Jagdeo and William waiting on me. Pastor Jagdeo was William's Pastor initially, before becoming mine too. He was kind, jovial, and a man of integrity who stood on biblical principles.

"Hi Pastor," I greeted him, extending my arm, receiving a firm handshake. He probably noticed I didn't even glance in William's direction.

"Hi Angelique, how're you? I haven't been seeing you at church, lately."

"I know, Pastor, but I plan to change that soon." Resting my pocketbook in a chair, I leaned against the wall. William and Pastor Jagdeo were sitting on the half circle sofa. *I can't believe he sat the man of God on the same sofa he and Roxanne desecrated.*

"I'm sorry to drop in on you without notice, Angelique, but your husband didn't want me to put it off one hour longer."

"Oh really? What's the sudden urgency?" I threw William a quick, but nasty look. He started nervously cracking his knuckles.

"If I'm not imposing, will you sit down for a couple minutes, Angelique?" Pastor Jagdeo said.

I took a seat opposite them on the smaller sofa, and wrapped my legs one over the other.

"Angelique, William explained that he made a mistake and it seems as if you intend to hold it against him for always. I do not know what the mistake is. . ."

"I can tell you," I interrupted, uncrossing my legs and sitting forward in one quick motion. Uncomfortably, William folded his arms, sat upright and daringly stared at me.

"I'm not certain that is important, Angelique," Pastor Jagdeo continued quickly. "What is important is, as Christians we need to forgive, and as the Bible says, 'seventy times seven.'"

"I know that well Pastor, but I cannot believe you're telling me it's not important for you to note that my husband brought one of his women into my home and on my bed. And of course, I also know they did not just lie in it. Neither did they just sit on the sofa both of you are sharing now." The pastor seemed confused; his jaw fell, and he quickly looked down at the sofa then up at me again. "If I recall clearly, the Bible also says we can put away the other, if one commits adultery."

"Pastor," William said getting up, "She is blowing this out of proportion."

"Oh yeah? So, I'm lying on you yet again?" I asked, getting to my feet also.

"Angie, not saying you lying, but you exaggerating the situation."

Our argument was heated. We only stopped when Pastor Jagdeo buried his face in his hands. After we stopped fussing, he looked up.

"I suppose both of you are ready to listen to me now," he said, looking from one to the other. I nodded and sat down again. William did likewise.

Pastor Jagdeo counseled us extensively. He condemned William's actions and recommended further counseling. He also let me know he wouldn't suggest I continue, or end the marriage; it was my decision, but he proposed I pray about it. Then he reminded us of our daughter and said whatever decisions we made, we needed to consider the impact it would have on her. Before Pastor Jagdeo left, William stood up and thanked him for coming and sharing with us. Then he turned to me.

"Angie," he said, "I know that you are probably tired of hearing me say I'm sorry, but please, for the last time, accept my apology. Can you find it in your heart to forgive me and we move on from here?"

I sat lost in thought; William and Pastor Jagdeo waiting for my response. Those ugly thoughts of him and Roxanne flashed across the screen of my mind.

"Angie?" William said with expectancy.

"I need some time." Rising to my feet, I left the room.

It was the morning of the start of the church's camp. I was still uncertain whether I should go, but eventually I decided it was probably the best place to be.

On day three of the meetings, the pastor preached a moving sermon. At the altar I cried out to the Lord, asking him to turn things around in our marriage and to help me forgive William. I started feeling better and the remainder of the camp meetings were spiritually uplifting.

Arriving home, I had a talk with William.

"If this is really what you want, then I will give our marriage another chance, but only on my terms. I expect to see big changes in your attitude, especially about absences from the home. Also, hear me and hear me well," I said, shaking a finger at him, "if you ever go back on your word or lift a finger to hit me, don't even waste your breath apologizing—this marriage will be over."

"Angie, I ain't going to grace you with lots of promises, but you'll see for yourself. Thanks for giving me another chance. I love you."

FOURTEEN

A Valentine to Remember

More than a year went by since the Roxanne incident. Bit by bit, I noticed positive changes in William. He was home after work most days and we started socializing again. He also began honoring his financial obligations. The only thing William didn't do, however, was go back to church. I hoped he would eventually.

Then it was Valentine's Day. William and I didn't make any plans, but while at work, I decided it would be good to prepare a dinner for two. With him being as unpredictable as the weather, it was unwise to go ahead and plan a dinner without informing him, so, I called William that morning from work.

"I have a good idea," I said.

"As usual," William laughed. "Go ahead, all ears."

"Since we have no plans for Valentine's, I'll prepare dinner for two. Think you can be home by 7:30?

"Sounds good to me. I'll be home before that," he said.

I left work at 3 and by 7 I had finished my dinner preparation with my two sisters' help. One of my brothers assisted, changing my dining room curtains to a rich red and white lace. A white linen tablecloth, red napkins with white ceramic holders, candles, and a vase of eight fresh red roses added a terrific splendor to the room. I chose the menu with William in mind. I placed the food in Pyrex dishes and left them in the oven to keep warm. It was a wonderful ambience.

"I thank y'all so much. I couldn't get through this alone," I said, handing Kianna to Gloria. I didn't want her disrupting our special evening. She would spend the night with my family.

"Angie, glad to help and glad you happy but..." Her voice trailed off. She took Kianna's hand and started for the door.

"Gloria, what is it?" I asked.

"Nothing man, I don't want upset you," she replied, lifting Kianna to her shoulders. Kianna loved heights.

"Well, you will have me worrying if you don't tell me. Promise. I won't get upset."

"Girl is only a thought—I only hope you don't go through all o' this for William and he don't show up," Gloria said, holding my gaze.

Gloria's words hit home, and I looked away, realizing she could be right.

"Nah, that won't happen. William knows I'm doing this, but thanks for your concern, Sis," I responded.

"Girl, for you sake, I hope you right," she said. We both laughed, then they were gone. For a moment I thought about what Gloria said. *No, Angie, don't spoil this evening.*

Think positive! I took my shower, then dressed in a two-piece sleep wear. I grabbed a book and sat down in the sitting room, waiting for him. It was seven thirty-five, but I wasn't anxious because he was seldom on time.

The barking of a dog outside startled me and I got up, heart racing. I glanced at the clock on the wall and was stunned. It was 10:45 PM. *Did I sleep that long? I must have been really tired. But William isn't home yet.* I became annoyed. *He had better have a good excuse.* Turning off the lights, I retired to bed, but couldn't sleep. I tossed and turned. The bedroom seemed hotter than usual, and I counted the hours, passing by. It wasn't until after 3 AM my counting stopped, and I drifted off into a fitful sleep, then woke up again. It was 5:15 AM and William's place beside me was still vacant. I can't describe the anguish I felt. I willed myself up and started to prepare for work. Passing the dining room on my way to the shower, I stopped and stared at the undisturbed Valentine's preparation.

"What a waste!" I sighed.

With a heavy heart and slow steps, I made my way upstairs to my parents' home to say goodbye to Kianna before leaving for work.

"Girl, you look beat. What happen?" Gloria asked. She stopped buttering toast and stared at me.

"Why something has to happen? Morning." I responded and continued to her room, where Kianna slept when she spent time with my family.

"Well the blind can tell—how was dinner?" she asked, walking away from the table and following at my heels, with the bread knife still in her hand.

"Please, Gloria, I don't want to discuss it."

"Y'all two ain't tired? What the argument 'bout so early in the morning?" my mother's voice came from behind.

"No argument, trying to find out from Angie why she look like that."

"Okay, okay," I said, leaning against the ice green painted wall. "Like you said, Gloria. After all we went through to prepare dinner, William ain't show up."

"Gosh, I'm sorry, Angie," my sister said, "Valentine's night of all the nights, he choose to spend away from he wife--not even part of the night, but the whole night. I couldn't have a husband like he. Don't worry, girl—the longest rope got an end." Gloria repeated one of my mother's sayings which means that in spite of how bad a situation, it will not last forever.

Mom stood there shaking her head from side to side. She didn't say a word.

After planting a kiss on Kianna's cheek, I said goodbye and hurried home to get my pocketbook before leaving for work. William was on his way in. We passed each other like strangers, yet, even strangers speak to each other sometimes. I sat on the bus and couldn't hold back the warm tears that rolled down my cheeks. *Why didn't I listen to my parents so many years ago? Why didn't I? I would have spared myself all this pain.*

FIFTEEN

Dark Night of the Soul

After being employed at the law firm for over six years, I started getting restless. The fact there was no room for promotion furthered my dissatisfaction. I successfully applied to fill a vacancy advertised in the *Chronicle* newspaper and was appointed project secretary of a large government pharmaceutical corporation. Benefits increased, and my salary tripled.

At the beginning of the fourth year of our marriage, after being ill for nearly a month, I visited the doctor and found out I was eight weeks pregnant. I was elated, and since Kianna was four, I felt there was a wide enough gap. Before this, I had longed for a son. On my way home from the doctor, I thought about William and was concerned, not knowing how he would react to the news. Anytime the talk of another child came up, William mostly said he had all he wanted in Kianna. Things were reasonably good between us for a while since the incident with Roxanne, and the Valentine's issue. We had a few disagreements, yes, but nothing out of the ordinary.

"So, what did the doctor say?" William asked, halfway through our dinner that night. A sense of fear suddenly gripped me, and I kept my eyes on my plate. I felt his eyes on me. Fear was replaced by anger. *Look, I really don't care if he's annoyed—this is his child too.*

"So, you can't say what the doctor said?" he asked again, setting the glass down on the table a little harder than usual.

"I'm pregnant," I replied, holding his gaze. For a short while he said nothing, only sat there, rhythmically tapping his fork on his plate. Then, suddenly, he got up and pushed his chair noisily away from him.

"Know that was the least thrilling news I've received in a loooong time," he said, heading to the kitchen.

"Sorry, but it takes two," I replied.

That time around, my pregnancy took a toll on me. I became sick often and wondered how it felt being well. I figured it had to be a boy since the pregnancy was totally different from my first. Unfortunately, the news of being pregnant seemed to have either frightened William or gave him an excuse to go roaming again. Many times, he was gone for an entire weekend, claiming he had to be in one county or another on work

---

I blamed myself for getting pregnant when I knew William never wanted another child.

Abused women blame themselves. Don't play the blaming game. It's not your fault. Further, having children should be a matter of discussion between parties, and when a decision against has been agreed upon adequate precaution should be taken.

---

assignments. I blamed myself for getting pregnant when I knew William never wanted another child, but I hoped the addition to our family would create a change of heart.

There were days when I missed Miriam. Just before I started my new job, her family moved to the Essequibo Islands. I had to travel tens of miles by speed boat to see her, so we didn't see each other often and telephones weren't that prevalent in the Essequibo region.

On Friday morning, February 11, 1988, around 2:20, my water broke and slight labor pains started. The morning was still, besides light traffic passing on the road. I looked across at William, sleeping soundly. I went to the bathroom, then returned to bed. There were at least six hours before the baby would be ready to make its way into the world—no need to wake William. About an hour later, a sharp pain ripped through my abdomen, causing me to bolt upright in the bed. The pain subsided; I got up, turned on the light, and retrieved my already-packed suitcase from the wardrobe.

"What time's it? Why would you turn on the light at this time?" William asked, shading his eyes with his hand.

"My water broke; it's 3:35," I responded, sitting down at the foot of the bed, unzipping the suitcase, making my final check.

"Gosh man! I now starting to get a good sleep," he sucked his teeth and turned over on his stomach. Quickly William dozed off again. I sat there looking at him. About ten minutes later, he woke up again.

"Shucks!" he said, sitting up hurriedly. "You wanna go to the hospital now, or can you hold on some more?"

"We can leave home around six," I responded.

"Then lie down and get some rest—turn off the light too."

By the time I switched off the light and returned to bed, he snored lightly.

I couldn't sleep. By five-thirty I was up again.

"Get up, William, get up," I said, shaking him.

"Uh uh, uh."

William got up, his mouth stretched twice its size, and until he made it into the shower, I could hear him suck his teeth every couple of minutes. Finally, the cab arrived, and we left home around six-thirty.

"Angie, hope you know I can't stay with you. I've got things to take care of. This accounting certificate I am studying for calls for more'n I ever bargained for," he said, riding in the car beside me.

"I didn't expect you to," I replied, staring at the moist dewy surface of the long, winding East Bank Public Road.

This wasn't my first pregnancy, so I wasn't overly anxious. I thought I knew exactly what to expect, but later found out how wrong I was. Although labor with Kianna was lengthy and extremely difficult, it was bearable. This time, however, excruciating pains ripped through my abdomen. I rolled on the bed, tossed, and cried out. Because of no dilation, the baby was still too high so my doctor induced labor for the entire night. Induction seemed to have tripled the pain, but proved futile.

Crying out in agony and tossing from side to side on my hospital bed, I visualized dying. The scene of my family and friends filing around my coffin haunted me all through that ordeal. During those moments, when I thought I was face-to-face with death, I made a vital decision—If I lived to walk out of that hospital, I was going to unearth all the strength and courage needed to walk away from an abusive marriage and a husband who cared nothing about me.

The following morning, the doctors made a quick decision to perform an emergency caesarian section because my baby's heartbeat had slowed. *I may have made my bed hard, but I didn't have to keep lying on it hard. I deserved to be happy.* Those were my thoughts as orderlies quickly wheeled me into the operating room.

When I regained consciousness, I was being rolled down the hospital corridors to my room. My body trembled violently. With one heave and a brisk movement, the orderlies transferred me gently from the stretcher onto the bed. Two nurses tenderly tucked my trembling body under a heavy blanket and attended to my needs.

"Congratulations on your son!" one said, smiling and adjusting the bed head.

"Thank you, Nursssse Fraser," I smiled weakly after reading her name badge. "I knew it had to be a boy, he was too…different from…my first pregnancy."

Mere words took intense effort and caused pain to my abdomen.

"No, no. Pleeease, don't talk, Mrs. Larrier, that will hurt the incision," she warned, gesturing with her hand.

"Where's he? Boy, he gave me licks! I have two pinches waiting for him when he gets here." I spoke between chattering teeth, ignoring Nurse Fraser's warning signal of her index finger over her lips.

"Oh, no such thing! He's too cute," the other nurse said, smiling. Her name badge read, Cadogon.

"He'll be with you within an hour. In the meantime, get some rest. We've got other patients, so see you later."

I lay in bed trying to stay awake, anxiously awaiting the nurse to bring my baby. During our few good times, William had said if it were a boy, he would name him after him, William Junior, but I had said William would be his middle name. I tried to picture what he looked like, but exhaustion probably took over because when the nurse eventually rolled in the baby, she remarked, "sleepy head, you've been out for the past two and a half hours. He's all yours now!"

I tried sitting up, but had to be assisted by the nurse because any slight movement triggered pain in the surgical area. But cuddling him in my arms, and kissing his pink rosy cheeks, made all the physical and emotional pain disappear. Gazing down at him I felt pangs of love for William, which I thought were dead. *It would be harder walking away than I thought.* He curled up and wriggled in my arms, and I concluded, he had his own features; chubby face, pink full lips and a flat nose—I couldn't see William or myself in him. He weighed seven pounds one ounce and was the picture of health and full of energy. When he cried, he opened his tiny mouth to the fullest and screamed with all his might.

I spent ten days in the hospital. Of the ten, William visited me twice. The day after Junior's birth was the first time. He continually sent messages with my family, saying he had to attend one class or another, and it would be critical if he was absent or late for any of them. During the time in hospital, I planned how I would execute the separation from William.

On day eight, William finally made his second visit.

"I'm homesick. I'm tired of being here," I complained, looking around the bare hospital room, which contained only the bed I lay on, a baby's crib, a cupboard, and two wooden chairs. William sat next to the bed, holding Junior.

"What nonsense you saying? You should be glad for the rest, girl. You ain't know the longer you stay in here is better for you?"

"Excuse me? Or you mean, *better for you*? Are you trying to say my being in here is giving you more time to do whatever you want? Well, Sweetie, don't let me stop you because whether I'm home or not, you still do what you want to do. I'll be speaking to my doctor on his next visit, about my discharge."

William sprang from the chair, placed Junior in the crib, and began pacing. His chest rose and fell with each furious breath. Suddenly, halting in mid-stride, he turned to me.

"I never told you I wanted another child! You were the one who went and got pregnant! Now you expect me to put aside all I have to do, to nurse you and a baby."

"Did I ever say that?" I said, raising my voice, and sitting up in the bed. "You are behaving as if I made this child alone."

"Now, Angelique, you listen to me…" William started, his eyes wild, holding out an index finger. A knock on the door intruded the moment. Gloria, Clement, and three of my other siblings entered. Gloria quickly glanced from one of us to the other. Her jaws fell.

"Did we interrupt something?"

"No, I was just leaving," William interjected. Then he briskly left the room, slamming the door behind him.

"What was that all about?" Eric asked, pointing after him at the closed door.

Exhausted, I gratefully sank back into the bed.

"What y'all have there to eat?" I asked, although not hungry.

Sighing, Gloria shook her head, removing the bag from her shoulder, rested it on the tiny cupboard-top and dived into it.

"Not your favorite, but as usual, Mom says it's good for you, especially now. Soup. Taste good too."

"Leave it on the cupboard, I'll eat it a little later," I said, looking across at the door, at the sound of another knock. Clement answered, letting in four of my co-workers.

Together with my siblings, they made the end of my visiting hours better than it started.

Finally, two days later I was discharged. I didn't bother to call William. My parents collected us after mid-day. Kianna, now four and a half years old, was overjoyed with her baby brother and wanted to hold him immediately. She wouldn't rest until I allowed her to sit and place Junior in her lap.

"Mommy, he so soft and he wriggling," she said, smiling. I took back Junior.

"You were like that when you were born," I smiled.

"Oh no, oh no," she said. "He is a boy. I am a girl."

We spent a few hours at my parents', and then went to our apartment. By this time, we had moved from below my parents' home to a bigger apartment--the second of three houses in the yard. Gloria and my younger sister, Ingrid, went with me and started putting things in order from the time they entered. William wasn't good at housekeeping.

Around 5:30 I heard William's keys being inserted into the door lock.

"Angie?" He called out with a note of surprise.

"Yes."

"You alright? he asked, entering the bedroom, wearing a broad smile.

"Yes, I'm fine," I replied, looking up at him. I was nursing Junior. He lightly stroked his head, looking down at him with an approving smile.

"Glad you're home, but I was expecting you more like tomorrow. We have a study meeting tonight at one of the guy's home in Campbellville. It wouldn't be for too long, so I'll go and be back pretty early."

"Do you have to go?"

"Yes. Why?"

"My stomach aches and I need some help with him while I get some rest. I don't think he will sleep anytime soon."

"You know something?" he paused. "I've noticed all you do lately is complain and fuss. That's the main reason why I didn't show up at the hospital all those days. Sometimes, I'm tired of it. You need to change your attitude."

"I've noticed all you do lately is complain and fuss. That's the main reason why I didn't show up at the hospital all those days..."

The abuser attributes blame. Don't settle for it.

I didn't respond. Tears stung the back of my eyelids. A part of me agreed with him, but another part didn't. Shortly after, William was ready again and he went his jolly way.

Adjusting to home after the hospital proved challenging and more than ever, I felt a deep sense of emptiness. William claimed he had to meet with his study group after work, when he didn't have a class. I still cooked for him and did his laundry, but when it came to making our marriage work, I simply stopped trying. Loneliness engulfed me and I longed for the end of my maternity leave. There were times in my life when I knew exactly what I should do, but couldn't get it done. During that time, I should have held firmer to my spiritual beliefs, but I didn't. Even attending church and being in communion with God, which I had once loved, didn't appear to fill the void anymore. I stopped going to church.

SIXTEEN

Even Kicked

It was a sunny Saturday morning, about one month after I came home from the hospital with Junior. I was preparing breakfast, while William got ready to leave home. Kianna was playing with her brother. Suddenly, there was a loud crash, sounding like it came from my parents' home. I left the breakfast and dashed to my parents'. There I found my brother, Steve, had been assisting Mom changing curtains in the sitting room, when his foot slipped, and he came crashing down with the China cabinet. Literally everything broke when the cabinet hit the floor. Thankfully, Steve only sustained a few minor cuts.

I returned home about ten minutes later.

"You so darn fast," William said, appearing at the bathroom door, white foam from the toothpaste around his mouth. "You doing something, leave it and gone, and mind other people business—darn fast!"

"Like yo' mother," I replied without thinking. That was one time I wished I could take back what I said. Shocked, William's head jerked back, and he looked at me spitefully.

"Oh! You telling me 'bout my mother, girl?" he said, rinsing his mouth quickly.

Shucks, ah gotta get outta here. I braced myself to run. It was too late! I darted toward the kitchen door, but William dashed from the bathroom, and the next thing I knew, Junior's hot water flask came sailing across the room. I dodged, and it went through the glass paned window. I tripped on Kianna's doll house and fell to the floor. William viciously kicked me several times—the tip of his shoes sending piercing pains to my side and back. I screamed, folding myself in the fetal position, attempting to shield my face with my hands. By then, Kianna and Junior were screaming.

William viciously kicked me several times – the tip of his shoes sending piercing pains to my side and back.

These actions should never be tolerated.

https://www.fionaharewood.com/resources

The next thing I knew, my mother was there wildly pelting blows on William with a flat piece of wood. She got a good few lashes in before two of my brothers came running in.

"Mom! Mom! No, no!" Steve shouted. He and Clement grabbed the wood, rescuing William.

"You makin' it a habit now. Always beating up on she because nobody don't get in y'all business. She ain't drop from a tree," my mother said, panting breathlessly. My brothers took her outside and then Steve returned alone. "Angie, you alright?" he asked, extending his arm towards me. My side and back ached. I took his arm and slowly got up. Kianna and Junior were still screaming.

For a minute or so, William appeared in shock, leaning against the concrete kitchen wall, his two hands hanging limply at his side, blood trickling slowly from his forehead. He then hurried to the bedroom, and a minute later came out again. With his shirt thrown on one shoulder, and mopping the cut on his forehead with a handkerchief, he left the house without saying a word. That was the last time William raised his hand to hit me or his foot to kick me.

About four weeks after that incident, I resumed work. The pharmaceutical project was behind schedule and everyone who could, was invited to work overtime. I couldn't really spare the time I had two babies to take care of, but I was comfortable with my mother babysitting for me, and I preferred to be at work. There were days when I was on the job from 7 AM and was scarcely home before 8 or 9 PM for five, sometimes six days a week. From the time I left home in the mornings, I was a totally different person; it seemed like I left all the cares behind. For most of the time I was busy at work and had a few great coworkers who kept me laughing. But when it was time to return home, I felt depressed. It was only God's mercies, my job, and my two children that kept me going.

About two months after I returned to work, the supervisor of the stores department, Raul, with whom I had developed a friendship, was leaving for Russia for studies. The staff planned what we called an *After Lunc*h—a party at a disco. Those were held basically on Saturdays, and they started around 1 PM. Being the church girl in the group, I told the others I would only attend because of my friend, Raul.

Without telling William, I went. It was my first time in a disco. At that time, the song "We've Only Just Begun (The Romance is Not Over)" by Glenn Jones was at the top of the charts and it was almost everyone's favorite. At that time, I was only into gospel music, but I couldn't resist that song when it played on the radio. While at the disco, that song started playing and Raul asked me to dance.

"You're crazy, I can't dance," I said.

"Come on, I will guide you."

It was my first dance and I did enjoy it. I had just sat down when Rick, another of my co-workers, touched me. Looking around, he pointed ahead. Turning my head, I followed his gaze and the direction he indicated. William and a group of friends, none of whom I knew, entered the disco. My heart began thumping wildly. They chose two tables in front of us. I was thankful for the dark disco with lights flashing on and off only at the dance floor area. William sat sideways, so had he searched the faces of the people at the table to his right he would have seen me. Thank God, he didn't. I wanted to pray, asking God not to let him see me, but was consumed by guilt. God is good, though. Within forty-five minutes, William and his crew got up and left. About an hour later, I made my way home.

For another six months, William and I lived under one roof and slept in the same bed, but we were strangers. We didn't quarrel much anymore because neither of us cared what the other did.

In November of that year, 1988, the job at the project came to an end. I was due to start working at the head office, but instead, I applied for my vacation and submitted my resignation.

PART TWO

A Fresh Start

SEVENTEEN

Bye-Bye Love

"Madam? What would you like?" The air hostess asked a little louder the second time. I heard her faintly before, but I was lost in thoughts.

"Um, so sorry," I said with a start, only then realizing my face was wet. I hurriedly wiped away the tears with the back of my hand.

"That's okay," the hostess replied, handing me a napkin. "Chicken, turkey, or fish?"

"No, thank you, I'll have a hot chocolate," I replied.

"Sure," she said, flashing a comforting smile then continued wheeling the dinner cart down the aisle of the MD83 aircraft.

For the last six months William and I spent together, no matter what he did, and how badly it hurt, I didn't cry anymore. Now, here I was, on an aircraft to Barbados, tears cascading down my cheeks. I felt numb and an incomparable sense of loss and loneliness tugged at my heart.

Informing my parents about my plans to leave my children with them and live abroad didn't go well at first. Leaving without the children was the toughest decision of my life, and even now, it still brings tears to my eyes.

"You don't have to go overseas to get rid o' William, Angie. You can come back home," Dad had said. Upon arriving home from work late that evening, I found Mom in bed. Her bedroom smelled like a hospital, from the Limacol she used on her forehead to relieve a headache. Dad was at his little desk at one corner of the bedroom, reading the newspaper. I dropped myself down in a wooden Morris chair by her bedside.

"Dad, I don't want to come back home. I need to be as far away as possible from all of this. Also, how I plan on leaving will make William really angry, and I don't want to risk his retaliation. And remember, I tried leaving him before but couldn't do it. I know the wisest thing would be to get out of this marriage, but I'm afraid if I stay here, it will be really hard. I may even reconcile with William. I believe distance and time between us is the answer. I really don't want to do this to my children, but I have to do it for me."

"Then take the children wit' yo'," Mom said, annoyance in her voice.

"Mom, I can't. I'm not even sure what to expect, and quite often I hear people complain of how difficult it can be living with other people, especially when you're away from your home country. Sometimes, they treat you as if your welcome has expired. If that happens, I don't want my children to be suffering with me. They will be better off with you all until I'm able to get things sorted out. Yes, Sarah promises to assist me with obtaining legal status in the country, but she's not sure how long that process will take. Kianna will not even be able to go to school without the legal documents. I cannot take her out of school.

Junior is only a baby. If I take him, who will care for him while I go job hunting and when I start working? It won't be sensible to take them with me now. I really need help from you both," I pleaded.

Mom sucked her teeth.

"You hear wha' I say? I not keepin' them," Mom had said. "Them children belong wit' their mother, at least."

"Okay, no problem. I'll leave them with a friend then because I cannot take them with me now." I got up and headed for the bedroom door.

"Which friend?" Mom had asked behind me.

"Agnes at my job," I said, continuing on my way out.

"Angie, don't get hasty. Come back," Dad had said.

I turned and leaned against the door frame, looking expectantly from one to the other.

"Evelyn," Dad started, "I believe it will be better fo' them pickney stay here. Is better fo' Angie settle first, then think 'bout carryin' them."

"Them children already ain't got no proper father, now you, their mother, goin' and leave them too." Mom sighed. "Anyway, if that is what you want to do, I ain't goin' stop you, but ah prefer they be with me than wit' anybody else. So, you plan divorcing William?"

"Yes. I'm finished with him. He doesn't care about me or the children and I will not continue in an unhappy marriage. Life is too short. After I'm settled in Barbados, I plan to return for my children. I will file my divorce then because I don't have the time to do it now."

"Okay." Her eyes held a faraway look.

"Is alright wit' me," Dad finished.

"Thanks, Mom and Dad." I hurried out before they changed their minds.

Three weeks before my resignation, I began executing my plans. The first thing I did was prepare Kianna for my absence.

"Kianna, Mommy has to tell you something, but you got to promise, never to tell Daddy," I said one night when I finished reading her a bedtime story.

"I not going tell he. Tell me," she said eagerly.

"Promise?" I asked.

"Yes, promise," she replied, sitting up with interest.

"Mommy has to go away for a while. I cannot take you and Junior with me. I have to leave you with Grandma and Granddad, but I will come back afterwards and get both of you. And while I am away, I will send you and Junior nice things, like clothes and toys and a tricycle."

"Toys and a tricycle!" she echoed, clapping her hands. "I want a yellow tricycle." She then knitted her eyebrows. "Why you got to go, though?"

"Mommy is tired of all the fighting and quarrelling with Daddy."

"Good. I glad he will not be able to beat you no more. And you know Mommy, I was real frighten' the day when he run you with the knife and you run up at Grandma. I hide behind the chair when I see he coming back 'cause I thought he would cut me with the knife." Kianna got off the bed and motioned me to follow her. She led me to the sitting room, showing where and how she hid. Those words and her actions tore at my heart, watching her huddle behind a chair.

"...Mommy, I was real frighten' the day when he run you with the knife and you run up at Grandma. I hide behind the chair when I see he coming back 'cause I thought he would cut me with the knife."

Every effort must be taken to shield our children from these unsafe situations.

https://www.fionaharewood.com/resources

"No, Daddy will never hurt you. You know he loves you and Junior."

"Yes, I know. I will miss you though, Mommy. But I will write you letters and send you postcards," she said, propping her jaw with one hand.

That was basically how our conversations went. Eventually, as soon as the topic came up between us, Kianna would be the one telling me of the plans. It tugged at my heart any time those talks came up, but I realized it had to be done. As promised, Kianna never uttered a word of those conversations to her dad. During the last week before my departure, I reinforced my anticipated absence more and more to her. She was only five years old at the time, but was smart and it amazed me, the things she understood. I tried never to poison her mind against her father, yet, I could never get out of my mind scenes of her screaming and running to seek shelter under the bed, or the table, when her dad and I used to fight.

Finally, it was the eve of that fateful day.

As usual, William wasn't around so I had ample time to execute my plans. I remember that last night before my departure so well. It was my final day at work. I had much to do, including picking up my plane ticket. It was 2 AM when I finally picked up my children from my parents' home and retired to bed. William arrived home at 2:30.

Later that morning, I dressed in my uniform for work, as usual. My flight was scheduled to leave Guyana for Barbados at 4 PM. William was having his breakfast on the morning of December 1st, 1988. He had a fresh haircut and wore a blue, fashionable plaid shirt with navy pants. I gave him some quick glances from behind and asked myself for the umpteenth time that morning—*Angelique, is this really what you want to do*? It was heart wrenching, and at that point I realized I still loved William, but I had to do what was best for my children and me. I slung my bag on my shoulder, Junior on my hip, and I held Kianna with my free hand.

"Come on Kianna and Junior, tell Daddy goodbye," I said, quickly looking across at William. Unaccustomed to any communication whatsoever from me, with a quick twist of his head, William stopped eating, then waved goodbye to his children, totally oblivious I was the one really saying goodbye to him. I smiled, watching Junior who had recently learned the goodbye gesture, wave wildly at his dad.

"Bye, Daddy," Kianna said, sliding out of my grasp and heading out the door. Reaching my parents' home, I felt weak and nervous. I knew if William had a hunch of what was about to take place, it would be disastrous. Mom said she was nervous too. My father took Kianna to school as usual, and promised to bring her home at mid-day. Eric and Steve hung around to help me. I lay down to calm myself and Mom kept a look out at the front window, to see when William left for work. We waited a half-hour after his departure before we did anything. I really don't believe in revenge, but it was payback time!

Mom, Eric, Steve, and I hurried to the apartment and we swiftly moved all my personal items to my parents' home. In the meantime, my pre-arranged buyers started arriving to collect their already-paid-for items which were mainly furniture. Strangely, from the time I went downstairs and started gathering the stuff, I felt a renewed vigor. I actually enjoyed clearing the apartment. Mom said her nervousness vanished too. By 11:15 AM I closed the door to the apartment William and I shared for the final time. The only things remaining were William's clothes and his books on the polished hardwood floor. Not even a cup was left from which to drink water, or a fork with which to eat. 'The longest rope has an end,' my sister and mother quoted ever so often, and William was the rope then.

The only large items remaining unsold were the refrigerator and bed. Knowing William like the palm of my hand, I made out a receipt as if I sold them to my mother.

That afternoon, my parents, my siblings, and my children were at Timehri International Airport to see me off. After checking in, we stood around chatting. I was aware of a lump in my throat, which seemed to grow larger by the moment. Eventually, it was time for our farewell. I hugged my daughter and my baby tightly, not wanting to let them go. Finally, I released them when the attendant's voice echoed on the intercom.

"This is the final call for departing passengers traveling on BW 989 to Bridgetown, Barbados. Please board at Gate 3."

Pulling my carry-on behind me, and without another word, I walked through the checkpoint not daring to look back.

"Ladies and gentlemen, we are now arriving at Grantley Adams International Airport." The flight attendant's words jolted me back to the present. Only then did I realize the attendant had long since brought my hot chocolate. It was cold by then. I returned it and thanked her as she completed her routine checks. Looking at my watch, I realized the flight was airborne for approximately 90 minutes.

The aircraft began its descent. Gazing down on the island which I would adopt as my new home, I determined that no matter how lonely or difficult it got, it was goodbye to William and all men, for always. This chapter of my life was closed—never to be reopened.

EIGHTEEN

Flying Fish And Cou Cou

Sarah and her husband met me at the airport in Barbados. Sarah was a family friend. We grew up together, although in different districts, and she was two years my senior. Besides being about four months pregnant, and noticeably thirty, Sarah's appearance hardly changed. She was Indian and had long, straight, black hair, which she wore mainly in a tight bun at the back of her head. She stood about 5-foot tall, with round features and light brown eyes. Charles, her husband was Barbadian, about five years her senior, dark, short, and stout. In spite of his quiet disposition, he was witty and made us laugh, possibly because his words were thickly coated, with his deep Barbadian accent.

It was a forty-five minute ride to the Barrow's home, which was in St. James Parish. That was my second visit to lovely Barbados, an island of 166 square miles and referred to as *The Gem of the Caribbean Sea*—it's national dish, flying fish and cou cou. During the ride, I sat motionless in the back seat of their vehicle, glad Sarah and Charles left me to my thoughts. The family lived in a quiet neighborhood, in a typical old-fashioned Barbadian chattel house.

I spoke with my family briefly the following morning by telephone, and my mother promised to write and keep me up-to-date with everything. Since Junior was only nine months old, he had no knowledge of what happened. But Mom said Kianna cried all the way home from the airport, but was nearly her usual self the following morning. She said they heard William cursing in the yard later that night, but nobody looked out.

It was strange being away from home, and the transition to living with others wasn't easy. Sarah was talkative as usual—I knew she was trying to make me feel at home, but it was difficult. I scarcely had time to myself since Charles had a cabinet making home-based business and Sarah assisted him. During those early days, I longed for nights to be alone and dreaded daytime when I was among people.

Six days after I arrived in Barbados, on a morning when the sun seemed to be playing peek-a-boo, I stood gazing through the window. I heard a whistle and saw the postman making his way down the narrow, grassy lane, leading to the house. Climbing the two steps to the cottage, he removed an airmail envelope from the top of the pile.

"Good morning," he said, ceasing his whistling and handing me the mail.

"Good morning. Thank you," I replied, my heart racing. Anxiously, I tore open the envelope, making my way to the bedroom.

"The girl get mail!" Sarah said, smiling from her sitting position in the undersized dining room.

"Girl, I only hope it contains good news," I replied, heading to the bedroom, flopping down on the bed. I unfolded the letter and started reading.

Hi Angie:

How are you? We miss you and we praying the day will soon come, when you will be able to look back at times like these and smile. In the meantime, you have to be strong. Let me bring you up-to-date with all the happenings:

Well my child, we made a stop and reached home after nine from the airport and judging from a dark apartment, we suspected William wasn't home. About midnight your father woke me up, saying, 'Evelyn, Evelyn, you hear that?' I sat up in bed and listened. William was in the yard cursing us loudly. He said we encouraged you to move out and leave him. That you don't have to come back, but he wants his children and his things you removed from the house. He also said he would bring the police to get them. We did not look out, and eventually we heard him no more.

Well about ten o'clock that Saturday morning, we heard a knock at the door. Everybody was at home and I was feeding Junior, so I shouted to Gloria to get the door. She came back, saying William and two policemen were there. I called your father and we went downstairs to them.

One of the Officers asked us if we were Mr. and Mrs. Castor. We said yes, they showed us their IDs, and introduced themselves. The one who said he was Officer Higgins asked us if we know William. I said yes, but your father said, he used to be our son-in-law. Officer Higgins explained that William reported to them, that you moved back home with his children and his furniture and he would like to have back his children and the items from the home.

In the meantime, Kianna appeared at the top of the stairs watching us. Your father told the officers you were not there, but the children were. They then asked us for you. We said we didn't know. Then they want to know how come you are our daughter and we don't know. Neither I nor your father answered. Girl, I was shocked at William's attitude. You should have heard him as if he knows anything about taking care of the children. These were his exact words.

"Well Officer, better yet, I want my children because these people are incapable of taking care of them and I demand my children be returned to me."

Angie, I could not believe your husband said that. Since when we became incapable of taking care of these children? Well my dear child, I couldn't do anything else. Although we tried to explain that it was your wish for the children to remain with us, they told us the law states, if the mother is not around, the father has sole right to his children.

I felt sick, but I read on.

The police gave us two hours to get the children and their belongings together and to deliver them to their father. Then they asked us about the furniture, and I told them we don't have anything belonging to William or Angelique in our home. Officer Prescott said they cannot take my word for it, and will have to search our home. They had a search warrant already prepared which they showed us. Girl, it's a lucky thing you made a receipt to me for the fridge and the bed.

Anyway, William and them came upstairs and started searching. Girl, I could see the disappointment in William's face, when he realized nothing was in the living room. When they reached the kitchen, and he saw the fridge, he quickly pointed it out to them, but this is what I said,

'Hold on Officer, hold on!' Girl, I went and get the receipts and present it. The officers read it then passed it to him. The color literally drained from his face and his mouth fell open. I thought he would faint. The officers then explained to him he would have to consult a lawyer if he needed to get back whatever household items he was claiming. You should have seen him when he left behind them—his two arms hanging at his side and like he barely wanted to lift his feet. But it ain't finish there. When they were leaving, one officer reminded us that within two hours the children should be with their father or it could cause problems for us. I couldn't help crying as I packed their things and put on their shoes. Actually, everybody was crying including your father, but I was praying at the same time.

I couldn't bear it any longer. I hugged the letter to my stomach and sobbed uncontrollably. The last thing I expected to hear was William had taken the children. I didn't even consider that possibility. I couldn't visualize a father as irresponsible as William taking care of our two children. Sarah heard my sobs and rushed into the bedroom.

"Wha' happen,' Angie? Wha' happen'?" she asked, bewildered, sitting next to me on the bed, tapping my shoulders. I didn't answer. I kept on crying. When Sarah realized she wasn't going to get a response, she grabbed the letter, stood up and started reading. Still sitting on the bed, with my back against the wall, I hugged my knees to my stomach, crying, rocking, to and fro.

"Angelique, If I was you, I woulda glad he refused to accept the children. At least they still with your parents, so I can't see why you crying like that," Sarah said, when she finished reading.

"What?" I asked, looking up with tear-stained face. "Did you say William refused to take the children?"

"Wait, why you asking me that? You didn't read the letter? Look it here," Sarah said, running her finger on a few lines on the now partly crumpled yellow pages. A teary smile covered my face, and I continued reading.

> *Well girl, I sent Gloria and Eric to take them. To my surprise, about twenty minutes later they returned with the children and said they knocked about three times before William opened the door. When he saw them, he immediately slammed the door in their faces without saying one word. Well, you know your sister. She said she couldn't believe he was for real, so they kept knocking and calling even though he had slammed the door. But he remained inside the apartment, as quiet as a mouse and did not show his face again. In the meantime, Kianna kept pulling at Gloria and Eric, telling them, 'Let's go back at Grandma, let's go back at Grandma.'*
>
> *Anyway, my child, I was really glad he did not accept them, and I now have my grandchildren with me. Later that day, we asked Kianna if she wants to go and live with her father. We all laughed at her response. She said she was glad her daddy didn't open the door when they went knocking because she does not want to live with him, she only wants to see him sometimes.*
>
> *Well my dear daughter, this is all for now. Be strong and take good care of yourself. Write soon.*
>
> *Mom.*

Relief flooded my soul. I refolded the letter and placed it into the partly disfigured envelope.

Initially, the Barrows were hospitable. I was helpful and since Sarah was pregnant, she was glad for the assistance. Although I kept myself busy, I found my days were extremely long and my nights even longer. Once in bed, the tears flowed, and an unbearable heartache overwhelmed me. Sleep became a stranger, and night after night I would lie awake for hours thinking of my children and family I left behind in Guyana. Those were days when I hoped and prayed for a better tomorrow. Yet at other times, I wished that tomorrow never came. Time and again, Sarah and Charles encouraged me to go out, make friends, and enjoy myself, but I only occasionally attended church with them.

Then one day something happened that made me stop, take stock, and start counting my blessings. It was early one morning in the same month of December 1988. I turned on the television to catch CNN news. I remember so vividly, the grim faces of the anchor man and woman, reporting the plane crash. Over 270 people, including 11 on the ground, were killed when a terrorist bomb blew apart an America bound Pan-Am Boeing 747, over the Scottish town of Lockerbie. I stood with my eyes glued to the television, my body shuddering. Somebody lost a mother in that crash. Somebody lost a father, a husband, a brother, a friend, a lover. Somebody would never see their child again. There will be empty seats at many families' dinner tables this Christmas. Entire families may have been wiped out, but due to the Creator's goodness and mercy toward me, I stood there, clothed in my right mind and full of life. My situation was dismal, but I knew *as long as there was life there was the hope* that someday, I would be reunited with my children and family. All wasn't lost.

After that, I began taking life one day at a time. Sarah filed an extension of time through the Immigration Department for me. I intended to apply for a work permit a few months later.

Sarah, being pregnant, was often too sick to work, so I was given her job at $100 a week. Even though I had no experience in this field, I gladly accepted. The trade was tedious, but I hung in there. My day began at 5:30 AM. House chores had to be finished so I could start working with Charles at 7:30 AM. I sanded, polished, and screwed on hinges and locks to mahogany furniture, such as wardrobes and headboards in the dusty workshop attached to the back of their house.

Charles primarily made the kitchen cabinets and cupboards, and I applied carpenter's glue to them. After the glue was partly dry, Charles would put on the laminate. My job, among other things, was to press on the laminate with a small piece of wood about six by five inches. That was my hardest task and the process took as much as an hour before the laminate stuck firmly.

At noon, I took a two-hour break from the workshop and used that time to prepare lunch for the family. Afterwards, I ate, then promptly returned to work, not stopping again until 6 PM. Even then, I often had to prepare dinner. After eating and taking a quick shower, I returned to the workshop by 7:30 to continue assisting Charles. My workday ended between 11 PM and 1:00 AM. Sometimes I was too tired to even climb into the bed. Those nights, I longed for my family, my hometown, and my job. It was the hardest I had ever worked in my life and the schedule stayed the same five days a week, but sometimes extended to six and seven days for nearly four months of my stay at the Barrows.

Charles was at first friendly, but then I noticed he took his jokes too far, and I realized I had overstayed my welcome at the Barrows'.

Four months later, I interviewed for a housekeeper position with the Mack family of four. I was hired and scheduled to start the new job in two weeks.

Charles was angry about my leaving and took every opportunity to quarrel about my work.

"Why is it that you so late? You should be out here even before me," he often said if I was a few minutes late in joining him at the shop. "Don't press that laminate so hard 'cause if you break it, it comin' out your pay." While fussing, among other things, he used to say he would call the immigration authorities for me. I eventually stopped working with Charles and started the housekeeping job. I then intensified my search for a new home.

A few months after I was in Barbados, Mom told me Simone, one of my coworkers from Ashmead Chambers, had left for Barbados shortly after I did. Before I left Guyana, Simone told me of her plans to join her fiancé in the St. James area of Barbados, but she wasn't sure of the date. My mother got me Simone's telephone number and we made contact. After work, instead of going home, I boarded the bus to Simone's home, and we went apartment hunting.

Tirelessly, we searched for any houses or apartments that appeared vacant or had a FOR RENT sign and made inquiries. Day after day, we continued our search, but to all our queries, the answer was no, or the rent was too high. After two exhausting weeks we gave up. Next, we utilized the newspapers, and Simone inquired of friends. There were quite a few apartments available in the newspapers, but all were too expensive. My wage from the housekeeping position was $80 a week and the cheapest studio apartment was $400 a month. I also had to consider other necessities such as utilities, food and transportation. This was going to be tougher than I anticipated.

NINETEEN

The Rescue Room

Two weekends after Simone and I linked up, she and Alex, her fiancé, invited me to a picnic. I felt carefree, riding in the back of their Suzuki, making our way to River Bay through the luscious countryside, to the breezy East Coast. The ride was nearly an hour.

"Angie, who'd think you and me would meet up here in Barbados? It's really good to have a friend nearby, when you're thousands of miles away from home," Simone said, turning halfway around in the front seat of the car. "I'm glad I found you. This way, you'll be able to assist us with our wedding plans."

"Glad I found you too; it was lonely before you came."

Alex was a body builder, and Simone invited me to one of his shows the following Tuesday night.

"Maybe I'll go if I get a ride, but I'll get back to you."

"Getting there ain't no problem, Angelique. We will pick you up, and here's a ticket too," Alex said, handing me the ticket.

"Thanks. So when's the wedding?"

"December—four months away. And in time for my twenty-ninth birthday," Simone replied beaming, her large brown eyes dancing happily.

"That's great. Congratulations to y'all, man."

"Angelique, she's driving me crazy with her everything-has-to-be-perfect attitude," Alex said, quickly glancing over at Simone.

"Angie, don't bother with him. You know how some men are. If I allow him to go to the altar in jeans and a T-shirt, he will certainly do so. I'm the one who has to make sure all's well. Leave arrangements to Alex, and when that day comes, we may have to call the pastor home to perform the ceremony." Simone said, laughing.

"Angie, girl, I can't wait for that day to come and go quickly so my life can be back to normal," Alex sneered.

I enjoyed the drive as we babbled on and on. The countryside was relaxing, and we sped past cows and sheep grazing lazily in lush, green pastures.

We arrived at River Bay, and immediately Simone and I left Alex. Like children, we raced our way through the noisy, colorful crowd to the top of the hill, overlooking the sea. The breathtakingly beautiful, endless expanse of blue water mesmerized me, and awe, coupled with fear, overcame me. The sea was calm, the sun's rays casting a shimmering glow to its surface. It appeared to greet the shore with vengeance, waving and lashing wildly against the rocky hill, causing a noisy swishing sound. After a while we descended the hill, making our way through the tantalizing aroma of barbecued chicken, steak, and burgers, rejoining Alex in the tree-shaded, grassy park.

Alex had already laid out the food on the portable table and a couple of his friends had joined him.

"Who these lovely ladies?" One of the men asked, sipping on a bottle of Banks Beer. The other coffee complexioned gentleman, short and muscular, about middle-aged, sat on the grass, eating. Upon seeing Simone, he hurriedly stood up and approached her, his lips parting into a smile revealing spacey, cream teeth. He wore a Hawaiian, short sleeved, three-quarter length pants suit, with a broad-brimmed straw hat and leather sandals.

"It's good seeing you again," he said, embracing Simone.

"So, wait, what really going on here? Only Cleve could get introduction and big hug?" The other bald headed, loud mouthed, tanned gentleman said. He appeared to be in his mid-forties.

"I can't understand you, Ronald? You can't wait?" Alex asked, taking a large bite of the Kentucky Fried chicken breast he held in his hand. "Ronald, this is Simone, and this is Angelique. Cleveland, Angelique," Alex said in a mocked rough tone, chewing vigorously on his KFC. He indicated Simone, then me. After eating, we sat around lazily on the grass, engaged in light conversation. I wasn't talking much. I stared at a little boy and girl playing catch. Instinctively, my thoughts drifted to Kianna and Junior. I wished they were here. It was nearly five months since I had left home, and anytime I thought about them, it felt like five years.

Lord, please, let the day come when I will be happily reunited with my family.

"We'll be back in a while," Alex announced before rising and slowly walking off with Ronald.

"Are you always this quiet?" I glanced to my left, and Cleveland's eyes locked with mine. I smiled. "How do you like Barbados?" he asked, a toothpick protruding from the corner of his mouth.

"I've not gone out much, but so far it's good. The scenery here is great. It's different from Guyana."

"Yes, I know. Guyana is beautiful in its own way, though," he said.

"You know Guyana? Have you been there?" I asked.

"Of course. I have a lot of Guyanese friends," Cleveland said.

"Oh really! Nice! I won't feel like a stranger around you anymore, then."

"Yes, he has Guyanese connections," Simone chimed in. "He knows lots of Guyanese people here too, right, Cleve?"

As if waiting to be prompted, Cleveland started telling us of his visits to Guyana and people he met. He said he liked Guyanese people, and always tried to lend a helping hand to all people, generally, wherever he saw it possible.

"Look, the fellas know I live alone," Cleveland said, "'cause my wife pick up sheself and went overseas years now. She left me in a big three-bedroom house. Sometimes people would contact me when they know of somebody who come in for holiday from Trinidad, St. Lucia, Guyana, or any of the islands, and need a place to stay. I rent out a room in my home sometimes."

"Oh, I didn't know you rent your room, Cleveland," Simone said.

"Yeah, man. You remember the last time you were here, a lady from Grenada was holidaying at me?"

"Yes, aaah Theresa," Simone snapped her fingers.

"She rented the room. Anytime you guys need assistance with anything, feel free to contact me, man," he continued. "If y'all want go partying or anything so, and Alex not available, call me. I still 'get down' yo' know," he laughed loudly, playfully slapping his hand against the grass.

"Well, Angie is a church girl. She don't party." Simone volunteered.

"Come on, partying is fun. We all need some o' that in our lives …"

I had stopped listening to them. I wondered whether I should ask Cleveland to rent me one of his rooms. At the same time, I assessed him. From his conversation, I liked him. I decided to wait until Simone and I were alone to ask her opinion.

About an hour later, Simone and I strolled around the park and basked on the hilltop again.

"Simone, you think it wise to ask Cleveland to rent me his room?"

"I thought about it too, and I planned to mention it to you."

"I'm sort of skeptical though. You think you know him enough to recommend that?"

"Really, I can't say I know him very well because I haven't dealt with him much. Anyway, we can ask Alex what he thinks. If he doesn't see a problem, you should go ahead and ask Cleveland to rent his room," Simone finished.

About an hour later, we made our way deeper into the park to find the others. Clouds gathered overhead, but the cool northeast winds were refreshing, rustling through the leaves of the trees. Alex had packed and was ready to leave. We bade Cleveland and Roland goodbye and joined Alex in the car. I sat in the rear, my back against one door, and my feet stretched out on the seat in front of me.

"Al, did you know Cleveland rents a room in his house?" Simone piped up.

"Yeah, he been doing that a while now. Why?"

"Think is a good idea for Angelique to rent his room?"

Alex paused for a moment before responding.

"I thought she looking for apartment. Angelique, if I did know you want' a room I'd recommend' it ever since. He don't really rent long term, but if I ask, I'm sure he will."

"Alex, you did not answer the question." Simone said.

"What question?" Alex asked, glancing briefly at Simone with a puzzled expression.

"Is it *a good idea* for her to do so?"

"Listen man, I know Cleve nearly fifteen years now. He's a cool fella. Angelique," Alex said, attempting to look at me in the rear-view mirror, "you ain't got to be 'fraid of anything."

"See, Angelique, I thought so, but I wanted to verify," Simone added.

"You know something, Angelique," Alex continued fluently, "the best way for a woman to earn respect from a man, is for that woman to first respect herself. I only meet you a couple o' weeks ago, and I'm a good judge of character……"

"Yeah, yeah, right," Simone interrupted.

Alex quickly looked over at her and smiled before continuing.

"And from what I see, you shouldn't have any problems with Cleve."

"Thanks Alex, you sure made me feel better. Would you mind asking him?"

"Not at all," Alex replied.

"…the best way for a woman to earn respect from a man, is for that woman to first respect herself. . . "

One of the ways to respect ourselves is to stop the first attempt of abuse.

While working the following day, I thought about the decision I made to rent Cleveland's room, if it was okay with him. I was still doubtful, in spite of Alex's confidence in Cleveland, but the more I thought about it, the more I felt it would be better than remaining at the Barrow's. If

I rent the room, I will still continue looking for a place, I told myself.

After work, I boarded the bus to Simone's. From the moment she answered the door, she smiled.

"As soon as you're ready, you have a new home, Angelique."

"Oh great! Did he mention cost?"

"He said you and him will discuss rent after you get there."

I sat down with a sigh of relief and we began making plans for my move to Cleveland's home.

I thanked Sarah and Charles for their hospitality. They didn't appear pleased and a coldness lingered in the air. Two days later, Simone and Alex helped me move into Cleveland's home in Britton's Hill, St. Michael.

"Alright, we' there!" Alex exclaimed, slowing his vehicle and parking at the side of the road. Exiting the vehicle, Alex stretched, then grabbed my belongings from the car's trunk. We walked up a narrow concreted walkway exploding with colorful hibiscus, oleander, and other flowering shrubs on both sides. The cream and brown wooden house, with a patio stretching the width of the house, was brightly lit and stood alone on a large piece of unfenced land. There was a motorcycle parked away from the side steps. The closest house was about 75 feet away.

"Hi, my brother," Cleveland greeted Alex, opening the door.

"Notice' like we get you at the right time," Alex said, bending halfway, picking up my suitcase and proceeding into the house.

"Yes, I was thinking you guys timed me perfectly. I just come from a business dinner the company had this evening. Cleveland hugged Simone briefly, then turned to me.

"Hi, Angelique, how you doin'? Welcome to your new home and I hope you enjoy it here," he said, smiling, hand outstretched.

"Thank you very much. I'm delighted you're allowing me to stay," I replied accepting his handshake.

"Glad I can help. Feel right at home. There's your room," he said pointing down the narrow hallway to a closed door on the right. "Let me know if I can help further. Anything to drink anyone?"

"Something light." Simone responded.

"A beer for me," Alex said, rubbing his shoulder and exercising his arms after taking the heavy suitcase to the bedroom.

"What about you, Angelique?" Cleveland asked, starting to make his way, presumably to the kitchen.

"Anything soft, thank you."

"Oh, Simone," Cleveland said, "you know this house better than me, show Angelique around."

"Okay, Cleve, but remember she is your tenant. Anyhow, I will oblige you the favor," Simone smiled. "Come on, Angelique," she said, grabbing my hand and leading me from the dining area, which contained a seven-piece wrought iron dinette set and a 19" color television on a black wrought-iron stand. We headed toward the sitting room.

The simple décor of the one floor three-bedroom cottage had the flair of a middle-class bachelor. The entire house was neatly kept, but dusty.

"Angelique, I think this is the thing for you," Simone said. We were standing, looking around the end bedroom which had my suitcase in a corner. The room was simple, spacious and comfortable. It consisted of a bed, a wardrobe, and a stand fan. In a corner, opposite the vanity, stood a writing desk, with reading lamp and an old, swivel chair. Cream tapestry window drapes matched the satin bed spread and shams. After examining the blue and white tiled bathroom situated at the end of the hallway, we joined Cleveland in the kitchen.

"You like the place?" Cleveland asked, filling glasses with ice.

"Yes, sure. I feel comfortable already. Thank you."

"I'm glad. That's the idea. Come, let's go to the dining room."

We each had our drink, but Alex and Simone had to make another stop before going home, so shortly after, they announced their departure.

"Angelique, you not scared to be alone?" Cleveland asked, finishing the last of his beer and resting his bottle on the tabletop, covered with blue and white checkered plastic. "I hang out a lot." Simone and Alex quickly turned their attention to me.

"Not at all," I lied, continuing my drink, avoiding any eye contact. I was unaccustomed to being alone, and in addition, this was a new home, so of course I was a tad uneasy.

"Good, 'cause I'm hardly ever home. It will be like you own this house. The neighbors around are friendly. You ain't got to be scared of anything. Oh," he paused, then gestured to the front of the house with his forefinger, "I sleep with the windows open, but you can close them if you wish." Cleveland then left with the others.

After they left, the house was as quiet as a tomb and I felt utterly alone. I quickly closed the windows and turned on the television. Within an hour, I finished unpacking, and the bedroom appeared as if I had lived there all my life. At 11:30, I finally retired and fell asleep the moment my tired body hit the bed. I hadn't rested well in a long time.

Hours later, I awoke to the sunlight streaming through the glass paned windows. I had forgotten to draw the curtains. *Shoot! It's nearly 7 o'clock and I have a longer journey to work this morning.* I sprang out of the bed, hurriedly made it, and then rushed to the bathroom.

On my way from the shower, Cleveland was in the kitchen.

"Morning, slept well?" he asked.

"More than well. If I don't be careful, I'll be late getting to work. Cleveland, I want to thank you…."

"I know you grateful, bo, don' bother with the speech," he interrupted, filling the kettle with water."

'Bo!' What do you mean by that? I heard you say it a lot at the picnic."

Cleveland laughed loudly.

"Well, a Guyanese would say I know you grateful, *man*. Right?"

"Yes."

"Then, 'bo' is used in the same way like *man*."

"I see. Okay, then, no speech, but you can at least tell me how much my rent is."

"I haven't really thought about it, but is $25 a week okay for you?"

"Sounds affordable, but you sure that is all?"

"You sound like a millionaire. Like I underestimate you, bo." He laughed loudly. "Yes Angelique, that is all. Now hurry and get ready for work. I may be able to assist you with living quarters, but I ain't got an extra job, bo."

TWENTY

Outta Here!

Living at Cleveland's worked out better than I expected. I enjoyed cleaning, so I kept the house tidy, and on weekends, I assisted him with his laundry. The first time he went home and noticed I cleaned the entire house, he was surprised and pleased.

"Wait! No Angelique, you didn't do my laundry too," he exclaimed from the laundry room when he went to put away his working shirt. Shortly after, he emerged from the bath clad in his black bathrobe grinning from ear to ear. I curled up in a chair in front of the television, eating a packet of potato chips.

"You so kind, Angelique. Thanks much, but you didn't have to do it."

"You're welcome, Cleveland. I know I didn't have to do it, but it's a pleasure."

Cleveland was not only my so-called landlord, we became friends. He wasn't home often, but whenever he was, we spoke endlessly on many topics. I shared personal things about my family with him and he told me about his wife and son. One evening when he returned home, he watched me apply rubbing alcohol to my forehead.

"What happen? You got a headache?" he asked, sitting down heavily on the sofa across from me.

"Yes, I worked hard today, but I'm not sure that's what gave me a headache."

"It's probably hard having to leave your office job in Guyana to come here and clean, ah?" He started taking off his shoes, then lifted his head to look at me. Our eyes met.

"You know, Cleveland, life is unpredictable. Had anyone told me I would end up working in a furniture shop, then cleaning bathrooms, scrubbing floors, pots and pans, for a living, I wouldn't have believed it. Anyway, being in a different country, with no working status, I have no choice. The good thing is, it's a way to help me remain independent. I don't look down on any type of job, and I also believe in an honest day's work for an honest day's pay."

"That's one way to look at it, Angelique. But I think I have a better way," Cleveland started. "If the world had a whole lot o' lawyers, doctors, engineers, teachers, and those people, who will empty the trash, do deliveries, mow the lawns, and perform those kinds o' tasks? That's why the Master made us all different. Just as our bodies cannot function effectively without all its members, a society cannot function efficiently without the various personnel. So, is senseless for anyone to look down on what another does."

"So true," I said, replacing the cork of the rubbing alcohol bottle and setting it down on the floor. "But on the other hand, I also think everyone should aim for the stars, and whatever one sets out to do, they should ensure it's done to the best of their ability. When I was much younger, I wanted to be a writer. I still believe I will write one day and become famous too!"

"Go for it, girl! The sky's the limit!" Cleveland said, looking at his watch and rising to his feet. "Hang in there, Angelique. Things will get better."

My job with the Mack family lasted just over three months before being forced to go job hunting again. I went to work as usual on a bright, sunny Wednesday morning in October. It was a good morning until around 11 AM when I heard Mr. Mack's car pull into the driveway. I was downstairs cooking. Soon after slamming the car door, he shouted for me from the yard.

"Angelique, bring yo' big [so and so] here and come and carry in these groceries."

I couldn't believe what the man said. *What does he know about me? No, he couldn't be speaking to me.* I folded my arms and leaned against the cupboard, debating whether to respond. Before I could make up my mind....

I couldn't believe what the man said. *What does he know about me? No, he couldn't be speaking to me.*

Verbal abuse can even be found on the job from so-called superiors. Take a stand against it.

"Angelique! Angelique!" He shouted again.

"Yes." I stepped from the kitchen into the dining room, my face as serious as a judge. At the same time, he entered through the side door.

"You ain't hear me calling you?" He asked smiling, presumptuously.

"You couldn't be calling me."

"Look, come and carry in the groceries," he said walking away, ignoring me.

I stood there biting on my lip, hurt and anger enveloping me. I resisted the urge to leave his groceries, take my bag, and leave his house.

When the devil's busy, he's really busy. The day seemed to drag on. While cleaning the sitting room upstairs, about 2:30 that afternoon Mr. Mack came up and went to his room and locked the door. I tried to hurriedly finish what I was doing. About ten minutes later, he shouted for me from the bedroom.

"Yes?" I answered coldly.

"I have two bottles of pills on the kitchen cupboard, downstairs; bring them with a glass of water."

I stopped cleaning, went downstairs, and got the tablets and water. When I returned, I noticed the door was ajar. I stood at the side of the door and knocked lightly with the tablet container, making a hollow rattling sound.

"Here is your water and pills," I said.

"Bring it," he responded.

My mind said, *don't go in there*, but I dismissed the thought and hesitantly proceeded into the bedroom. I was unprepared for what met my eyes. Mr. Mack lay sprawled on his bed, his light-brown, old, wrinkled body, exposed. His face fixed in a devilish smile while motioning me towards him. For a fraction of a second, I stopped and stared. My hands were outstretched, still grasping the tablet container and the glass. They both fell to the carpeted floor and I darted from the bedroom as fast as a deer. I ran to the downstairs dressing room, intending to

Mr. Mack lay sprawled on his bed, his light-brown, old, wrinkled body, exposed.

Sexual abuse can be found even in your work environment. Take steps to eradicate it.

change my clothes, but instead, I grabbed my bag and got out of there as fast as I could.

When I got home, I called Mrs. Mack at her salon and explained why I wouldn't continue working for them.

"Good heavens! What am I hearing this afternoon?" She paused before continuing. "I won't even say I don't believe it because that's how lawless the man is. Angelique, I do apologize. I will drop off your check."

Arriving home that afternoon, I met a letter from my mother. We wrote each other every week, and as my daughter promised, every time I opened my mother's lengthy letters, there was a short note from Kianna. In previous letters, my mother told me that some days were up for Kianna, while others were down. A few times she found Kianna covered under a blanket, crying. When she asked her why she was crying, she said she wanted to go with her mommy. Mom also mentioned that there were times when she was frighteningly quiet, but Mom felt that the times when Kianna was that care-free little girl outweighed the depressing times. Mom also said that Junior, although he was irritable sometimes, grew more accustomed to them every day. Every letter Kianna wrote, she would start and end by telling me she and Junior loved me and wanted to come with me. I earnestly looked forward to hearing from them, but those letters tore at the core of my heart and caused tears and depression.

It was bitter-sweet receiving pictures of them. Only by photographs I watched Kianna and Junior grow up. Being away from my children and family took a toll on me because I was mostly sad and alone. I didn't feel like going on with life, but I knew I had to hang in there, or come crashing down on two innocent children. I didn't go to church often, but I prayed a lot and that's what kept me holding on.

I prayed a lot and that's what kept me holding on.

Prayer changes things. Pray yourself out of anything, even abusive relationships. Your partner may even change, as a result of prayer.

Strangely though, when I opened the letter that afternoon, unlike other times, there was no note from Kianna. I wondered if she got tired of writing or forgot about me.

Hi Angie,

How are you doing? How is your new home? I received your last letter and as usual it's like having you near me when I'm reading them. Your children are doing well. Junior is very busy now. He is now able to say a few words and wants to be rude already. You should see his actions when anyone annoys him. I had to bar him from the kitchen because he is always emptying the cupboards. The other day, I went into the kitchen and saw him sitting in front of the cupboard with the frying pan turned down on his head.

Kianna loves to play. Before I started writing this letter, I told her I was writing you, so she should write her letter. She asked when I was going to mail it. I said tomorrow. You know what your child told me? I must go ahead and write because her friends were waiting on her to play hide-and-seek. She said she will send her letter the next time I am writing. Then she collected her hat and left.

Well child, your father had to evict William. Can you imagine since you left here—more than six months ago, he refused to pay any rent? Did I tell you he moved his sister

Melissa into the house with him? She brought all her furniture. Your father sent him a notice to quit and he did not respond, so after one month, your father filed for possession of his property. The case came up in court and William did not show up. The Magistrate postponed it twice and he still did not show up. Eventually, the Magistrate granted your father's request and issued an eviction order.

You know your father can be something else. The court's personnel turned up a morning when Melissa was alone at home. She knew nothing of the happenings, but the officer didn't listen. She and all their belongings were placed at the side of the road. I was embarrassed for her and William. Well you know some neighbors were sorry for him and said we shouldn't have done it. They fail to realize Eric Castor Snr. don't mix matters. People don't know, but they like to get into other people business. They won't see mortgage, rates, and taxes have to be paid for these properties. If your father didn't need another source of income, he wouldn't have rented out the houses. Anyway, when William passes here now, he puts his head straight. Kianna normally shouts for him, and sometimes he would wave, but at other times, he acts as if he didn't hear her.

Girl, he looks bad too. He wears one outfit over and over. Gloria said she heard he lost his job also. It's sad. Look, I haven't cooked yet for the day so I will end here. Love you and take care of yourself.

Mom.

I finished reading and sat back on the sofa with the letter on my stomach. My mind was way back in Guyana . . .

"Another letter eh? Bad news?" Cleveland asked behind me. I sat up, startled.

"I didn't hear you come in."

"I realized that," he said. "I'm starved." He went to the bathroom, washed his hands, then proceeded to the kitchen.

"Angelique, I got chicken lo-mein. Want some?" he shouted from the kitchen.

"A little. Thanks."

"So how the family and children?" he asked, standing at the dining table and emptying the contents from the Styrofoam container into two plates.

"They're okay, I guess."

"Hmmm. Don't sound too enthused to me, and being so lost in thought when I came in, I know you're worrying about something. You're gonna come to the table or you want yours there?"

"I'll come." I got up, walked to the table, and sat opposite Cleveland.

"Wanna talk about it?" He asked, wrapping long strands of noodles around his fork and placing them in his mouth.

"Today wasn't one of my better days. I think adults can be selfish sometimes."

"And why you say that?"

"Anytime my mother tells me about my children, I think about the situation in which their father and I have placed them. Too often when adults cannot get along together, they tend to make vital decisions, without stopping to consider their consequences. Usually it's too late when we realize our children are the ones being hurt. I heard a pastor preached one time and he

---

. . .children are the broken pieces in a broken marriage.

We should all aim to save our relationships before it gets to the broken stages.

Children may suffer psychological effects, resulting from Divorce. Both children and parents can be helped.

https://www.fionaharewood.com/resources

---

mentioned that *children are the broken pieces in a broken marriage*. That's so true."

"Hmmm. I get where you coming from, but first lemme correct you. Not *all* adults act that way."

"I know Cleveland, but I wish William and I had worked out our differences. That way, our children wouldn't have to suffer because of our selfishness."

"Yes, working through our problems will have less impact on our kids. They will grow up happier and mature into wonderful adults."

"It's sad, really sad." I began eating. "And, on a lighter note," I paused, then put another forkful of noodles into my mouth. "I walked off my job, today."

"Really? Why?" Cleveland asked. He stopped eating, looked at me and rested his fork on the plate. I briefly outlined what occurred between Mr. Mack and me.

"No, the bastard ain't do that! You kidding me! You want me go get him?"

"No. Don't. I'll find another job."

"Angelique, if you was my daughter, I would've find he and knock he out, bo. Stone cold! Please, don't think all Bajan men are like him, you hear? That's disgusting!" Cleveland said, shaking his head.

"Angelique, listen to me," he continued. "Better days are ahead. Mark my words, and always remember, *behind every dark cloud, there is a silver lining*."

"Angelique, listen to me," "Better days are ahead. Mark my words, and always remember, *behind every dark cloud, there is a silver lining*."

People in abusive relationships should look towards a better day . . thinking that way gives inner strength needed to find help or leave that relationship, if necessary.

TWENTY ONE

Writing Brings Healing

I rolled over and burrowed my face deeper into the soft foam pillow. I was in no hurry to get out of bed. It was my first week without a job. I tuned to the gospel station Faith FM and heard the song "One Day at a Time," followed by a medley. I sat up in bed and started bopping my head and tapping my feet to the music. Even though I had no income, it felt good being away from the hustle and bustle of a busy day.

During my two weeks without a job, after job hunting, I spent my free time watching television, reading novels, and writing to my family and friends. Writing made me feel better. Reading was my favorite, and I enjoyed suspense, court scenes, and mysteries. I stayed clear of love stories because the memories of my failed marriage were still painful.

Around 10:30 that morning I heard a shuffling at the door. I sprung out of bed in time to see an airmail envelope slide under the door and stop at my feet. Great! Mail from home! Quickly I tore open the envelope and started reading.

Well my dear daughter:

How are you? I received your last letter. It is always great receiving your mail. We do miss you very much and are praying the day will come soon when we will see you again. It may seem, every letter opens the very same way, but it's only because we really miss you. No one, or nothing can ever take your place. It brings tears to my eyes ever so often when I think about you, but God is good and I do know, someday you will be happy again.

It may surprise you to know, William came to me regarding his children. He probably now miss them. I was sitting on the front porch one afternoon last week, when he stopped and asked to talk with me. As usual, he did loads of apologizing. He asked me how you were. I told him the last time I heard from you, you were alright. He then asked if I will allow him to visit the children and take them out sometimes. I told him I had to talk with your father, which I did. Your father vowed he would never speak to William again and he does not want him in his house. However, he said they are his children and he has no problem with him seeing them, but it has to be downstairs. Your father also told me to tell William, whenever he takes them out, he has to ensure they are back by a certain time.

Since then, he came by twice. He did not take them anywhere, but he brought snacks and played ball with them. Kianna and Junior were excited. William is something else though because it's now nearly eight months since you left, and he always acted as if they didn't exist. Now, when he is seeing them, he brings them snacks. He probably thinks they can exist off of potato chips and corn curls. He does not seem interested in how they eat or wear clothes. I did not bother to tell him anything though. This is all for now. Write soon.

Love you,
Mom.

Later that evening I sat watching television when the program *Ideas Becoming Reality* started. The host, Sharon Corbin, interviews people who are making a difference in society. That afternoon two authors were on the show. I became caught up with the interview. The authors were Barbadians who resided in the United Kingdom. They were sensational and caught my attention, especially when they said, "Writing sometimes brings healing from emotional hurt." By the end of the program, I was inspired.

It was a night when even the leaves on the trees were still. Outside was even hotter than inside. *Gosh! I feel like stripping my clothes.* Eventually I went to my room, turned on the fan, threw myself on the bed, and allowed the partly hot air to blow over me. Laying there, the authors' words came back to me.

"Writing can sometimes bring you emotional healing."

I thought about my babies and began turning words over in my mind, trying to form a poem about my darling son and daughter. The verse became too long to remember. I hurriedly jumped up from the bed, and grabbed a pencil and a notebook. That night, I started a few lines to my first poem.

Like two armored and shining knights,
My babies brighten up my life,
And though we are far apart, I pray we will never part,
For you two hold the golden key to the gates of my broken heart.

It sounded good to my ears, and I felt closer to my children than at any other time. From then on, when I wanted to feel close to my family, I locked myself in my room and started writing. I began putting words, then sentences, then paragraphs together in what I hoped would be my first book. Next, I thought of the day my best seller would be released.

Three weeks after walking off the Mack's job, I accepted another housekeeper position with the Singh family. Mrs. Singh gave me the job when she realized I was from Guyana, her home country. The job was from 8:00 to 1:30—five days a week at a wage of $60. My tasks included extensive cleaning and laundry.

I was married to that job for a long time, although it barely stopped short of slavery. Mrs. Singh was always at home and checked on me frequently. When something wasn't done to her liking, she asked me to re-do it.

The job proved harder than the Mack's job, and many days I went home with sore hands, an aching back, and thighs. The good thing about it—I was out at 1:30 PM sharp, although there was not a minute to rest.

Sometimes I went home after work. Other days, I stopped by Simone's. We'd watch videos or simply hang out and chat in her tiny sitting room. Soon, another woman joined us.

Simone and Lynette were friends from Guyana, and they met at the neighborhood park. Lynette came to Barbados and lived with her boyfriend, James, at his mother's home. She was the fun type and hated being in a house for too long. About 7:30 one evening, I was leaving Simone's when Lynette showed up. She stood just over 5-foot, was well-covered, and chocolate-brown in complexion. Her perfect white teeth further enhanced her attractive smile, while her finger-wave hairstyle showed off her oval-shaped face. Lynette wore a red halter top and stretch jeans which fit as if she'd hung them and jumped right in. Red high-heeled slippers and silver accessories complimented her outfit.

"Wha' y'all doing this evening? I in a partying mood. James gone to St. Vincent and coming back this weekend. I tired being in the house. Tonight is the young people's night at the 357 Disco—half price and all! Le' we go in there, man," Lynette said.

"Sounds good to me. Especially since I haven't party in a while," Simone said. "Angie, what're you gonna do? Stay home and watch the four corners of Cleveland's house? Come ooon! Let's go, man," Simone urged, dancing around the sitting room to the tempo of T.C.'s calypso song, "Put a Woman in Front."

"Sorry, y'all know I don't party and I'm tired. All I want is my bed. Y'all go. Have fun," I said, putting on my shoes.

"Angelique, you can be a real spoil sport. This is how you intend to continue living? You can't be like that," Simone started preaching.

"Angelique, I know you dance at church, so wha' happen' wit' dancing at a party? Is the same dancing," Lynette chimed in.

"Oh no, it's not! It can never be the same dancing," I answered.

"I know, Angelique, that's only a joke, but you need to lighten up. I can't get it how you could live like that—pretty boring."

Listening to them, I began reasoning within.

It's true you know. I live a dull life. If I die now, I can't even say I enjoyed anything. Partying one or two times cannot do a thing to me. Look how many people usually party and nothing happens to them. Some of them even happier'n me. . .

"So?" Simone stood in front of me, her head cocked to one side, her eyes fixed on me.

"What would I wear?" I asked, looking down at the faded jeans and light blue T-shirt I wore to work that day.

"Good! So you coming along, right? You'll find something to wear."

"We still got time. Simone can dress, and then we can all go at your place and wait on you to get ready," Lynette said.

"Way to gooo!" Simone said, excitedly connecting upraised palms with Lynette.

"Shucks!" Simone said, stopping abruptly. A pair of worried brown eyes searched ours.

"What?" I asked.

"Since Alex left for Trinidad last week, he calls me about three times every night."

"Wha' time normally is his last call?" Lynette asked.

"Probably after 12:00 or so."

"And before that?"

"He called not too long ago. He may call again about 9:30."

"Good, I got it cover'," Lynette said, smiling mischievously. "We goin' wait fo' his second call. While you talking wit' him, yawn and make some tired sounds. That way, when he calls at midnight and you don't answer the phone, he goin' think you sleeping because you was tired when he last call'.

"That's it! That's it!" Simone said. "Lemme go and see what I will wear. I haven't a clue what he's doing on his so-called business trip anyway." Simone did a happy dance, both arms held high and swaying her hips; then she hurried to the wardrobe.

"I very glad James is away," Lynette remarked.

At 9:45 PM Alex called. Already dressed in a black and white striped strap top with black pants, black and white high-heeled slippers and silver accessories, Simone grabbed the telephone. Lynette and I were tickled with the act Simone put on while talking with Alex. Yawning audibly, she stretched, making some tired sounds from the back of her throat. We were forced to go outside, lest our giggles alerted Alex.

Ten minutes later, we were on our way to my place. While I showered, Simone and Lynette rummaged through my clothes to find me a suitable party outfit. They came up with a low waist, black and white dress, sleeveless, and carried four cut-outs down the back. At the top of each cut-out was a tiny black bow. I had never worn the dress, but I loved it from the moment I saw it and had bought it for $60. I wore it with matching black high heeled slippers. After Simone applied my makeup, I was pleased.

We arrived at the 357 Disco just after 11:30. The smoky atmosphere was gorgeous with its flickering, colored crystal ball lights. Butterflies relentlessly fluttered in my stomach as I tried blocking out the side of me which condemned my actions. My anxiety disappeared when the pulsating rhythm of Ras Iley's "Cat Attack," then Red Plastic Bag's "Ah Raising Meh Own Cock" devoured me.

Lynette led the way to the bar.

"You okay, Angie?" she asked. "You look nervous. Relax, man. You goin' see you will enjoy it."

"I'm okay," I replied, already enjoying the music.

". . . I can do wit' something to drink," Lynette was saying. "I'll order. Wha' you guys want?"

"Scotch on the rocks," Simone replied.

"Wha' 'bout you Angie?" Lynette asked.

"Don't know. Something soft."

"Gimme a break! You don't mean a Sprite or nothing like that, right?" Simone teased.

"Yep, anything so. Sprite, ginger-ale, orange juice," I responded, matter-of-factly.

"Look, Lynette, get her some sort of wine or something," Simone insisted.

"Then you both will drink it," I said, dismissing them. I started singing, tapping my feet and bopping my head to The Mighty Gabby's, "House Call From Dr. Cassandra."

"Good, you now look like you in the party spirit," Lynette joked.

We were enjoying our drinks and engaging in light conversation when the DJ changed the mood to some vivacious dub.

"Come on guys, let's not waste good music." Simone said, getting up. A swarm of revelers flooded the already crowded dance floor.

"Angie, come on." Lynette pulled at my arm, sliding off her stool.

"No, Lynette. You go ahead," I replied, attempting to shout above the music. She paid no attention to me. The next thing I knew, she pulled me to the dance floor. I couldn't just stand there. Lynette started dubbing, and I too did my thing. Somehow it felt good, and my feet didn't tangle as I anticipated.

It was as if being of African descent, music automatically flowed through my veins. My inexperience didn't stop me. I got down on the dance floor to soca, dub, and reggae.

"Thought you couldn't dance!" Simone shouted. She had found a partner and they were having fun.

"I thought so too," Lynette shouted back. I paid no attention to them—It was time to 'hold up yuh hand if yuh love Botha and jump around if yuh love Mandela.'

I was enjoying every minute of it. It was then Lynette's turn to be surprised. The DJ changed back to soca.

"I tired girl. Le' we take a break."

"Not yet. I'm enjoying this. I love soca," I replied, holding my hands high and gyrating my body to the rhythm of "Da Beech Is Mine."

"I can't believe this! Honestly, I can't believe this! Angelique, I gotta sit down," Lynette said, smiling, shaking her head, waving goodbye.

Shortly after Lynette left, a fella came from nowhere and started dancing with me. I didn't mind, so I continued dancing. He tried asking my name while we danced but I wasn't interested in holding a conversation. I wanted to dance. I gestured no, then tugged lightly at the end of one ear. He eventually gave up, but remained my dance partner for that session. I only stopped when the ballroom dancing started. I knew that one called for practice.

Simone and Lynette teased me when we left the disco. They said I was sly and refused to believe I only partied once before when my co-worker was leaving Guyana. We took one taxi and it dropped me off first. I finally crept into bed at 4:15 AM. I was tired and hoped I would be able to wake up to go to work later that morning.

I did wake up in time, thanks to my body clock—mostly I wake up before sunrise even if I had a late night. My head throbbed and my entire body ached. It were as if I did a body fitness crash course. Being Friday and pay day, I couldn't afford to stay home. I made it to work and eagerly looked forward to the end of the workday.

TWENTY TWO

No Christmas For Me

I wasn't prepared for applying for the work permit on my own. Since it didn't work out with the Barrows who had promised to file for the papers, I had to figure out a way to obtain those necessary documents. Without a work permit and legal status in the country it was impossible to find a job in my field. Furthermore, I was unable to travel in and out of the island, so, reuniting with my children seemed hopeless.

Filing the application for a work permit proved difficult, so I found a lawyer. My appointment with the lawyer was successful. He said he would be able to file an application on my behalf, but my task was to find five hundred dollars. Besides his consultation fees of one hundred dollars, I hadn't any money. I promised to return with a deposit as soon as it was possible. Obtaining the work permit became even more urgent after learning that Lynette and her boyfriend had a quarrel, and his mother called the immigration authorities. Lynette was held in the immigration prison for a while and then sent home.

After meeting with the lawyer, I made my way to Simone's house. During the ride, the five hundred dollars I had to raise for the counsel's representation weighed heavily on me. My financial situation deteriorated, and even though my parents told me they would finance my children's upkeep, I never left it solely to them. I sent them money whenever possible and also bought Junior and Kianna little things, like vitamins, toys, and clothes. Although I wasn't there in person, I knew those were special moments when they received something from me. I planned to work and save the lawyer's fee because I really needed to find myself a better paying and less strenuous job. I missed my children most of all and wanted to be able to see them soon. At times, I considered having my parents send the children for a holiday, but airfares were expensive. Also, I would've preferred to be living on my own before I allowed my children to visit.

My second Christmas away from home approached quickly. I remembered feeling Christmas in the air in Guyana. It was a sentiment one couldn't really explain, but it were as if cares were far away. Burdens seemed lighter, everyone was busy with Christmas cleaning, shopping, giving, sharing—it was always a marvelous time. From November 15th of every year, stores were decorated, and Christmas carols played continuously. Since I left home, Christmas became one of the saddest times. I couldn't stand listening to Christmas carols, especially Dolly Parton's, "I'll Be Home With Bells

On." Occasionally, tears welled in my eyes when I entered a toy store and saw excited children with their parents fussing about the toys they wanted. I didn't sense that joyous and wonderful feeling anymore, possibly because I was thousands of miles from home and family.

I didn't allow my feelings to deter me from shopping for my children and family. I had started saving meager amounts each week and had enough to buy their presents. I shopped for clothes and toys for the children. Some of my siblings had special requests, but Mom and Dad said I didn't have to get them anything. I ignored them. They were doing so much for me I had to get them something. I made a special effort to get Kianna a bicycle, since she was too old for the tricycle I promised her. By December 1st, I gift wrapped everybody's presents, packed them in a large box, and sent it along. The joy they shared with me after receiving the package was enough to make me happier than I had felt in a long time. Junior was still too young to understand, but Kianna was ecstatic.

TWENTY THREE

Winds of Change

I awoke about 5 AM one cool morning in mid-January feeling refreshed. I lay on the bed in the dark bedroom with my eyes closed. My mind drifted home and the tears began trickling down. How I longed for my children. Many times, I contemplated going back to Guyana, but decided against it because I hadn't achieved anything, and I refused to return being worse off than I left. Returning to Guyana meant starting all over again. Besides, about three months after I migrated, Guyana began experiencing inflation, and its economy took a nosedive. Prices skyrocketed and many people lost their jobs. It was difficult for those in the job market to obtain employment. Returning home empty handed was simply an option I couldn't afford. I sat up in bed and reminded myself of the legal fees I had to raise before going back to the attorney. Time slipped by. My children were getting older, and we were growing further and further apart.

Reaching to the lampstand, I turned on the light, read my Bible, prayed, then got up and looked out the bedroom window. The captivating orange colored sunrise in the east ascended slowly, greeting the dawn of a brand new day. Sparrows flew gracefully overhead, chirping melodiously. The morning air mixed with fresh dew drops was stimulating, causing me to inhale and exhale great gulps of fresh air. In spite of my problems, I was thankful to be alive and healthy. After a long, warm shower, I grabbed the remote and sat down in front of the television. Flicking channel after channel proved futile. I got up and looked outside again. It was a beautiful day. It would've been wasted indoors. A couple passed by. The gentleman had a towel thrown over his shoulders and the woman wore a bathing suit with a towel wrapped around her lower body. It was indeed a great morning for the beach.

As quickly as the thought entered my mind, I rushed to my room, pulled opened the drawer, and retrieved my tiger print, one-piece bathing suit. I seldom had the urge to go to the beach.

After dressing, I did some half turns, examining myself in the mirror. I hadn't changed much since I left Guyana, besides gaining about ten pounds in mostly the right places. Weighing in at about 120 pounds, I stood 5-foot, 3-inches tall. I put on my shorts and T-shirt over the swimsuit, grabbed a towel, and took a brisk 20-minute walk down to Brown's Beach.

Approaching the seashore I slowed my pace, looking around for a place to leave my belongings. I noticed an empty bench about 20 feet away. I took off my shirt and shorts, left them on the bench, placed my bathing cap on my head, and proceeded to the edge of the wide vastness of blue water. Testing the water, I stood there, allowing the waves to wash over my feet.

A group of men were to the far right.

"Well, hello, there."

"Good morning."

"Sure beautiful sight on a great morning."

"You're welcome to join us over here...."

I smiled and continued on my way into the sea. The water was a tad chilly. I picked a spot a short way off from the majority of swimmers. I couldn't swim, so I was careful not to stray far from shore. Wetting my face and allowing the salty water to cover up to my shoulders felt good. Then I kept a look-out for the forceful waves that came minutes apart, lest they cover my head and carry me like they were taking the sand. From the moment my body was partly submerged in the water, I knew I'd be at the beach for a long time. It was that good.

The beach became more crowded. I watched children playing with their dog and a ball, and then my attention turned to four professional swimmers, racing each other, diving and back stroking. Suddenly, a man emerged with noisy splashes, about five feet from me. He flashed me a smile, revealing a gold front tooth which glittered in the sunlight. I didn't return the smile, but held his gaze for a few seconds.

"Hi, you enjoying the water this morning?" he said, cheerily.

I nodded, then immediately focused my attention again on the children and their dog. I heard nothing else from him, and looking around, he was gone. After another 20 minutes or so, I felt tired, but I wasn't ready to go home. I left the sea and walked for a couple yards on the shore, then sat down on the sand.

I smiled, my mind drifting back to when Kianna and I had visited Barbados three years earlier. We tried to build a sandcastle, together, on that same beach. Kianna became upset when some restless waves washed it partly away.

"A dollar for your thoughts," a voice said beside me.

I looked up into the eyes of the gentleman who spoke to me while in the water.

"They're priceless," I replied, and continued playing in the sand.

"You mind me joining you?" he asked, then sat down before I had a chance to reply.

Even now, I cannot remember how the conversation went between us, but I recalled thinking that he seemed different than other guys I'd met. They scarcely hesitate to compliment a lady on how good she looks, whether true or not, especially while she is wearing a bathing suit. But here was this guy, carrying on a lively conversation, yet he hardly even seemed to notice my body or what I was wearing. I relaxed. A while later the sun overhead started beating down on my bare back with a vengeance.

"I'm going back into the sea," I said, rising to my feet.

"Alright. I going home," he said. He got up and we headed in opposite directions.

After spending another uneventful half hour in the water, I decided it was time to go home. I paddled out of the water, headed for the beach house, and showered quickly. I towel dried myself while still in my bathing suit, then put on my shorts and T-shirt. Walking up the embankment away from the sea made me realize how tired I was. Checking the pocket of my shorts I retrieved four dollar bills I had placed there. Instead of walking home, I made a quick decision to wait for the bus. I crossed the road to the bus stop, hoping I didn't have to wait long.

It was not quite three minutes when my newly found acquaintance joined me again.

"So, you leaving?" he asked, smiling. At the same time, he buttoned his shirt, hiding his dark, hairy chest.

"Yep, I've had enough. You seem to have a habit of appearing out of nowhere. Where'd you come from?" I asked, looking around at the cluttered convenience store behind me.

"In the store."

"I'm sure I looked in there while crossing the road, but I didn't see anyone."

"Remember, you can't always see everything. So sorry, I talked with you and didn't even introduce myself. I'm Ricardo, Ricardo Coppin," he said, holding out his hand.

I smiled, accepting his firm handshake.

"I'm Angelique."

"Nice name, never heard it before. Which bus you' waiting on?"

"Forde's Road," I replied, looking down the road. The road was clear.

"Angelique, is alright if I ask you something?" Ricardo cocked his head sideways, looking at me intently.

I returned his stare for a moment.

"If I recall clearly, you asked a couple of things so far and never once asked permission. Why ask now?"

"You got an interesting personality." He smiled. "I believe we can become friends. Just friends," he reiterated, smiling broadly. "And that is, if you ain't have a jealous husband or boyfriend because I don't want anybody shooting me."

Without responding, I folded my arms and shifted from one foot to the other, then allowed my eyes to pick him apart. What a pity we're not made to see beyond the physical. He stood about two inches taller than me, dark brown and burly. He couldn't be more than three years my senior. He was not what one would call handsome, but he was soft-spoken and there was something about the way he looked at me, with light brown, imploring eyes.

"….I know how ladies are, but I can give you mine."

"Ah…. give me what?" I asked, puzzled.

"Short concentration span or your thoughts far? My number." His face took on a serious expression. He patted his shirt, then pants pockets as if looking for something.

"You got a pen?"

"No."

"Cheeze um! Just the day I ain't got a piece of paper or a pen," he remarked, slapping his forehead lightly. "Okay, then pleeease try to remember this and as soon as you reach home, write it down then you can call me whenever - 42-52-168, 42 -52 -168," Ricardo said. After that, following everything Ricardo said, he repeated those numbers in the same syllables - 42-52 -168, causing them to remain in my brain, whether I wanted them there or not. He sounded so funny, I looked at him fixedly and smiled, but he was serious.

"There's my bus," I said, looking up the road.

Ricardo searched frantically around him. He dashed across the road and grabbed a small piece of white paper, fluttering in the wind. I scarcely believe he observed the traffic rules before darting across the road again prior to the minivan stopping. He quickly picked up a little rock. I got on the bus and the driver was about to continue on his journey when Ricardo shouted, "Driver, wait—wait, wait! Please!"

Looking back, Ricardo had rested the paper against the opened door of the bus and printed on it with the stone. The driver stared suspiciously at him. Within a couple of seconds, he was finished, then he hopped on the bus.

"A minute driver, a minute, please," Ricardo said, his eyes anxiously searching among the then alerted passengers.

I was already seated. He walked midway into the bus and handed me the folded piece of paper.

"Thanks very much driver, thanks," he said, hopping off the bus, leaving the curious passengers gazing from him to me with puzzled facial expressions.

"That had to be really important," the gentleman sitting next to me remarked.

I immediately unfolded the paper and looked at it. Remarkably, the imprints of the number, as Ricardo was saying it – 42-52-168 were visible. I thought of him and his actions for a long time. Two things about him impressed me--his seriousness and the extent to which he went to get me his number. If I ever contacted him, I was aware it could get serious, but was I ready for another relationship? I didn't even want to answer the question. It was Sunday and a house needed cleaning.

I had a late breakfast, and then cleaned the entire house. After doing Cleveland's and my laundry, I cooked. Surprisingly, that day Cleveland was home early.

"Hi Angelique, how you doing? The house looks good. I thank you so much."

"You're welcome, but forget it. It's I who must thank you," I replied casually.

"Heard from home lately? Then again, I shouldn't ask that, 'cause you get a letter every week. Your mother is like you—loves to write."

"That's true. Sometimes her letters are three and four pages long, back and front. I enjoy reading them, although at times they bring me bad news and make me sad."

The ringing of the telephone interrupted our conversation. Cleveland answered it.

"Hi Simone, what's up? Looking for Angelique? She right here. Oh, there's a show this evening? I didn't know that. No, I plan' to retire early this evening. I have two good movies. I was about to ask Angelique if she wan' watch them with me. Hold on."

Cleveland turned his attention to me.

"Simone and Alex asking if you feel like taking in a body building show this evening. 8 o'clock. Still got time," he said, looking at the clock on the wall.

"Not sure…I'm tired. I was at the beach this morning."

"You actually went to the beach?" Cleveland interrupted in amazement. "You alone?"

"Yep," I said nodding my head.

"Good fo' you, bo. You should do that more often. Anyway, think you can make the show? Simone lookin' fo' company while Alex on stage showing the world what belong to her," he laughed loudly.

"Ask her what time they'll collect me."

"Yes, she sound like she gon' make it. What time y'all could pick her up? No, bo, I in for the night. Y'all go and enjoy y'all self. 7:30 alright, Angelique?"

"Yes, that's good."

Then one of Cleveland's friends, Dave, shouted for him.

"Is Angelique home? I want her to meet my wife. She is Guyanese like her."

Dave and Grace entered and an almost two-hour conversation struck up between us. Talking with Grace, it felt like I knew her all my life. I was glad to learn that they lived only two blocks away.

Later that evening, Simone and Alex picked me up as planned, and we enjoyed the show. Ricardo was forgotten, and I didn't even mention him to Simone when she asked me during the show how come I went to the beach by myself.

Sometimes I preferred being alone, especially during those moments when memories overwhelmed me, and I couldn't hold back tears. Weekends were particularly unhappy. They appeared long, possibly because I always stayed at home. I visited neither Simone nor Grace on weekends since both of their husbands worked during the week, so I allowed them their quality time.

It was now three weeks since I had gone to the beach. After my chores, I retrieved my writing notebook. One author on the show, *Ideas Becoming Reality*, said it was easier writing about what you know, so, I decided I would base my storyline around my life. My story became interesting and I was enjoying writing it. After about two hours, my eyes and fingers became tired. I took a television break then chatted on the phone for a while with Simone and Grace. Afterwards, I sat on the porch, watching as couples got into their cars, while others boarded mini-buses and went out. Boredom was replaced by loneliness. I felt like going somewhere, but not alone. Ricardo's happy smile and imploring eyes flashed across the screen of my mind. Thinking about him, his number came to me exactly as he had repeated it—42-52-168. I toyed with the number in my mind for a while, contemplating calling him.

I sprang off the porch rail, walked to the telephone, and purposely lifted the receiver. I began scolding myself while listening to the telephone, ringing at the other end. What if his wife or girlfriend answers? Considering hanging up, a male voice answered.

"Hello, good evening."

"Good evening. May I speak with Ricardo, please?"

"This voice sounds familiar," the person at the other end of the line said as if trying to jog his memory. After a short pause, he queried: "Angelique?"

"Unlike me, you don't forget voices, do you?" I responded.

"Wow! This gotta be my lucky night! I wait' patiently for this call, but after two weeks past' and I didn't hear you, I start feeling that you ain't gonna call. So, how you doing? Glad you call', man," Ricardo went on, excitement growing in his voice.

We talked endlessly. After a while, I forgot being bored or lonely. I was also thankful Cleveland wasn't home because I didn't have to think about sharing the telephone. I learned a great deal about Ricardo, including the fact that he lived in the St. Thomas area with two sisters and a brother. They shared the family's home, since his parents passed away. He also had another brother, married, and lived elsewhere. Ricardo was a mason in the construction industry and lived a basically quiet life. Smoking, drinking, or partying wasn't part of his lifestyle. He loved nature, enjoyed movies, and the beach. I eventually hung up after midnight and I had a date for the following night, although at the time we couldn't decide where we'd go.

The following day, I was more excited at the thought of having someplace to go, than with whom I was going. I chose an orange skirt suit. I was not too eager for Ricardo to know where I lived yet, so we arranged to meet downtown at 7 PM. Not wanting to be the first to arrive, I left for the 20 minute ride, ten minutes prior to the meeting time. A smile parted his lips on seeing me.

"I can tell you hate waiting, so you made me wait, instead," Ricardo said.

"You got it! Waiting is not my hobby," I responded, smiling.

"No problem, but I always on time."

"I'll try to remember that."

"Okay," Ricardo said, looking at his watch. "Feel like taking in a movie? The cinema is two blocks away. The last show starts at 8:30—it's now 7:25."

"What's showing?"

Pump Up the Volume with Christian Slater. My sister said it is good."

"Okay."

"Let's go to Cheffette's and get something to eat. You mind if we order take away?" he asked.

"Not at all, but I'll have something light," I responded.

As soon as we made it to our seats in the balcony, the national anthem started. The movie was good and we both were absorbed in it, but we still found time to chat and get to know a little more about each other.

Exiting the cinema, Ricardo asked, "You had a good evening?"

"Yes. Thanks to you."

"Can we do this again?" he asked, looking at me. I avoided his eyes. They made me uncomfortable. When he looked at me, it were as if he saw a part of me I preferred to keep hidden.

"Probably," I responded.

"And you sure there ain't nobody to get annoyed if we do this often?"

"On my part, no. What about you?" I held his gaze. We were standing at the corner of the crowded and noisy Roebuck Street. Cab drivers were shouting above the mass of people, trying to attract passengers.

"You wouldn't have a problem with me. If I had anybody else, I wouldn't be here with you," he said with that serious countenance I was beginning to learn. My sixth sense told me he was truthful. "It's after midnight. Let me take you home?"

"No, I'll be fine. Taxis are right across the road," I said, pointing to the waiting cabs, lining the corner of the street.

"Now, that will make me worry. Will you call me as soon as you get in?" We crossed over the road.

"Taxi?" one of the cab drivers asked, approaching us.

"Yes, a minute though," Ricardo answered.

"Really, it will be all right, but I'll call if you insist."

"Then I insist," Ricardo said, faking firmness.

Laughing, I boarded the taxi. Ricardo paid the man before I even said where I was going.

"She's going Britton's Hill. Is that enough?" he asked the driver.

"Yeah, yeah. Thanks man," the driver said starting the engine.

After a couple more dates and telephone conversations, Ricardo expressed his feelings to me.

"Angelique, from day one I saw you on the beach, I felt something for you I ain't feel for nobody in a long time. I love you."

I didn't respond, only forced a smile. It was a Friday evening, about one month after our first date. We were sitting in Queen's Park, in Bridgetown. I had the feeling that Ricardo was sincere from the first time we met—the way he took time trying to make me remember his telephone number without even asking for mine. When we were together, I was the focus of his attention—the way he looked at me, listened to everything I said, wanting to know all he could about not only me, but my family, my children, my interests. When he realized I wasn't ready, he didn't pressure me for sex, although a few times I sensed his impatience. He saw my financial needs and was generous in meeting them. This was enough for me.

But when I searched my heart, even though I enjoyed Ricardo's company and liked him, I was not in love with him. To some extent, I preferred it that way. I reasoned to myself—after the painful experience with my first marriage, being loved may be the better way to go. I loved William unconditionally and what did I receive? I don't think he ever loved me back. One major problem in our relationship—William was a taker and hardly gave anything—neither to the relationship, me, nor the children. I did the loving and everything else to make our union work. When I left him, I vowed I'd never love another man. If Ricardo wants me, I suppose he would have to be the one doing the loving.

"What you thinking? Did you hear me?" Ricardo asked.

"I wish I can be honest with you, without hurting your feelings."

Ricardo sighed, his eyes boring into mine.

"What happen? You got somebody else? That's the only thing would hurt me."

"Nothing like that," I held his gaze.

"Then I could deal with anything else," he smiled.

"Since I met you, you've been good to me. You're a nice person and deserve someone who'll love you, care for you, look out for you, and everything else, but I'm not sure I'm that person."

Ricardo sat there staring at me and I felt uncomfortable, saying what I needed to say.

"I may care for you and even look out for you, but I cannot say at this moment that I love you. I really don't want to waste your time or hurt you."

Ricardo took my hand. "Angie," he said, "Ain't no hurry. I can wait. Real love grows. I had a broken relationship too, and at one time I thought that way, but I got over it and I feel the time has come for me to move on. You will get there too."

Ricardo and I began seeing each other more often. Eventually he met my few friends. It was a sunny day at the horse races—Barbados Cockspur Gold Cup. The Garrison Savannah, the race course, came alive, exploding in colors. Horse racing fans congregated to watch and bet on their favorite horses, while others like me, went for the fun of it. Ricardo and I made plans to meet at the Garrison and he was already waiting at the main gate when I got there with Cleveland, Alex, Simone, and Grace. I introduced them all to Ricardo, and Cleveland was the last.

"You seem an alright fella, from what I heard," Cleveland turned and looked at me, still shaking Ricardo's hand, smiling, broadly. "But lemme tell you, don't hurt my friend, or you will answer to me. She is like my daughter now, okay?"

"I don't say much, man. Time will tell," Ricardo responded, with upraised hands and smiling. At that moment, the commentator announced the start of the first race and we all headed in the direction of the finishing line.

One evening during conversation, Ricardo looked up from the newspapers he was browsing, a broad smile on his face.

"My sister, Susan, is asking about you."

"Oh really? She's always nice on the phone. "Is she the mother-figure since your Mom is no longer around?"

"Naah," he responded, shaking his head. "She is the last and she twenty-four. She cool. I want you to meet all o' them. My family is small."

Shortly after this exchange, I met three of Ricardo's siblings. His baby sister, Susan, looked a lot like him—skinny, but a tad shorter. Not long into our conversation, Wayne, Ricardo's oldest brother, said, "Once Ricardo says he loves you, we love you. I'm glad he's dating again. I was getting worried." He laughed.

I soon learned, men will be men, and they will wait only so long before they make their sexual intentions known. Sometimes when we were together, we would engage in light petting, but then there were times when his petting got too intense and I would wriggle my way out of his embrace and caresses. Ricardo didn't understand, but I couldn't give myself wholly to someone for whom I felt no real love; and even though I hardly went to church, there were still some things I felt uncomfortable doing, knowing they were wrong.

We were going steady for another four months when Ricardo asked me to marry him. I loved the fact that he made me the focal point of his life. I also found him fair, loving, honest, and helpful, yet talking about marriage was uncomfortable. When I searched deep within, love still wasn't there. Although I had willed myself never to love again, I thought Ricardo deserved to be loved, and I hoped I would grow to love him some day.

"It's too soon," I protested. "I can't marry you now, Ricardo."

"So how long more will you keep putting me off? Angie, you should know I'm not seeing anybody else. I don't want anybody but you," he pleaded. "What do I have to do to prove my love for you?" Ricardo sounded as if his heart would break. We were huddled close on the boardwalk, watching the moonlight beaming down on the surging Bridgetown Sea.

"I'm still a married woman. You don't expect me to commit to you while I'm still married, do you?" I freed myself from his embrace and walked a few steps away. He followed me.

"All you gotta do is go back home and get your divorce, Angie. Money is no problem, I will pay your airfare and for the divorce."

"No, I don't want you doing that. My divorce is not your problem."

"Angie, I didn't say it was my problem and I didn't mean to offend you, but it goin' take you too long to save the money you need. Le' me help you. That's all I asking. When you get the divorce, we'll be free to move on with our lives."

"Ricardo, I need to think about this a little more. I never planned on ending one marriage to start another. How will that look?"

"How you mean *how will that look*? You checking for people and what they will say? This is you and me. Don't listen to other people."

"What if as soon as you get me where you want me you start showing your true colors? The real you. This is how most relationships start—blissful! And then, after a few mornings all hell breaks loose. I don't want to deal with that anymore."

"So, you think I acting? I ain't the person I pretending to be? As soon as I get you where I want you, Prince Charming goin' turn back to the wicked frog? Angie, that hurts! That definitely hurts!" Ricardo said, flopping himself down on a nearby bench.

"Ricardo, I'm sorry, I never meant to hurt you and I do appreciate all you've done and what you're trying to do," I said, sitting next to him. "I need some more time. Is that too much to ask?"

We said nothing for a while.

"No, it ain't too much to ask," Ricardo eventually said, breaking the silence. "How much time?" He asked, running his hand through my hair.

"It's now August, so possibly by December I can travel back home."

"So, does that mean you'll allow me to help you with the airfare and the money for the divorce? 'Cause with that little bit of money you working for, I don't see you raising that amount in four months."

"Yes. I will let you. And thank you, Ricardo."

"Not a problem at all. This is what I tried to tell you all the time. Then, when you get back, we will talk about getting *married*."

"Hmmm. Why does that word still do something to me when I hear it?"

"Don't worry – this time it will be different. So, when you be coming back if you go in December?"

"If the divorce goes uncontested, I should be back within six months."

"Six months! Boy that goin' be a long wait." Ricardo gazed into nothingness. "But at least is a start." He drew me close and kissed me—a long lingering kiss.

TWENTY FOUR

Putting the Past to Rest

For the first time in three Christmases, I joyfully sang along with Christmas carols on the radio. "I'll Be Home With Bells On" had become my favorite. On that bright sunny morning of December 18, 1990, even the air had a different and much more beautiful aroma. It was a *home scent!*

"Boy, I never see you so happy," Ricardo remarked, watching me pack, a sad expression on his face.

"Come on, now. Why are you sad? Thought this was what you wanted me to do," I said.

"Yes, yes," he sighed, despondently. "I want you to go and get things straighten' out, but you got no idea how it will be without you."

"I know, and I thank you so much for making a difference in my life." I stopped packing, walked across the floor, sat next to him and held his hand. "Mark my words. Time will fly quickly. But we've had great times and whenever you miss me, remember those times. Especially last night." We both smiled at the memory.

"The wait was worth it." Ricardo had remarked after we were both spent.

LI 363 departed Grantley Adams International Airport at 9:20 AM touching down at Timehri International two hours later. Unlike an overcast Barbados, which I had left only a short while ago, the sun appeared in all its glory over Timehri. After the flight attendants tested the aircraft's stairs, I was among the first out of the door, down the stairs, across the tarmac, and at the immigration counters.

Making my way out of the exit, I saw a sea of happy faces—people awaiting their relatives. My eyes quickly searched the excited and noisy crowd. Hands waved from within the crowd and I heard Gloria's voice.

"Angie! Angie!" Looking to my right, there they were. Kianna broke free from her grandmother and raced towards me.

"Mommy, Mommy, I'm so glad you' back," she shouted, her eager eyes dancing with delight. With outstretched arms she jumped up and grabbed me around my neck. We almost fell. Her head reached my shoulders. Her long, thick plaits were decorated with bubbles and bows. I felt a hug from behind. Still clinging to Kianna, I spun around. It was Gloria, and behind her, three of my siblings.

Lots of hugs and kisses were exchanged.

It was an unspeakable joy being home, but reuniting with my children and family was all too overwhelming.

Tears stung my eyelids. Thankfully, this time they were tears of joy.

My parents were basically the same, even though there were small signs of aging evident. It was a great airport reunion, yet, all through that, one person held tightly to his grandmother and wouldn't let go. His bright eyes seemed to be asking, *Who is this woman, and what is going on here?*

"Junior, baby," I said, smiling and holding out my arms. "Come to Mommy."

He would have none of it. He turned away, holding steadfast to my mother. I tried taking him, but he started crying, hanging on to his grandmother for dear life. Junior was no longer the little nine-month-old baby I left behind. Almost three years old, he was dark skinned, with a low haircut and looked like his dad.

Minutes later, my luggage was packed into the mini-van and we were on our way home. Only two years had passed since I left, but it seemed longer. The country's beauty with its many new buildings, well-kept winding roads, and sun-burnt landscape ambushed me while driving along the East Bank road.

Later that evening, there was quite a celebration among my family and close friends. Mom went to the extreme to ensure the menu consisted of foods I liked.

"So, Angie, how was Barbados?" Mariam asked.

"Girl, we got to talk, but overall, good because at least I am here sooner than I expected."

Before Miriam could reply, Carol, who was back in Guyana from Grenada, joined us.

We then pulled chairs to the porch and sat down, ate Demico ice cream, and chatted like old times.

Eventually, it was bedtime. Mom brought Junior and tried tucking him into bed with me, but the child cried pitifully. "Grandma, I don't want sleep with that lady. Grandma, I don't want sleep with that lady."

Yes, it hurt, but I couldn't be annoyed with him. I was mad at myself. I felt terrible about making the decision to leave my babies. Their father's attitude had nothing to do with them. For more than a week, I observed Junior play and talk with everybody in the family, but he still kept his distance from me. One night, we were all sitting in the living room when Kianna took a large framed photograph of me from the divider and held it up.

"Come Junior, come," she called.

Junior ran across the living room to his sister.

"Who is this?" Kianna asked, pointing to the photograph.

"That my Mommy," he said, clapping his hands, smiling.

"Well, that lady," Kianna said, pointing to me, "is the same Mommy as in this picture. Why won't you go to her? Come on and go to her." Kianna lifted him, attempting to hand him over to me. He screamed and wriggled free of her grasp.

"Angie, this is strange, and I know you must be feel bad, but he goin' come aroun'" my mother said. "Junior loves watching at pictures, so every opportunity we get, we use that photo and some others to point you to him. Kianna usually get yo' album and you should see how she and he does be bending over it, turning pages. Girl, Kianna enjoys showing you off to him. And I would tell he, Junior, this is you Mommy. She gone away, but she comin' back to take you and Kianna with she. Angie, you should see how excited he would get when we show he them pictures. A few times, I notice he passed there and stop and gaze' at the photo. At times, he would point to it and say 'Mommy, Mommy.' Then at other times he would just gaze at it, with a kinda faraway look in he eyes. Girl, when he does that, I would feel sad."

"I'm not bothered," I lied. "He'll get over it quicker than we expect."

I felt bad, but I understood my mother was the only mother Junior knew, and I was certain it would take time, patience, and lots of love to eventually win my son. There was one consolation—It was my mother to whom he gave his affections.

Being home again unearthed many memories. The most painful were those of William and me. To my dismay, those covered up hurts were like fresh bleeding wounds. William somehow learned I was home and three days after my arrival, he showed up. I refused to see him in spite of pleadings from my sister and mother.

"Angie, all he keeps telling me is that he change and he only asking for a fresh start with he wife and family," my mother said.

"Mom, that is hard to believe," I said. "And I maintain, if he was a changed man, as he claims, he'd start supporting his children. But it doesn't seem to matter to him how they survive."

"Angie, at least you can go and see what he wants," Gloria said.

"Suppose that will be the last time I go out there? Y'all know if he has a gun or something? Look, I don't trust the man. I'm finished with him, and I'm not going to say one word to him. I'm finished."

Finally, my mother went and told William I refused to see or talk with him.

A short while later, I left the bedroom and went to join Mom and Gloria in the living room. I looked out the window and saw William leaned against the wooden fence, his shoulders heaving up and down from sobs. I stared at him long and hard. I wasn't convinced. That's when I knew I had stopped loving William Larrier.

"He is my grandchildren's father and I just sorry things had to be like this between y'all," she sobbed.

Our actions have a domino effect. It doesn't only affect us. Hence, we must pray for guidance in our choices.

Turning away from the window, I saw, to my aggravation, my mother, sitting on the sofa crying too.

"Mom, what're you crying for?" I asked, irritation creeping into my voice.

"He is my grandchildren's father and I sorry things had to be like this between y'all," she sobbed.

"I thought it was only yesterday we were watching *The Oprah Show* when we felt sorry for those battered and abused women who went back into relationships they had previously given up," I reminded my mother. "Look at that woman who showed a picture of her badly damaged scalp and reported that her husband swung her around by her hair, causing chunks of it to remain in his hand. She had left him for a while, but months later she went back with him, only to be beaten yet again. While Oprah cried, you remember what she asked the woman? 'After all of this, why do you go back? Why do you go back?' Mom, that show helped me make up my mind. I am not going back with William. I believe it's time for me to move forward, not backward."

"I know," Mom said, blowing her nose on a napkin Gloria handed her. "Ah sorry how things work' out between y'all."

"Well, I'm sorry too, Mom. It's crying time for him now. I've shed enough tears. And who was the cause?" With a shrug of my shoulders, I sat down and focused on a comedy show on the television.

William told friends and relatives of my rejection of him and many people said I was wrong. I looked like the villain. Everyone seemed to have forgotten about my years of pain and suffering at William's hand. It seemed as if nobody cared or even remembered the heartaches that caused me to leave my children, family, and everything I loved, to live alone in another country. It was an exceptionally difficult decision, but nobody cared.

William told his friends and relatives of my rejection of him, and many people told me I was wrong. I looked like the villain.

Do what you need to do with a clear conscience. You are the one in the situation.

My father was the only person who stood by me with my decision. Although my mother and siblings were speaking to William, my dad never spoke to him again—not while I was gone, neither when I returned. A few days after William showed up at my parents' home, my father received a letter.

"Evelyn, ain't this absurd? Wha' he really think it is at all?" Dad said, holding out the opened letter he had received and read.

"Wha' you mean?" Mom asked. She took the letter, read it, and then passed it to me.

I shook my head upon completion and handed the letter back to my father. It was an apology from William to my dad on how he treated me, along with a request for my father's assistance to help him reunite his family.

"I not in that," Dad said, crumpling the paper in his hand, and throwing it at Junior. Junior ran after it, kicking it around the living room.

Ricardo called me every day for the first two weeks while I was in Guyana.

"Do you know what your phone bill will look like?" I asked one evening while we chatted.

"No problem, Angie. I miss you and I can't wait until you get back," he said.

"It's always nice while one is making overseas calls, but when the bill comes you wish you didn't stay that long on the phone, or even make the call," I warned him.

Ricardo laughed heartily.

"Okay, Angie, I understand, and we may need that same money when you get back, so I will bear my loneliness."

"Once a week will be good."

After that, I heard from Ricardo once or twice a week. When I told my family about him, they were happy for me.

"Angie, yo' older now, and from the terrible experience you went through with William, I don't think you will make another wrong choice. I give you me blessing," Mom said. We were sitting on the porch enjoying the cool night's breeze and watching the traffic pass slowly by.

"From how he talk' wit' me on the phone, he sound alright. But who wouldn't sound alright. Ah only hope he not another William," Dad joked.

"He will get a taste of what William get," Gloria butted in. "I never see a big man cry so. All the bad he used to play." She threw back her head, letting out her contagious laughter.

"You laughing? You better take warning!" Mom cautioned.

"Ah getting a Bajan brother-in-law," Gloria laughed again.

"So, wha' yo' plan doing with the children, Angie?" Dad asked. "Yo' mother was thinking, since yo' goin' into a second marriage, it might be better for you to leave the children with we. Sometimes second marriage with children don't work too good. You could always let them come and holiday i--."

"Oh no, no Dad. I can't do that. My children belong with me. It was hard enough for all of us these three years. I already made it clear to Ricardo, and he said he has no problem. The only thing is, I will have to return without them for a second time. After we are married, I will be able to file for permanent residence for them. It may take about a year, but I plan to have them join us as soon as those papers are processed."

"We ain't have no problem with that, once you know is okay with the young man and yo' ain't carrying we grand-children fo' nobody to ill-treat them," my mother said, a worried expression on her face.

"Mom, they are my children. I don't think anyone would love them more than I do. You actually believe I will allow them to be mistreated?" I got up from the plastic outdoor chair and faced my parents. "If you do, then you don't know your daughter."

"Angie, we tryin' to tell you, in life things happen, and you already had some rough times. You have to be careful. But yo' know somethin'—your life reminds me of a river—never smooth!"

"What Mom? You and these sayings. What is this about *river never smooth* now?"

"Think 'bout it, a river is always active, and sometimes turbulent too," she started. "You find water flowin' really fast at the source of a river and a lot of erosion happen there. That can mean life is rough. When yo' get to the middle of the river, it is wider, and start slowing down—that can mean life is calmer; when the river meet the sea, it move slowest because of a wide smooth channel. But all through a river there is action—some parts very rough, some not so rough, and then it looks like it barely moving—that part is when life is good, but it is always some kind of movement. At this time, you life is a lil' calm. In life, everybody got a share of good times, bad times and uncertainties."

"Hmmm, I guess the many ripples and waves contribute to life. Wow! that makes so much sense. But where you learn all of that though?"

"What? Yo' think I ain't went to school," she smiled. "Anyway, Angie, Whateve' we can assist with, we will," my mother finished.

"Thanks, Mom and Dad," I said, hugging them both.

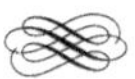

Three weeks after arriving in Guyana, I served William with the divorce petition. My father, a marshal, and I delivered it at his parents' home. I was sad. It was painful to have it all end this way. I had loved this man for a long time.

William was angry at receiving the petition, so he showed up at my parents' home on many occasions and publicly threatened me.

A few weeks after serving the petition, I stood on the road in front of our home, waiting for transportation to Georgetown. My mother was on the porch.

"Yo' notice' William down there?" she asked.

I focused my attention in the direction she indicated and sure enough, William was there with two friends about 150 yards away.

"Angie, be careful," she warned. "You can neve' tell wha he might do."

"I don't see a cause for concern. He doesn't seem to be going anywhere. Does he?" I asked.

"Grandma, Grandma, come quick. Junior pinching my ears and his nails need clipping," Kianna screamed from inside.

"You hear wha' goin' on there?" Mom asked, hurrying inside to rescue Kianna from her brother. After she left the porch, a mini-van pulled up and I boarded the front seat next to the driver. A woman who was also waiting for transportation climbed in and sat next to me. To my dismay, as soon as the van drove off, William darted between two oncoming vehicles, crossed the road and stopped the van. He hopped on and sat in a back seat. I considered getting off, but quickly changed my mind. After all, my stop was the final one and William dared not try anything in the heart of Georgetown City. I hoped my mother didn't see him get on the van, causing her to worry.

The journey was uneventful. The mini-van arrived at its final destination, in Georgetown and William got off before me. I didn't see where he went. Instantly, I became scared. I was on my way to a 1:30 PM appointment with my attorney. While walking past Demico House, the fast food joint which also housed a motel and bar, I heard quick steps behind me. I looked around and my eyes locked with William's. He grabbed my wrist firmly and started pulling me in the opposite direction.

"You did what you had to do. Left me and went away and now you back, you think you high and mighty? Well, I now ready to teach you a lesson you will never forget," he hissed in my ear.

My wrist hurt from his grip. I had no idea where he intended to take me, or what he meant to do. Not wanting to attract attention, I didn't scream, but I knew I had to think quickly. Frantically, I looked around for a policeman. There was none. Pulling me for about twenty yards, he continued issuing threats. Suddenly, a traffic policeman emerged from a side street riding his motorcycle slowly. William also saw him. He grabbed my shoulders and turned me around roughly. Whatever the cost, I knew I had to get the policeman's attention.

"Police! Police! Help! Help!" I screamed, trying to free myself of William's grasp. I refused to continue walking but he started pushing me. Looking back, I saw the police heading toward us. Within a few seconds he was at my rescue.

"Madam, why do you need help? Who is this man?" he asked, eyeing William.

"He's my husband, but we're separated and in divorce court. He's assaulting me," I said, rubbing my sore wrist, humiliated by the quickly growing crowd.

"What do you have to say for yourself, Sir?" The officer asked William.

"This woman and I were living together, and she stole all my jewels and lots of other things and went away. I only trying to find out when she bringing back my property," he said, giving me some up and down eye movements.

The crowd erupted in loud chatter, some of the men taking William's side of the issue while a few women were on my side.

"Man, you should beat in she tail."

"Fo' what? She right."

"That is how the women are."

"Nobody don't run from good. If he was good, she would o' neve' left he."

"It should o' be me, she woulda know…."

"Hello! Hello!" the policeman shouted, clapping his hands to get the crowd's attention. "How y'all get in the people story?"

Instantly, the crowd became silent and a few people started walking away. By that time, another policeman joined us. The officers stepped a little way off and had a short conversation. The crowd started voicing their opinion again.

When the policemen rejoined us, the traffic officer cautioned us. "It's a serious offense to obstruct the peace." He paused before continuing. "Right now, I working in the line of traffic so I ask' my colleague to deal with the two of you," he said indicating his fellow co-worker.

"I'm Corporal Bradshaw," the new officer volunteered. "I going have to ask you all to accompany me to Brickdam Station."

We started up the road for the ten minute walk to the station. A few people from the crowd followed too. At the station, I gave a statement of the incident and the sergeant warned William against such behavior.

"You may leave now, Madam. We will detain Mr. Larrier for about an hour until we think you have reached your destination," the sergeant said.

Too scared and embarrassed to continue my journey, I returned home.

Upon my arrival, Mom opened the door.

"How come you back so quickly?"

"So, I guess you didn't see when William boarded the same bus?"

"What? No, I ain't see," she said, knitting her brow and taking a seat on the step.

"Same thing I was tellin' you. He better don't make me got to deal with he." She pouted her mouth and propped her jaw with one hand. "So, wha' really happen?"

Taking a seat next to my mother on the steps, I related the incident between William and me. Mom erupted in anger, but for the most part, she shook her head.

Following that incident, whenever I had to leave home, I made sure someone was with me.

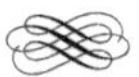

I hired my ex-boss, Mr. Crumwell, to represent me in my divorce case. The hearing was fixed for the last Friday in February of 1991 before The Honorable Justice Peter Chang. The weather that day mirrored my inner feelings. The rain came down in torrents intermittently, and outside was slippery, overcast, and gloomy. I half expected William to contest the divorce, but up to the day before the hearing, Mr. Crumwell said there was no response filed to the petition.

"Next case, please," Justice Chang said for about the fifth time that morning.

"Angelique Larrier v. William Larrier," the Marshal's voice boomed throughout the quiet courtroom. Mr. Crumwell stood up. I followed suit.

"Your Honor, I represent the petitioner in this matter," Mr. Crumwell informed the judge, opening his attaché and pulling out a legal sized manila folder. The black bold writing at the front read, Larrier and Larrier. "No Answer was filed in response to the petition, Sir."

"Orderly, kindly call three times for Mr. Larrier," Justice Chang instructed. The orderly stepped into the court's corridor.

"William Larrier! William Larrier! William Larrier!" he shouted with authority, his voice echoing into the courtroom and down the corridors.

Dressed in a black, well-tailored skirt suit, black high heels, and simple silver accessories, I held firmly to the back of the heavy wooden bench in front of me, aiming to steady my trembling hands. While working with lawyers, I enjoyed being a spectator in court. During that time, I don't think it ever crossed my mind that one day I would be on the other side of a courtroom. I remembered my mother's words, 'Life is a funny game.'

"No answer, no appearance, Sir," the orderly informed the judge. He retraced his steps and took up his position again on the right side of the judge's bench.

"Mr. Crumwell, you may proceed with this matter, uncontested," the judge said.

After about ten minutes, Justice Chang granted me the divorce and full custody of the children. Walking away from the courthouse with my lawyer, relief washed over me.

"In six weeks, the decree nisi will be made absolute. After that, you can marry again, Angelique," Mr. Crumwell said, glancing across at me, smiling mischievously. We were making our way across the spacious concreted courtyard and back to his chambers.

"Who told you I'm looking to get married?" I asked, returning his smile, though still nervous.

"Give me a break! What you trying to tell me? That all this time you in Barbados and ain't find a Bajan man yet?" he said, laughing.

"You probably know what you're talking about," I finished.

"Indeed I do, and I will hear sooner or later. Whatever you do, don't forget my invitation. I can travel to Barbados for the wedding," Mr. Crumwell teased.

Eventually, Junior and I started bonding. Everywhere I went, providing Kianna was not at school, I took her. Junior didn't want to be left out, so he became my friend. He started talking with me, showing me his toys, and including me in his little games. He didn't address me, though. When he wanted my attention, he approached me and lightly tapped me. Sometimes, I pretended not to notice him, hoping he would address me by saying, "Mommy," but he didn't. *In his time, that will happen.* I was thankful for small mercies.

With lots of time to spare and since the computer industry was booming, I completed a five-month full-time diploma course in computer technology. Most of the secretarial vacancies I saw in the newspapers in Barbados required computer literacy, and I intended to move on from cleaning homes one day.

Finally, the day came when my business in Guyana was completed. My departure this time wasn't as sad. It wasn't easy parting this time around, but there was no dark cloud, rather, a spirit of hope.

TWENTY FIVE

Eleven Days

Six months after I left Barbados, I returned. Ricardo met me at the airport. Not having had obtained a work permit while living on the island made it difficult to re-enter. I had violated immigration laws. The immigration officer interrogated me for a while, then told me to have a seat. I had heard that once they ask you to sit, you will be sent back to your country on the next flight out. I was scared, but instead of sitting in the seat she indicated, I stepped aside, giving way to other passengers, praying continually. Finally, I became the only person standing behind the counter. My prayers were answered. The officer stamped my passport with permission to remain on the island for *eleven* days.

Making my way out of the customs area, I felt Ricardo's tight embrace before seeing him.

"Gosh!" he said excitedly, "This is the best day of my life. I use' to think this day would never come." He then stepped back, his eyes piercing into mine. "You don't look too pleased though. What happen?"

"Tell me," I partly yelled, "what will I do with *eleven* days?"

"What *eleven* days you talking 'bout?" he asked absent-mindedly, standing back, looking me over and smiling broadly.

"Here, look!" I pointed out the stamp in my passport.

"That's good time. Enough to get marry. What you fretting 'bout?" He bent down, picked up my two suitcases, and gestured with his head to the taxi cabs.

"What? In *eleven* days! You gotta be kidding," I said, half running to keep up with his brisk steps.

"I couldn't wait for this day, Angie. I so glad you're back...." Ricardo went on and on about how good I looked and how much he missed me, showing the least worry about my concerns. We were sitting in the back seat of the yellow airport cab. My complaining was like throwing water on a duck's back, so I gave up.

"You look good too." I smiled.

Ricardo had hardly changed over the last six months and seemed to have been taking good care of himself. His dark brown complexion glowed, he appeared a little brawnier, but those imploring eyes still unnerved me.

"Ehm! What's with the new polo shirt and jeans?" I asked playfully, pulling at his sleeves.

"I tried to look good for you. So, you notice'," he replied, kissing my neck.

"We're not alone in this cab, you know." I slid to the end of the seat.

Ricardo's older sister had given him a piece of land, and he had started building a house on it for us, but in the meantime, we stayed with her and her two children.

We spent the evening chatting, unpacking my stuff, and planning my eleven days. That night, lying in bed, I was almost happy. Pieces of my life were beginning to be put back together. *Very soon I'll be whole agai*n—or nearly whole. I only wished I felt the same way toward Ricardo, as I did for William all those years ago. It is said that true love doesn't happen overnight. True love grows. I longed for that day because I felt as if I was short-changing both Ricardo and myself of something really special.

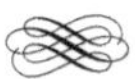

Obtaining a marriage license proved difficult. Some Barbadians believed Guyanese women married Barbadian men to obtain status in the country, then divorced them once they received citizenship. So, the immigration authorities started making it extremely difficult for Guyanese to acquire marriage licenses.

"Are you sure this is not a business wedding like all the others?" Mrs. Red, the immigration officer asked, looking at me sternly. She sat behind her untidy desk which was piled high with worn dog-eared manila folders. I stared back into her large, brown, hostile eyes. Her hair, dyed like her name implied, appeared as if she first combed it, then proceeded to scatter it wildly about her head. She was fair in complexion and heavy set.

I have better things to do besides marry a man for business, I wanted to snap back. Instead, I politely replied, "No, madam. It's not a business wedding."

"That is what y'all say. After all, you overstayed in the country before."

"Look, it seems as if nothing I say will convince you, so the ball's in your court," I said, shrugging my shoulders. She then turned her attention to Ricardo.

"Are you sure you want to do this?" she asked.

"Yes, I know what I want. Why you making this so difficult?" Ricardo asked, holding her gaze.

"Okay, hope you don't come back in here a few mornings from now asking us to throw her off the island because that will be too late."

On an early misty Thursday morning in May, Ricardo and I walked into the little Adventist church, situated at the top of a hill in St. Michael, Barbados. This was in absolute contrast to my first wedding day when I was madly in love with my fiancé. It was a grand affair and I was a proud bride, in a flowing white gown, hosting nearly seventy-five guests. On the other hand, here I was, on a Thursday—the most unromantic day of the week. With no fuss, I wore a peach organza and satin, low-waist, knee-length dress. It had three-quarter sleeves with little diamante stones scattered at the front. I had it made for a cousin's wedding while I was in Guyana. A cluster of cream forget-me-nots stuck into one side of my loose flowing curls, and I carried a simple bouquet of cream, silk roses. Off-white high-heels and imitation pearl accessories accentuated my attire. Ricardo wore an off-white dinner suit with identical patent leather shoes. Susan, Ricardo's sister, and Dave, Grace's husband, were our witnesses. The pastor was already at the church when we arrived.

"Wow! You guys are not joking at all," the pastor commented, slightly pulling up his jacket sleeve, looking at his watch. "Six o'clock on the dot! We can get started right away."

We smiled our approval.

"Y'all look smashing," Dave said, lifting his camera from around his neck, adjusting the lens.

"You can all approach the altar when you're ready," the pastor said.

It was difficult describing what I felt at that moment. I repeated my wedding vows and although I wasn't head over heels in love with Ricardo, I respected him for the person he was. There was a man who hardly knew anything about me but was willing to allow me to share his life, and at the same time, afford me the opportunity to start all over again. I was truly grateful.

"I, Angelique Castor, take thee, Ricardo Coppin, to be my lawfully wedded husband." I meant every word I pledged to Ricardo in the presence of God, the pastor, and our witnesses. This was my second marriage—one I had never bargained for. *This has to work! I will make it work. I know I will grow to love him.* Those were some of the thoughts that kept flipping over and over in my mind.

We did nothing special following the ceremony. Dave and Grace returned to their homes, and we prepared a simple lunch.

It was adjustment time again. I was accustomed to doing things my way, but now I was back to sharing my bed and everything else. Ricardo was cool and easy to please, acting as if his only desire was to satisfy me. Then I discovered Ricardo had an insatiable sexual appetite. Making love two or three times a night was still not good enough for him. If he had his way, we would be spending most of the times we were home, in bed. At first, I didn't worry.

My next move was to find a job. I still had no work permit, so I started asking among my few friends and acquaintances about vacancies. It wasn't long before one of Simone's contacts called and said her supervisor needed a general housekeeper. She recommended me and the job became mine. It was from 8 AM to 1 PM, five days a week at $100 per week.

Within two months of the marriage, I became pregnant. Initially, I was unhappy because I wasn't settled and had just gotten a job, but I accepted it because Ricardo was excited. Also, since I was twenty-nine, I felt it was better to have my last child and get over that stage of my life.

"Angie, I want at least one child from you," Ricardo used to say.

"You need to rephrase that sentence," I used to correct him. "Not at least one child, *only one* child."

"That's okay, you got two already, so we'll have three," he used to say.

Sometime during the first year of our marriage, we started visiting a small Pentecostal church about two blocks from where we lived. The services were invigorating, and the people were friendly, so we continued going for about three months, every Sunday night. Eventually, Ricardo made the decision to be baptized. I was excited and it moved me to re-dedicate my life. I always believed in that saying, 'a family that prays together, stays together' and I knew with both of us on the same path, our marriage was bound to work. It was my heart's desire to have a successful marriage.

Later that year, I was moved from housekeeper to billing clerk with a small picture framing company, a job I'd heard about through an acquaintance. The job was by far less strenuous than cleaning, and being pregnant, I was glad to make the switch, but I looked forward to the day when I would be able to settle into a real career.

Just over a year from filing the necessary documents, I received citizenship and the children became permanent residents of Barbados. But there came another setback. The following year Kianna, then ten, would be taking the common entrance examination. In the Caribbean and Guyana, that exam is critical in the life of a primary school student. The exam enables children to be placed in high schools, and those scoring top marks are allocated to the highest graded schools. The educational system in Guyana and the Caribbean is basically the same and students start high school around age twelve. Kianna did well academically, and my family felt I should allow her to remain in Guyana to complete her exams, then move her to Barbados to start high school. I agreed. So, the wait for our permanent reunion continued, but I was able to travel to see them and they were able to holiday in Barbados whenever possible.

TWENTY SIX

Stranger In My Bed

Something inside me turned with sluggish excitement while the doctor examined me. Later, the ultrasound showed a baby girl. Ricardo was elated. For the most part, this pregnancy caused me to remember when I carried Kianna, being full of life, and I was hardly sick. Sometimes, I even forgot I was pregnant. By this time, we had moved to our half-finished house next to Ricardo's older sister.

It was three weeks before our baby's due date. I no longer worked because I was fired. My employer didn't like the fact that I had to be out of the office for monthly, then biweekly pregnancy checks. He was also upset that on Fridays, payday, while all the other employees didn't mind waiting until 6 to 7 PM for their checks, I would request mine by 5:30 when I thought I had a long enough day.

After completing my evening chores, habitually, I curled up in front of the television and watched the 7 PM news. Most times Ricardo and I watched the news together, but sometimes he was late getting home. That evening, the news ended around 8 PM with an episode about a man whom a female police officer successfully chased for miles in Bridgetown before being apprehended. He harassed women and touched them indecently, but he was finally caught. *That man has to be really sick,* I concluded at the end of the news.

Later that evening, engrossed in a movie, I heard the 9 PM bus stop. I quickly got up and peered into the darkness as Ricardo still didn't get home. After the bus proceeded on its journey, I waited at the door for about three minutes. Ricardo didn't come on that bus, either. Somebody probably invited him out and he didn't get a chance to call, I thought. For the next two hours, I checked every time I heard a bus come by. The wait became unbearable and I was becoming more worried by the minute. It was unlike Ricardo to stay out that late without informing me.

The last bus at midnight sped past our stop, and I knew that was cause for concern. I speculated on whether something was wrong because there had to be some serious reasons which prevented Ricardo from being home, or even calling. I eventually fell asleep in the chair. I awoke again at 5:00 AM. Ricardo was still not at home.

I jumped up hurriedly, washed my face, pushed my feet into my slippers, locked the door behind me, then made my way into the partly dark and chilly morning to Ricardo's younger sister's home. Susan answered the door, wrapping her duster around her.

"Why you out here so early?" she asked, concern evident in her eyes.

"Ricardo didn't come home last night," I said, stepping into the house.

"That's strange, he ain't call, either?" she asked, bracing against the closed door.

We began contemplating the cause for Ricardo's strange behavior, but couldn't come up with anything. By daybreak, we started making phone calls to his brothers, a few relatives, and the hospital, but to no avail. At 8 AM, I placed a call to his job. His supervisor said he didn't show up for work the day before.

"But he left home to go to work," I argued with the foreman.

"I'm not disputing that, Mrs. Coppin. All I'm saying is he did not show up here. That is unlike Ricardo though. If you hear anything further, please let us know," Mr. Reynolds said.

I replaced the receiver. Whatever happened to Ricardo had to have occurred the previous day and I knew nothing. I felt as if I was falling to pieces. My baby seemed to share my dismay. She became restless and began turning. I thought I was going into labor. Holding my protruding stomach, I sat slowly down on the brown loveseat.

"Angelique, you alright?" Susan asked, quickly glancing over at me, then rushing to her bedroom, returning almost immediately with a bottle of rubbing alcohol and cotton wool. She poured the liquid on the cotton wool then started mopping my face, pausing at my nose, allowing the strong scent to drift up my nostrils.

It was a few minutes before I became myself again.

Susan called out from work so we could go looking for Ricardo.

"I ain't want you fatiguing yourself, Angelique. You stay home in case Ricardo call and I will go," Susan instructed.

"No, I'm coming too."

"You sure you okay? I ain't want you delivering on the road, you know."

"I'll be fine," I said, heading home to shower and get dressed. Where we'd go looking neither of us knew, but we realized something had to be done, and soon.

In less than an hour, making my way out of the house, two police cars pulled up at our entrance. They braked noisily. Five policemen quickly alighted from the cars and I watched as two of them roughly pulled a man out of the back seat of one of the cars. His clothes were caked with blood and dirt. He seemed badly hurt and was hardly able to walk. The portion of his face that was visible appeared badly swollen. By that time, Susan had joined me at the door. *Who on earth is that?*

"Oh Gheez!" Susan exclaimed, placing her hand over her mouth, her eyes wide. "That's Ricardo!"

My legs became weak and I felt faint, struggling to keep up with Susan, who was hurrying toward the policemen.

"You all know this man?" one officer asked, looking at us, indicating a scarcely recognizable Ricardo. Ricardo hung his head and limped on one foot, then braced against the side of the car. By that time, a crowd had gathered while others were hastening to the scene.

"Yes," Susan replied.

"That's my husband," I managed. My knees wobbled like jelly, and I held on to Susan.

"Well, he told us he has a wife, but we didn't believe a man with a wife would degrade himself to such an extent," one of the officers said.

"Madam, we have a warrant here and would like to search your home," another officer added quickly, holding out a white sheet of paper.

I couldn't believe my ears. I paid no attention to him or the paper he handed me.

"Will somebody tell me what is going on? Why do you want to search our home?"

"Officer, what is the problem? What did my brother do?" Susan asked.

I stepped towards Ricardo. "Ricardo, what happened? Why're they holding you?"

Ricardo didn't respond. He stood there, hands limp at his side and head bent.

"Madam, obviously you will not like what you're about to hear, but we have to tell it to you anyway. We have a warrant to search your home for any evidence of pornographic magazines, pictures, etcetera."

"Pornographic magazines and pictures!" I echoed him. "But why?" I attempted to scream, but it felt as if the words were stuck in my throat.

"Madam, taking into consideration the offence your husband is accused of, if we find porn in your home, it will be used to strengthen our evidence against him when this case goes to court," an officer informed me.

"I need to sit down, Officer," I said.

Making my way to the house, Susan assisted me, and I sat heavily on the bottom step. The crowd started following close behind us, but two of the officers kept them out of earshot. Listening to the officer relating the incident which resulted in Ricardo's arrest, it slowly dawned on me.

The man I heard about on the evening news the previous night was none other than my husband—the man harassing women and touching them indecently.

TWENTY SEVEN

Guilty Without Evidence

The weeks and months following that fateful day were a living nightmare. After the police officers were satisfied with their search, the police took Ricardo back to the station. The next day, he appeared before the magistrate and bail was denied because his charges included resisting arrest and assaulting a police officer. Ricardo claimed he had no recollection of what happened on the day in question, so the magistrate committed him to the hospital for psychiatric evaluation. One week later, he made another court appearance and was released on bail with surety.

The media was outside the courthouse, but fortunately, I saw the photographer before he saw me. There was no way I would be photographed in light of such an incident. The photographer snapped a photo of Ricardo and his siblings descending the courthouse stairs. That photograph made the front page of the *Daily Nation*, the island's main newspaper, the following day.

"Angelique, how come we all there and you not?" Susan asked.

"Right there, but possibly behind everyone else," I remarked.

"Ricardo, it's been four days since you've been home and you haven't said anything about this incident," I said, bathing his swelling and bruises with warm water.

"I tell you, I don't remember nothing," Ricardo snapped.

"How come you can't remember anything? Can't you at least try?" I nagged him.

"I cannot remember anything," Ricardo maintained.

"Were you feeling sick that morning when you left home? Did you lose consciousness or something? According to what the police said, this did not only happen one morning. This is not making sense to me, Ricardo."

"Angelique, I can't understand why you acting as if you don't believe me. I say I can't remember anything," Ricardo finished.

I didn't believe Ricardo, although I wanted to. For the first time, I started to question his integrity, as

I didn't believe Ricardo, although I wanted to. For the first time, I started to question his integrity, as scenes of our sex life flashed before me.

It is best practice, before planning a marriage, to find out about the individual and their family. You may do so by spending time with the family, getting premarital counseling, taking inventory tests, etc.

https://www.fionaharewood.com/resources

scenes of our sex life flashed before me. Ricardo never seemed to be satisfied during our love making and would go on and on if I allowed him. Did I leave an abusive husband to settle for a rapist? Embarrassed and confused, I didn't know how to handle the situation. Simone and Grace called me a few times, and I admitted I was too humiliated to talk about the incident.

"Angie, I know Ricardo is you husband, but I really think you should pack your child and find somewhere to go. This is embarrassing. I don't know I could live with somebody after that. But, is you husband and you in it, so, you got to know," Grace said.

A few days later, I tried talking with Susan.

"I cannot get over this incident with Ricardo, Susan. He keeps saying he cannot remember anything."

Susan was hand washing some clothes at the concrete sink in the fenced backyard.

"I really don't know how he get heself in that. Is so embarrassing. My coworker saw me in the papers and wanted to know how come I got a brother like him."

"Was he ever involved in anything like this before?"

"Not that I know of," Susan said, vigorously rubbing the collar of a white shirt. "He was always quiet and didn't get into trouble. But when we were younger, a few times I caught him peeping at me while I was showering, and our mother beat him."

That is probably still a part of him. What on earth have I gotten myself into?

My sister called me one evening, not long after the incident. I hardly heard from my family via telephone due to the high cost of overseas calls. Anytime they called, it was either something special such as my birthday or to deliver serious news. This time, Gloria's voice had a worried tone.

"I calling from my job. You remember Shane, who work' with me at CARICOM Secretariat?" she asked.

"Yes. You mean the guy from Barbados."

"Yes. Well, you know we only see Ricardo in your wedding photos, so we ain't really know he. Shane normally get newspapers from home and he show' me a picture which he said he certain is you husband and he family. The article talk' about Ricardo being lock' up for something indecent. The only thing we sure 'bout is the name, but the photo is not that clear."

My stomach churned. I grabbed the telephone and sat down in the closest chair.

I didn't know what to say.

"Angie, you there?" Gloria asked.

"Yes. Did Mom and Dad see the newspapers too?"

"Yes, I took it home."

"Oh shucks!"

"So, Angie, is true? I'm so sorry."

"Gloria, tell Mom I'll write her."

"Angie, don't go yet—you there?"

"Yes."

"Mom also told me to tell you she had a dream."

"What dream, now?"

"About Ricardo."

"Oh?" I asked, becoming more alarmed. Most of my mother's dreams happened. If she had good dreams, we didn't worry, but we hated it when she dreamed about bad things.

"What was the dream?"

"A couple weeks after y'all were married, she said she dream Ricardo sitting at a table in the house as if repairing something. She said the strange thing about the dream is he was wearing a pair of dark sunglasses. And you know Mom—the interpreter of her dreams!" Gloria chuckled lightly. "She said the dark sunglasses mean that Ricardo may not be who he is pretending to be. She thinks that he probably hiding his true self."

"What?" I screamed into the telephone.

"Angie, I sorry if I upset you, but don't worry. Things will work out. Love you."

"Love you too. Bye." It were as if the energy drained from my body.

Due to stress and fatigue, I went into labor one week early and Romaine entered this world via caesarian section like Junior. It was sad she came at that time, but her appearance brought much needed joy, and started a brand new era. From the moment we received the results of the ultrasound, we had chosen her name. Romaine weighed in at 6 pounds 7 ounces; light in complexion, with little pink lips, bright eyes, and a round face. She had a head full of hair which extended to her forehead. Ricardo held her.

"Thank you, Angie. Thank you," he said with a teary smile.

The nurses concluded Romaine was far from ladylike. She screamed continuously and was always searching with her mouth for something to eat.

Arriving home, Romaine kept us busy, and Ricardo's situation was shelved for a time, but soon, he was back worrying about what would be the outcome of his case. I often wondered if I would have more ridiculous surprises from him. The more I thought about it, the more terrified I became of the future. I wanted to take Romaine and leave Ricardo, but that wasn't an easy task as it dawned on me,

I would be running again. I couldn't run from every situation. I also worried that people would think I only married Ricardo to become a citizen. *What if he was telling the truth? What if he was sick and needed my help?* Still, my experience with Ricardo's insatiable sexual appetite kept gnawing away at the back of my mind. I concluded that Ricardo was an actor because during our dating days he was a totally different individual.

I wanted to take Romaine and leave Ricardo, but that wasn't an easy task as it dawned on me I would be running again. I couldn't run from every situation.

In instances like these find help; find a counselor.

I also worried that people would think I only married Ricardo to become a citizen.

Never worry about what people think, especially when you have a clear conscience. Your actions will not please everybody.

Being in Barbados, away from family, made me realize how much assistance my family, especially Mom, lent with Kianna and Junior when they were babies. Ricardo encouraged me to remain at home and take care of Romaine, as opposed to putting her in day care and going back to work. That wasn't a feasible idea for more than one reason.

First, I couldn't forget I was both mother and father to two other children, and second, since Ricardo's incident, he was sick and didn't work for about a month. When he returned to the job, he was laid off. Fortunately, he found small jobs here and there. Our savings were depleted, and financially it became a struggle. So, reluctantly, at ten weeks, we placed Romaine in daycare and I accepted a part time job as secretary assistant with a small insurance company, earning $125 a week.

With Ricardo's court date drawing closer, it was a tense time. I lost my appetite and suffered many sleepless nights. Ricardo also lost considerable weight. On the day of the hearing, within less than 90 minutes, Mr. King, Ricardo's lawyer, succeeded in having all charges dismissed, due to a technicality. We breathed a sigh of relief, but the dismissal of the case didn't end all of Ricardo's legal problems.

Romaine was two years old when Mom and the children visited us in Barbados for the first time. Ten-year-old Kianna, and Junior, then six, loved their baby sister. They didn't let Romaine out of their sight and their grandmother doted on them all. Kianna and Junior were excited to visit, and made the best of it, although we had one incident with Junior.

One evening, Ricardo was leaving to go to the corner store.

"Ricardo," Junior shouted, "You going to the store? I want come with you?"

Before Ricardo responded, Mom addressed Junior.

"Junior, I tell you, call he 'Daddy' or 'Uncle Ricardo.' You can't call he Ricardo."

"He not my daddy. My daddy at home," Junior said, pouting, holding his pair of shoes in his hand. Ricardo looked down at him, smiling.

"Okay, then call he Uncle Ricardo. You ain't hear yo' sister calling he uncle?"

"He ain't my uncle, neither. Uncle Eric, Uncle Steve, Uncle Clement and them is my uncle."

"So, what you want call he?" Mom asked.

"I ain't want call he nothing, so I ain't goin' call he," he said, flinging his shoes to the floor, then running to the bedroom.

"That's alright, Mrs. Castor, I have no problem with that," Ricardo said.

"Oh no, he must show some respect for adults," I chimed in. "Junior!" I called after him. He appeared, leaning against the bedroom door frame, still pouting.

"This is Uncle Ricardo," I said, gesturing toward Ricardo. "And from now on, whenever you have to speak to him, you will say Uncle Ricardo," I said, shaking my index finger at him. He bent his head, then crawled into his grandmother's lap. Ricardo went ahead to the store. *This is reality, I suppose, and some of the pains of not having one father for all my children.*

This is reality, I suppose, and some of the pains of not having one father for all my children.

It is not good having several children for several men. Things happen, but it would be better if we count the cost.

I believe on the surface, Mom accepted Ricardo, but within she was worried, especially after his arrest and the fact that I chose not to discuss the incident with her. She said the dream she had about Ricardo shortly after we were married came forcibly back to her while visiting with us.

I had just finished ironing clothes around 6:45 that Sunday morning for all of us to attend church.

Bam! bam! bam! It was a loud, startling knock on the front door.

Ricardo was preparing breakfast, and my mother and the children were in the bedroom.

"Who could that be?" I asked. Ricardo gazed at the closed door.

I proceeded to the door.

"Who's there?" I asked.

"Police! Open!" a loud authoritative voice said.

I froze. Quickly, I regained my composure and opened the wooden louver window at the side of the door. Four uniformed policemen lined the front of the house with rifles drawn. Another two darted to each side of the house while three or four more were making their way to the house. Most of them had rifles. By that time Ricardo was at the door, opening it.

"We're looking for Ricardo Coppin," one officer said.

"Why?" I asked sharply, before Ricardo answered. They ignored me.

"I am Ricardo Coppin," Ricardo answered.

"We have a warrant for your arrest."

I felt cold and hot all at the same time. My mother approached the living room with Kianna trailing behind her. Seeing the officers, she knitted her brows and her mouth fell slightly open.

"Where were you last night?" one of the officers asked Ricardo.

"Home."

"All night?" He inquired, writing in his notebook. In the meantime, a female and a male officer entered our home and started looking around.

"Yes, I was right here all night." Ricardo said, disgust clouding his face.

"Madam, can you say where your husband was all last night?" The officer asked.

"Yes, and he told you." I said, turning and walking towards the dining room. I shouted to him over my shoulders, "He was at home."

"You don't have to adopt an attitude. We are just doing our job," the officer said. "You see, last night a woman was raped on Brandon's Beach and your husband is a suspect."

I hurriedly turned around, retracing my steps.

"What?" Ricardo asked, hooking one thumb in his pants waist and nervously running the other hand through his hair. "Everybody here can tell you, I been home all the time. From Friday evening when I come in from work, I didn't leave here to go anywhere."

"That is true," my mother volunteered.

"Sir, we believe you, but we still have to do our job. Put on your clothes and come with us down to the station for further questioning," the officer said.

"You gotta be kidding!" Why I gotta go to the station? I ain't do nothing, and I ain't going to no station," Ricardo said.

"Sir, I'm going to say this for the last time," the officer said coldly, pointing his pen at Ricardo. "You either come with us obediently, or we will have no problem carrying you."

Ricardo sucked his teeth hard and stormed off in the direction of the bedroom.

"This is really not fair," I started. "Because of that one incident, it seems as if every time there is a problem you people will come and take my husband away. This is really not fair."

"Life, in general, isn't fair, madam," the officer responded, shrugging his shoulders.

Then I remembered the two officers who had stormed into the house. I made my way to the bedroom. They were going through a set of drawers.

"What are you looking for again?" I asked angrily. "You wouldn't find pornography in this house."

The male officer laughed.

"What a lovely dress! Like you were all going to church?" The female officer asked, indicating the clothes on hangers, admiring the rose-pink silk dress I had chosen to wear that morning. I turned and left the room.

The police left with Ricardo shortly after. Neighbors formed little groups on the road while some looked out of their windows.

"Where Uncle Ricardo going?" Kianna asked.

"He'll be back soon," I said. All the while, I wondered how I would explain this scenario to my mother.

"But, Angie, you never answer when I write you concerning that newspaper article Gloria friend show her," Mom said. I was serving breakfast.

"It was embarrassing."

"Wha' really happen?"

We left the children at the dining table and entered the living room. I quickly filled her in on the first episode.

"So, you think he do it?" She asked.

"Mom, I don't know what to believe, but at the same time, I'm not closing my eyes to it."

"While the police was here, I remember the dream I had 'bout him. Can you remember the dream with Ricardo wearing sunglasses while working in the house? I believe that dream telling we that he pretending, or he acting. He is not who he making you believe he is," Mom said.

This situation with Ricardo and the police was shameful. *I guess I should expect this since I married a man I knew nothing about.*

After that incident, Mom appeared uncomfortable at our home. She looked over her shoulders frequently, became startled at any knock at the door, and was overprotective of Kianna and Junior when Ricardo was around. On her scheduled departure, I was sad to see her and the children leave, but I knew she would be happier at her own home.

The incident of the police showing up at our home was the first of five over the next year. Whenever a sexual assault was reported, the police stormed our home, much to our humiliation, if they were unable to immediately find the true perpetrator. Quite a few times, Ricardo was taken away to the police station for questioning and then released after the authorities were satisfied he wasn't involved. I became well-known at the station because whenever they took Ricardo, I went with him, and refused to leave unless they were sending him home.

"You don't have anything to do at home?" an officer asked me once, while I waited on them as they grilled Ricardo.

"No. You came and obstruct my home, and anytime you do that you will have to put up with me," I replied, sitting back in the chair, crossing my legs.

That was the last time they took Ricardo.

TWENTY EIGHT

Reunited

We had some setbacks. Ricardo's older sister and I didn't get along and she demanded the land on which the house was built—the land she had gifted her brother. Consequently, Ricardo rented a piece of land in Sugar Hill, a part of the countryside in Barbados, so he could move the house. He was a hardworking man and spent a few weeks laying the foundation for the house. When the groundwork was completed, early one Sunday morning, with the help of some friends, he broke down the house by sections and within a day it was rebuilt at our new location. It was basically the four wooden walls and the floor that were set up before we moved back in later that evening. Sugar Hill then became our new home. The house was located at the top of a steep hill and we all had our share of falls, either climbing up or down the hill.

As long as there's life, there's hope. Kianna and Junior finally joined us in Barbados. They were 12 and 8 years old, respectively.

"I'm so glad to be with you, Mommy." Kianna said, hugging me, smiling. "I now have to find a new school and new friends."

"I'm glad you and Junior are with me at last. I'll try my best to get you in a great high school like the one you passed for in Guyana. And friends? You'll soon have lots of them."

Ingrid, my younger sister, travelled with the children to help make their transition easy, but it was a bumpy road for Junior, who had difficulties adjusting.

"I want go back with Grandma and Granddad," he cried often. He even got sick. "Junior, why are you crying?" I asked him one day as he held on to Ingrid. "Tell me what I can do to make you stop crying."

He stopped crying briefly and with the back of one hand, wiped away some tears.

"I want go home with Grandma, Granddad and Daddy," he said, looking at me expectantly. I thought about his answer, wondering if I should send him back. It broke my heart to see him so unhappy.

"But this is home for you and Kianna, now. I will let you both go and see them sometimes."

"No, I want Kianna and me go back and live with Grandma and Granddad now," he insisted.

"Okay, so you want to go when Auntie Ingrid is going back?" I watched his eyes light up.

"Yes, me and Kianna want go back with Auntie Ingrid," he said.

"No, Junior, I staying right here," Kianna's voice came from the kitchen. I didn't even realize she was listening. Junior started crying again, louder this time. I stretched my hands towards him, and he came.

"Junior, Kianna don't want to go back. You want me to send you alone with Auntie Ingrid?" I asked.

"No, I want Kianna come too," he cried.

I had my answer. Wherever Kianna was, there he wanted to be. It would be only a matter of time before he settled in.

"He will get used to it, Angie, give him some time. Give he time and shower he with lots of love. Even though they spend a lot of time with us, nobody can take your place," Ingrid said.

"What will I do without you, Sis? Thanks." At 21, Ingrid had matured into a beautiful young woman. Her flawless skin glowed and she was skinny like I used to be.

At that time, Romaine was three and as terrible as a three-year-old could be. Ricardo spoiled her and she was always into mischief. After a few days, she became familiar with Kianna and Junior and she began fighting with them. She even tried hitting Kianna. Anything Junior had she took away, making him cry. Romaine got punished many times a day. The first major fight between Ricardo and I was because of her.

It was a Saturday morning. After breakfast, I gave them each a mango, then I left the kitchen and went to join Ricardo and Ingrid in the living room. Suddenly, Junior screamed.

Rushing to the kitchen, I saw Kianna trying to release Romaine's teeth from Junior's thigh. Junior bawled. I repeatedly slapped Romaine before she stopped biting him.

"What happen'?" I asked Kianna. I took an ice cube from the freezer and applied it to the teeth marks on Junior's thigh.

"Romaine finish' her mango first," Kianna started, pointing at Romaine, a mean expression on her face. "Then she get up and went over to Junior, trying to take his mango.

Junior didn't give her and the two of them start fighting. Before I could stop them, Romaine started biting Junior."

By that time Ingrid and Ricardo were in the kitchen. I put Junior on a chair and knelt down in front of Romaine who stood there, a smirk on her face.

"This is your brother," I said, holding out her little hand while pointing to Junior. "He is far older than you. Do not," I said, slapping her hand hard after every word, "hit--him--again." She started screaming, then proceeded to hit her head against the cupboard--a gesture she engaged in when unable to have her own way. I slapped her on her hand again.

"I can't understand how all of this come about." Ricardo shouted. "As soon as anything, you always hitting on her and don't hit the others." He picked her up and left the kitchen. I followed him.

"The others don't get into any one's way," I replied, "so I don't have the cause to hit them. But be sure, if they deserve lashes, they will definitely get some. None of this would happen if you had listened to me and trained her in the first place. Anytime I try to discipline her, you always get into it. You better be careful, or you will hold your head and bawl for her one of these days," I said.

"I can' understand. Suddenly since they come, you acting as if she ain't yours."

"What?" I interrupted him. I felt as if I popped a blood vessel. "I can't believe you said that. Yes, you did! But let me tell you something." I stepped in front of him, "I was the one in those hospital beds all three times for them, so don't you ever utter words like those to me again. You're only father of one, but I am mother of three, and I felt the pain for each and every one of them. Don't you say that to me again."

"I ain't got nothing to say to you, again. I going make sure Ro don't play with them anymore."

"You will do no such thing," I warned him. "You're treading on dangerous ground."

"Angie, y'all stop man. Them is only children. Soon from now, y'all will see how good they will play together again," Ingrid said.

For nearly two days after that, Ricardo kept to himself and hardly said anything to anyone. For a while, that kind of behavior was a norm among the children and Ricardo always became upset when the children fought and Romaine ended up crying. I began feeling as if he resented my children. As time went on, I felt torn between them all. The only thing I could do was pray and talk with them, especially Kianna and Junior, since they were older. *Another reason I should have had one father for my children. I should have waited until my children were grown to have another marital relationship.* It wasn't easy having children from different fathers under one roof.

> *Another reason I should have had one father for my children. I should have waited until my children were grown to have another marital relationship.* It just wasn't easy having children from different fathers under one roof.
>
> **Prayer saw us through this rough time.**

Soon it was time for Ingrid to leave. She was a great help during that month, and I was sad to see her go. We all went to the airport. I expected Junior to protest, but he only cried a little. When Ingrid waved goodbye, he sadly gazed at her. Kianna didn't cry, but tears settled in her eyes.

TWENTY NINE

Proving Myself

Financially, it became a struggle. We were now a family of five, and it was difficult to make ends meet. Both Kianna and Junior attended public schools, but we had daycare expenses for Romaine. Our combined wages were $450 a week. Ricardo stayed clear of debt, so he built the house himself from his wages. He preferred not to borrow from the bank. Due to this decision, there was hardly enough money for even the necessary food items. Life became like punishment.

It was time for me to find a better paying job. I began networking and sending out applications, responding to vacancies. Around that time, our new pastor oversaw a massive cleanup and refurbishing effort at the church. Members who were able to donate money or time did so. Ricardo helped with painting and some masonry work while I made new drapes.

I arrived at the church early one evening when two other members and I planned to hang the drapes. Pastor

Perkins, standing about five feet seven inches tall, dark, and medium built, was at the church too.

"Hello Sister Coppin, how are you this afternoon?" he asked.

"I'm fine, thank you. How are you?"

"Besides tired, I'm blessed. It was hectic at work today, so I think I will retire early tonight. How was work for you today?" he asked.

"Today I didn't work. I only work Mondays, Wednesdays, and Fridays."

"I didn't know that. Your husband told me you work for an insurance company. Are you still there?"

"Yes, I am, but job hunting right now. I need a full-time job."

"I'm glad you told me. You do secretarial work, right?"

I nodded.

"I will keep a look out for you," Pastor Perkins finished.

Two weeks later, I was at home with Romaine when the telephone rang.

"Can you get here at BWIA within three hours?" Pastor Perkins asked, a sense of urgency in his voice.

"What's going on?" I asked.

"And look your best. We have a vacancy. You will be interviewed by the vice president, the area manager, and HR."

"Wow! God be praised! Thank you!" I shouted. "I'll be there."

"Three other people are also being interviewed, but providing it's God's will for you to have the job, it will be yours," Pastor Perkins said. Then he was gone.

Two and a half hours after Pastor Perkins' phone call, I sat in the reception area of BWIA West Indian Airlines. I was nervous, but occasionally my heart did some excited somersaults as if something good was about to happen. Pastor Perkins worked as sales manager for the airlines. Even when I spoke with him about my need of a job, I never expected to have an interview at the airline. I thought he may know someone who needed a full-time cashier or receptionist, but it never entered my mind that my first interview would be at a prestigious airline.

"God, I thank you for giving me this job," I prayed even before the interview started. While I waited, Pastor Perkins joined me briefly.

"I see you made it in good time, and you look professional too," he remarked. "They are interviewing for a receptionist. I only found out this morning, so I told my boss about you and asked her if they will consider one more person. He said yes, and that's when I called you."

"I thank you so much, Pas…. Mr. Perkins—I have to remember to leave Pastor Perkins for when we're at church." We laughed.

The secretary showed me to the room on the left, labeled V.P. Marketing. With my heart thumping wildly and with sweaty palms, I entered the spacious office with its exquisite décor and navy wall-to-wall carpeting. The carpet's color cast a soft reflection on the crystal chandelier hanging over the conference table, while several framed photographs of Heathrow Airport and some other busy airports hung from one wall. The vice president's workstation overlooked the beautiful scenery of a busy Bridgetown. The focal attraction of her brightly polished desk were three model BWEE aircrafts—a Tri-Star, the MD83, and the newly acquired airbus. They stood in take-off positions as if ready for the sky.

Mrs. Moore, vice president of marketing, first introduced herself, followed by Mrs. Bishop, area manager, then Mrs. Austin, human resources officer. They were all sitting around the glass top conference table. Besides the vice president who had an authoritative air, the others appeared reasonably friendly and made me feel at ease.

"So why do you want to work for BWIA?" Mrs. Moore asked.

"I know I will be a valuable asset to your airline," I started, sitting back in the chair and holding her gaze intently. "Although I never had a job as a receptionist, having worked in many secretarial positions, reception has always been a crucial part of my assignments. I also know a receptionist's manner in dealing with a customer can either build or break a company, and of course, I will be here to build your business, Ma'am," I finished, continuing to hold her uncomfortable stare.

She continued looking at me fixedly.

"May I see your certificates?" she asked, finally.

After examining my certificates, the human resources officer asked for proof of my citizenship and then explained what the job entailed.

"We will get back to you, and thank you for attending," the V.P. said, rising to her feet. The others followed suit, and quite soon, I was on my way home.

I could barely wait for Ricardo to come home to share my good news.

After serving dinner, I joined Ricardo at the table. "I received a call for an interview today, Ricardo."

"Oh? Who called?"

"BWIA."

"Really?" he asked, "I didn't know you applied there."

"I didn't, but I told Pastor Perkins I'm looking for a job. There was a vacancy and he called me."

"That's good! I'm glad. So how it went?" he asked.

"The interview was okay, but I have to wait on them to get back to me. Gosh, I can't wait. I have the feeling I will get through. I'm praying." I said.

"The only thing is, Ro will have to be at the daycare all week," Ricardo said.

"Hey, that's no problem. She will be well taken care of and she is almost three, so I don't see a cause for worry."

"Alright." He finished abruptly.

One week later, I received that long-awaited telephone call.

"Mrs. Coppin?" An unfamiliar voice said when I answered the telephone.

"Yes."

"This is Mrs. Austin, human resources officer, BWIA." I held my breath. "I mailed you a letter today, but I'm not certain it will reach you in time, so I'm calling to offer you the position of receptionist with BWIA West Indian Airways. Will you accept this offer?"

I took a deep breath then responded, "Yes, Mrs. Austin. I accept. Thank you."

"You may report for work at 8 AM on Monday. Thank you for accepting. Bye now."

"Thank you, Lord, Thank you, Lord!" I shouted, replacing the telephone receiver.

While I worked at the lawyer's office and the pharmaceutical corporation in Guyana, I was content in both jobs. But at BWIA, I was ecstatic. I enjoyed every minute of my employment. At first, I found some of the staff standoffish. Passing through the reservations department while saying good morning, only a few responded, while others stared at me as if I were from Mars. I was the only junior staff in administration, so it wasn't easy making friends, but everyone was polite. Pastor Perkins made me feel at home. He was one of the nicest people I met in Barbados. Anytime I passed by his office in the sales department, smiling he would say, "Look at the girl whom the Lord loves." Later, I found a few friends in the reservations department.

According to my job offer, I was temporary receptionist with a probationary period of three months and a salary of $1500 a month. That was a tremendous jump from the five hundred dollars which I earned at the insurance company. The letter also stated that after my probationary period, my family and I would be entitled to a limited amount of free travel, and an unlimited amount of ten percent space available travel, meaning, after exhausting our free travel, we could travel on BWIA and other airlines, paying only ten percent of the fare. Life was beginning to get better!

In the meantime, I made a mental note to improve my wardrobe. *It would've been better being employed in the reservations department where they wear uniforms. Anyway, I have a great job and that's what matters.*

For the first two weeks, I basically answered the telephones. It was Wednesday of the third week of my new employment. The VP herself sought me out.

"Mrs. Coppin, my secretary is at lunch and I need to have this document typed and faxed to our head office in Trinidad, right away," she said, handing me a lengthy handwritten spreadsheet. "Think you can get this done within half an hour?"

"Sure, Mrs. Moore," I confidently replied, although my heart started skipping beats and my hands became sweaty.

"Bring it to my office when you're finished," she instructed, retracing her steps.

Lord this is my test, help me to pass it, I prayed.

I opened the Excel program on the computer and started typing, while simultaneously taking all the incoming calls for the administration and sales departments. Twenty-five minutes later I walked into the vice president's office and handed her a manila folder with her finished spreadsheet, along with the original.

"What? You're finished already and you didn't even check with me regarding my handwriting? Not many people around here can read my scribbles," she said, reading through the document and collating it with the original. Quickly, she scrawled her signature at the bottom of the spreadsheet, then returned it to me with a fax number.

"Send it right away, please. Thank you very much, Mrs. Coppin."

You're welcome, Mrs. Moore," I responded, proceeding to the fax machine.

A few days later, Pastor Perkins approached my desk, a broad smile spread across his face.

"The V.P. told me you were her savior the other day, Angelique."

"Oh yeah?"

"Yes, she did. Keep up the good work," he remarked, hurrying down the corridor.

Following that task, I did miscellaneous jobs for other officers who needed assistance. I loved it, as the added work provided experience, and also broke the monotony.

Things began falling into place, little by little. Kianna settled in and she loved her school and friends. Junior was doing well, also. Ricardo was a great help with Romaine. Together, we took her to the daycare on our way to work, and we met at the daycare in the evenings.

Even though life appeared to be getting better, Ricardo's incident was always at the back of my mind. I didn't know what to believe. I also suspected Ricardo wasn't being altogether truthful when he said he couldn't recall what happened that day when he was taken into police custody. Also, whenever I tried discussing the issue with him, he dismissed me, so we didn't talk about it. It bothered me that I was married to someone who would do such a terrible thing. I only hoped that if Ricardo was guilty, he would never attempt such a monstrous act again. At times, I wondered if he would ever molest any of my two daughters, in particular Kianna because she wasn't his child. *What a terrible thing to ponder, but it's difficult to control the mind.* Although I gave him the benefit of the doubt, I found myself being extra watchful over my girls.

After being on the job for about nine weeks, the vice president summoned me early one Monday morning. Upon entering her office, the area manager and the human resources officer were there.

". . . my secretary is due to retire in six weeks. Unfortunately, she has an emergency and is forced to start pre-retirement leave as of today," the vice president continued with a flow of words. "We already have a replacement, but that person is not due before the next six weeks. Do you think you will be able to manage this office until the new secretary arrives?"

They all looked at me searchingly. I silently considered my response. *This is a good opportunity to prove my worth. But what if I fail?*

"Who will be training me?" I asked.

They all looked at each other, then back at me.

"We will be able to assist with any questions you have, but for the most part, you will have to manage on your own," the vice president said, looking at me fixedly. "I know it is a great deal to ask, but you will have to continue with your normal work, also. See, we're short-staffed, and cannot hire anyone at the moment. As you may know, the airline has gone through some strenuous financial difficulties."

God, you got to help me, I prayed.

"I will manage," I replied, nodding my head. The vice president sat back in relief and the area manager and the human resources officer smiled.

"Thank you, Mrs. Coppin," Mrs, Austin started. "You will receive your usual salary, overtime, and an acting allowance.

"We know this may call for many extra hours on your part, but do what you have to do, and from now, you may occupy Mrs. Boyce's seat," the vice president said.

I left the office with mixed emotions. It was indeed a privilege to be asked to work for the VP's office. They had to see something in me to even consider it, but on the other hand, I wondered if I would be able to cope. The late hours and Ricardo having to collect Romaine plagued my mind.

My mother always said, "Nothing good comes easy and in order to achieve anything, sacrifice precedes it." There were days when I was at work from as early as 6:30 AM and most nights, I locked the doors to the airline's office, sometimes as late as 9 PM. Many days, I forego lunch, and most evenings, the guard and I were the only persons in the building.

The job consisted of administrative duties, only on a higher, larger, and more confidential scale. The vice president was in charge of the Barbados office and seven marketing offices, located in five islands and two countries. To cope, I tried to be at my desk extremely early to get a jump start before my boss's arrival. I utilized those early hours to become familiar with the filing system, computer programs, and to complete odds and ends which were left over from the day before. In the evenings, when the office was quiet, I concentrated on drafting answers to complaints from dissatisfied passengers, compiling flight delay reports, typing, and other tasks which needed close attention. It was challenging to complete these tasks with phones ringing, intercoms buzzing, clients and passengers waiting for assistance, etcetera. Being a self-learner was to my advantage, and despite the heavy workload and extremely long hours, I enjoyed every minute of my job. My reward came when I saw my superiors beaming with amazement and the wonderful comments I received. They couldn't understand how I did it. My acting allowance and overtime also made it all worthwhile.

On the contrary, problems started at home. Ricardo could not see why I was so engrossed in my job. I understood his concerns, and tried to explain that it was only for a couple of weeks, but he wouldn't listen.

"You gotta have a man," Ricardo said, in response to my "Good evening, Rick," on entering the house. I was stunned. Worse, he said it in Kianna's presence. Those words hit me like a ton of bricks. Bracing against the closed door, I allowed my bag to slide from my weary shoulders to the floor. In my wildest dreams, I never expected to be accused of such a thing. I opened my mouth to respond, but Kianna looked at me. Instead, I dragged my tired feet to the bedroom and checked on Junior and Romaine, who were asleep.

"You gotta have a man," Ricardo said, in response to my "Good evening, Rick,"

Verbal abuse takes various forms. It's terrible when a spouse accuses the other of having an affair. Get help and rise above verbal abuse.

https://www.fionaharewood.com/resources

Later that night, I tried talking to Ricardo, but he wouldn't listen and continued accusing me of having an affair. It was only the second week since I had accepted my new assignment. I still had another four weeks. That night, I tried to figure out a compromise, a way to be home earlier, while still managing my workload. It was almost impossible to leave before 8:00 PM since the vice president and the area manager stayed until around 7 PM. If I leave shortly after them, my mornings would be hectic. An idea came to me. *If this is how he will behave, I will leave the job. I can't put up with him accusing me like this. This may even cause us to separate.*

"Ricardo," I said, tapping him on his shoulder, ensuring he was still awake.

"Yes."

"I've decided to leave the job."

"Man that is the best thing to do. You can always find another 8 – 4. Ro miss you, and I alone got to be struggling with her," he complained.

I turned my back to him and tried sleeping, but couldn't. It had taken me over four years to get the job I wanted, after scrubbing floors, cleaning people's toilets, and doing other miscellaneous work. I loved my job and was enjoying it. There was no place for boredom, and every day I learned something new, not forgetting the salary and benefits

"Man that is the best thing to do. You can always find another 8 – 4. Ro miss you, and I alone got to be struggling with her,"

Watch out for the petty excuses. It is financial abuse when a family is undergoing economic struggles and a spouse selfishly encourages his wife to leave her job.

https://www.fionaharewood.com/resources

it yielded for my entire family. Ricardo was selfish, unfair, and insecure.

The following morning, I awoke at 4:30 and started cooking as usual so Ricardo and the children could get something to eat when they returned home. Then I had my shower and started dressing.

"So, you will let this week be your last?" Ricardo asked, sitting up in bed.

"There will be no last. I will remain there until my services are no longer needed, or, until the time comes for me to move on. That time is not yet," I said, sitting on the bed, putting on my stockings.

"I expected that. It got to be that the boss got you or something," he said.

"Yes, the boss got me. It sure took you long to figure that out," I retorted, getting up instantly and leaving the bedroom.

The weeks went by and Ricardo continued his nagging. Sometimes, I ignored him, but at other times, I didn't, and we started quarrelling frequently in the children's presence. Our relationship became strained, and I noticed Ricardo began shouting at Junior for little or nothing.

"Ricardo, I warned you before, when you gonna' start testing with my children, you are treading on dangerous ground. Junior did nothing for you to shout at him like that," I said coldly one morning after an incident.

"Ricardo, I warned you before, when you gonna' start testing with my children, you are treading on dangerous ground. Junior did nothing for you to shout at him like that," I said coldly . . . "He is so stupid . . ."

Shield your children from this kind of verbal abuse which can lead to physical abuse.

https://www.fionaharewood.com/resources

"He is so stupid, I asked he to bring Romaine's shoe and up to now he can't find it!" Ricardo screamed. Then he sucked his teeth, got up, and marched into the bedroom to get the shoe.

"Consider that statement again, then put yourself in his place, and tell me who is more stupid, you idiot," I said, following after him.

"You calling me idiot? You calling me idiot?" He blurted out, spinning around and rushing at me with an outstretched palm. I darted towards the kitchen and grabbed the first thing my hand rested on.

"Dare touch me this morning, and I will open your head with this rolling pin," I said, breathing heavily, holding the round wooden kitchen tool in mid-air. The children started screaming and running in the midst of us. Ricardo regained his composure, picked up Romaine, and headed to the living room.

"In case you didn't know, when I left William Larrier, I vowed another man will not hit me and get away with it," I informed him. "If ever you lift your hand and hit me, don't you ever turn your back to me after that," I threatened.

I was sorry after speaking those words and apologized later, but I learned that if you allow a partner to hit you once, you will be hit always. It is better to curb it before it even starts, but there may be better ways to do so. For days later, we said nothing to each other, and I noticed at church time Ricardo found something else to do or simply said he wasn't going.

I learned that if you allow a partner to hit you once, you will be hit always. It was better to curb it before it even starts, . . .

Seek help for physical abuse.

https://www.fionaharewood.com/resources

At the end of my six weeks at work, the new secretary took up her position.

"Mrs. Coppin, it was great having you on our team. I only hope the new secretary is as good as you are or nearly," the vice president said on my last day as her assistant.

"Thank you, Mrs. Moore," I replied. "I'm sure she will be."

"We will all see," she finished.

With the assignment of the new secretary, my job became less strenuous, but ours were never a normal 40-hour week. My long hours reduced considerably, but I often worked until 6 PM. Ricardo became a little more relaxed but was still insecure.

After another year, a vacancy arose for the position of secretary to the area manager of Barbados and St. Vincent. I was amongst a pool of applicants, and to my delight, the position became mine.

That year, Ricardo, the children, and I spent Christmas in Guyana. It was a great reunion, especially for Junior. Ricardo loved it too—except for the food. He hated our white rice and the way we stir-fried our vegetables. He was accustomed to beans, rice, and steamed vegetables.

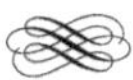

By then, William had re-married and had a son. We still didn't talk to each other. On one occasion, I answered the phone and he was at the other end.

"Mrs. Coppin, how are you?" he inquired.

"Who do you want?" I asked. Emotionally, contact with him didn't hurt as before, but I still hated him for the heartaches he caused me. The forgiving spirit wasn't there as yet, although I was convicted and knew I needed to forgive.

"Wait, you still so hostile?" I didn't hear the end of his sentence. I promptly slammed the telephone down.

"Who was that?" Mom asked, hearing the phone ringing again almost instantly.

"You better get it," I said.

"Hello," she answered. "Oh, was you? Boy, don' worry with Angie, she nerves bad. Le' me ask she." Mom turned her attention to me.

"William want the children spend two days with he."

"Once he plans to bring them back," I replied.

"Is okay William. When you goin' come fo' them?" she asked. "Alright, we going get them ready," Mom informed him.

Kianna and Junior were excited to be with their dad and his family. At the end of their stay, William returned them.

"Mommy, I want come at my daddy every time school close," Junior said on entering the house.

"Oh yes, Mommy," Kianna chimed in, "Daddy said you must send us to spend all the holidays with he because we are with you all the time, and he hardly get to see us."

Now whose fault is that? And he probably paying the airfares.

"Okay, okay, I will see what I can do." I said, hugging them.

You *never miss the water 'till the well runs dry.*

THIRTY

Broken Trust

Progress slowed considerably when we moved into the unfinished house at St. Joseph. It was a simple white wooden house in need of painting. Ricardo adopted a negative attitude and there was no rush to complete the house. He didn't see any urgency, but I needed the convenience of a finished home. I convinced Ricardo to allow me to take a loan from the bank to finish the house, since he was determined not to create any debt for himself. I went ahead, borrowed the money, and started repaying it, alone.

While I continued working with the airline,

Whenever we argued over something, especially if I worked late, he accused me of having an affair. Then he started listening to some of his co-workers who had nothing good to say about Guyanese women.

Don't ignore it if your partner accuses you of cheating – it is a form of domestic violence.

https://www.fionaharewood.com/resources

Ricardo's insecurities grew progressively worse. Whenever we argued over something, especially if I worked late, he accused me of having an affair. Then he started listening to some of his co-workers who had nothing good to say about Guyanese women. One day I found him going through my documents—birth certificate, citizenship certificate, and passport.

"What're you looking for, Rick?" I asked, hardly paying attention to him.

"I want to keep your passport because the fellas at work tell me that y'all Guyanese does up and go y'all way when y'all ready," he said, without looking up. He continued going through the drawer. Ricardo's directness always stunned me—he never polished what he needed to say.

"You didn't mean that," I began, approaching him, attempting to grab the documents he had removed from the drawer. "Are you allowing your co-workers to tell you how to run our home? Why don't you be a man and think for yourself?"

"I not letting them tell me how to do nothing, but they right, 'cause a man at work, his wife is Guyanese, and she pick up herself and gone 'long and leave he," he said, slamming the drawer shut, then throwing himself on the bed.

It was no use arguing with Ricardo. He was one of those people with whom you couldn't reason. *It certainly took me long to realize that.*

"You need to get to know this Guyanese woman," I responded.

Then, in bed, Ricardo became more and more demanding and aggressive. At Easter, I took the children, including Romaine, to spend two of their three weeks' vacation in

Guyana. I spent one day away and returned on Sunday because I had to work on Monday. After a long time of not attending church, Ricardo decided to go with me that evening. The pastor preached a reviving sermon, causing me to commit to doing more for God.

Later that night, we made love, and I fell asleep. It wasn't an hour later, and Ricardo was waking me. He wanted to have sex again.

"Ricardo, my weekend was hectic. I'm also tired from the plane ride. I can't do that again."

"You always crying out and complaining," he said, anger rising in his voice. "I can never have a good time with you." He started wrestling with me.

"I cannot understand you. You're so unreasonable!" I shouted. With all the strength I could muster, I rolled from under him, hurriedly got up, and darted for the children's bedroom. He caught up with me before I could lock the door. Ricardo grabbed me roughly, slapped me repeatedly, threw me on the children's bed, and raped me. When he was finished, he apologized profusely. He was my husband, but I felt violated and dirty.

"Angie, I'm sorry. I didn't mean to do that, but you always saying no when I want my sex real bad."

I was exhausted, but I lay on the children's bed next to him and stared at the ceiling until the early hours of the morning. He slept like a baby beside me. Ricardo made a mistake when he hit me. I had warned him. I wasn't going to allow him to physically abuse me like William did.

I had warned him. I wasn't going to allow him to physically abuse me like William did.

In order for abuse to cease, the victim must stick to his or her word/threat.

That morning, I got up and prepared for work, then I stuffed my toothbrush and a change of clothes into my tiny handbag. I planned to return while he was at work to collect my clothes and anything else I needed.

"I gone," I mumbled on my way out, without even looking at him or stopping to share a goodbye kiss.

"Angie, you still annoyed…" he began, but I was through the door.

I planned on staying with Grace and Dave for a few days. I called Grace at work.

"Hi Angie," she said. "How was the trip? Good you get back in time for work."

"Actually, I got in yesterday mid-day." Getting back on time was my concern prior to leaving because travelling as staff, we were easily bumped when flights were full.

It goin' be a good two weeks break for you and Ricardo with the children gone."

"Not really," I said. "And I wanna know if it's okay with you and Dave for me to stay over at your place until the children return?"

"Huh? Wha' happen? This ain't sound right," she blurted out, concern edged in her voice.

"I can't tell you that now…"

"Okay, okay," she said, "No problem. Come on up after work. You know Dave wouldn't mind."

I thanked her and hung up the telephone.

Without telling Ricardo, I spent the night at Grace. The following day, he called me four times but every time I heard his voice, I hung up the telephone. During lunch, Grace had one of her friends drive us to my house to get some of my clothes. To our surprise, the windows were open and music was blaring.

"He home, Angie," Grace said. "I suggest you don't go fo' any clothes now because he may want to hit you again and trust me, I ain't goin' stand by and see he hit you."

"So, what will I wear to work for the rest of the week? He has to learn a lesson. I don't plan on going home before the children get back," I said.

An idea struck me.

"Take me back to work. I will deal with him later this evening."

"What you planning to do?" Grace asked.

"Watch me girl. I will teach him a lesson he will never forget."

That evening around 6 PM, Grace and I went to St. Joseph's Police Station.

"How may I help you, ladies?" an officer asked from behind his desk when we walked into the otherwise empty station.

"I have a problem with my husband," I started. "I don't really plan to leave him, but I need to be away from him for a while. I need assistance getting my clothes from the house."

"What kind of problem, madam? You need to be specific as we don't like interfering in domestic matters," the officer responded, looking at me searchingly.

I explained the situation with Ricardo and me.

"Is he violent?"

"I wouldn't say so."

"Has he ever had any problems with the police?"

"One time, and that resulted in the police showing up at our home pretty often after that."

"Oh?" The officer said. He folded his arms at the back of his head, then sat back in his chair. "I need to know about that." At that moment, four other officers walked in.

I told the officer about Ricardo's incident with the police and what triggered it.

"Gentlemen," he said rising from his seat and turning to the other officers, "we have some work to do. From what I hear, this man may be dangerous because he resisted arrest previously." The officer buzzed someone on his intercom and spoke. Shortly after, Grace and I left the station with two vans and eight policemen.

Ricardo was sitting in the patio when we arrived. His mouth fell open.

"Angie you bring police for me?"

"Yes. I warned you about hitting me. I want my clothes."

"Yes. I warned you about hitting me. I want my clothes."

Victims must find strength to face their abusers. Go with a trusted individual if you cannot do it alone.

One officer explained to Ricardo the reason for their visit. Quietly and calmly, Ricardo spoke to the officers, admitting he was wrong and he told them to ask me to stay. The officers were sympathetic with him. Three of them spoke to me, while the others kept talking with him.

"Your husband seems really sorry for what he did. He said he will never hit you or molest you for sex again. We think you should give him a chance and stay home," one officer said.

"Wait a minute! I don't believe you guys taking his side," I said, shaking my head in disgust. "I didn't bring y'all here to pacify things. I asked y'all to intervene so I can get my clothes and that's it, nothing else. May I go inside and get my stuff?"

"Sure madam, if that's what you want, but we still think you should make up with your husband."

"No. He needs some time to consider his ways. When the children return, I will be back. He should learn his lesson by then."

I entered the bedroom and started collecting my clothes and some toiletries. Ricardo followed behind me while the officers stayed in the living room. I could feel his breath on the side of my face as he pleaded with me to stay. I quickly grabbed a few things and left the bedroom.

"Wait!" one of the officers said when I emerged with my stuffed bag. "We left you two alone, hoping the man would be able to talk you into staying, but you stubborn, man."

"I'm ready to leave," I replied, walking out the door and down the stairs. Grace joined me outside and we were offered a ride to the bus stop.

After two days, Ricardo was at Grace's home every night for a week. For the first few nights I refused to speak with him. He pleaded with Grace, saying how sorry he was and asked her to tell me to go home. After a week, I returned home, mainly because I wanted Ricardo to stop bothering Grace.

Some people never change. Before the children returned, Ricardo was back to his old habit. Sex, once a night, was not enough for him. So, we went back to our routine of quarrelling and fighting.

THIRTY ONE

That Sixth Sense

I took the children to church whenever I went, but one Sunday night, Kianna asked to stay home to complete a project she had for school the following day. I couldn't stay away from church because I had a part in the program that evening. It was also raining, so I told Ricardo I would leave the children home.

"No problem," he said. "I ain't plan on going anywhere." He was ironing some clothes for work.

I returned home within three hours. The children were still up. Ricardo was in the bedroom. I decided to get something to eat before tucking Romaine into bed. Kianna was then almost 13 and still small for her age. Normally she didn't say much, but there were times when I could tell something was bothering her. While eating, I noticed she kept looking at the bedroom door, and even though she said she had an assignment, she didn't seem to be doing much of that.

"What happen?" I asked. She didn't respond, but got up and went to the bedroom. I stared after her, and wondered if she was annoyed I went to church and left her at home. After my meal, I went to the children's bedroom and found her sitting at the edge of the bed, staring at the floor. I sat down next to her, placing my arm around her shoulders. Glancing over at Romaine, I noticed she was asleep.

"I know, you're annoyed with me because I went to church and leave you home," I said, eyeing her closely.

She shook her head.

"Then what's the matter? Remember you can tell Mommy anything," I said, removing my arm from her shoulders and turning to face her. The frown on her face was replaced with nervousness. She unfolded her hands and wrapped her nightgown's hem around her fingers.

"I want tell you something, but I don't want cause any trouble," my daughter said, glancing quickly over her shoulders to the bedroom door.

I froze. It was as if a sixth sense instantly revealed what she intended to say. My stomach churned, my heart began racing and I felt hot. I wished I was having a bad dream, but I wasn't. Kianna was looking at me nervously.

"Go ahead. Tell me," I gasped, "There will be no trouble. I promise."

She seemed to gain some courage and began skeptically. "Junior was doing his homework in the living room and me and Romaine were lying in the bed. I was reading so I could get the answers for the questions I was working on. Then Uncle

---

"Uncle Ricardo lay on me and started kissing me on my mouth like the people do on TV. I try to fight him off, but he was too heavy…"

Waiting around without support could cause damaging scars water cannot wash away.

Ricardo come and lie down in the bed with us and he started to play with Romaine. After a while, Romaine said she was hungry, and Uncle Ricardo called Junior and tell him take Romaine and get her cookies. As soon as they left the room—" Kianna stopped speaking, glanced at me, then lowered her eyes and started to chew on her nightgown hem. I gently removed the material from her mouth and placed my arm around her shoulders.

"Yes, I'm listening. Go on," I urged. By this time, my heart thumped wildly.

"As soon as Junior and Romaine left the bedroom," my daughter continued, "Uncle Ricardo lay on me and started kissing me on my mouth like the people do on TV. I try to fight him off, but he was too heavy. Then quickly after, Romaine push' the door and he came off me. Then he get off the bed and left the bedroom. Not too long before you come home, he tell me I must not tell you anything, or he will beat me," she finished.

Shame washed over me. I didn't know what to say, neither could I utter a word to make her feel better. It was clear I had failed Kianna by bringing her into this situation. My parents' words turned over and over in my mind. "*Angie yo' could leave the children with us. A second marriage is not always easy with children of a previous marriage.*" I hugged my daughter tightly and prayed silently.

Dear God, how do I handle this? What do I do?

"*Angie yo' could leave the children with us. A second marriage is not always easy with children of a previous marriage.*"

Sometimes we wait too long, hoping for change. Faith without works is DEAD! Take action!

I felt sick and disappointed in myself. Frustration enveloped me and a bitter anger grew within me. I felt an urge to rush to the bedroom and choke Ricardo until his eyes popped out of his head, but I remembered I promised Kianna there would be no trouble. Tears streamed down my face.

Dear God, what do I do?

"Kianna," I started, looking at her directly. "I am glad you told me this. It was probably hard for you to tell me, but I'm glad you did. Also, I'm really sorry to put you through this. I promise I will protect you from now on. I will never ever leave any of you alone with him again. I will look for another house and we will move out and leave him here. But I want you to do something for me.

"What?" she asked looking up at me.

"Keep this incident a secret between you and me. This is shameful, and I really don't want to tell this to anyone."

"Okay," she said.

When I retired to bed, Ricardo was asleep. I tossed and turned wondering how to deal with the situation. I didn't want to betray my daughter's trust by starting a fight with Ricardo. By morning, I felt weighed down by a heavy burden. I went to work but left before 10 AM telling my boss I wasn't well. Yet, I couldn't go home. I chose all the desolate streets and walked and walked and walked, then I found myself near our assistant pastor's house. She worked part-time and I hoped she was at home that day. I walked up to her house and knocked on the door. Waiting for a response, the tears came in torrents.

Sister Gladys opened the door with her usual smile, but it quickly vanished, and she hugged me and led me inside.

"Want some tea or something?" she asked.

"No thanks," I sobbed. "I'll be okay."

"Give me a couple o' minutes. I have something on the stove," she said, hurrying to the kitchen.

I looked up and saw a picture hanging on the wall. It was of a cat clutching for dear life on a breaking rope. Under that picture the words said--*Lord, Help Me To Hang In There!*

I was certain that picture was there all the time, but I never saw it before. It was grace that caused me to see it at the appropriate time. I had to hang in there. If I had chosen to let go, I would have come crashing down on three innocent children.

A loud knock on the door interrupted my thoughts. Sister Gladys looked through the eyepiece before answering.

"Angelique," she whispered, "it's Sister Barbara. You wouldn't mind her being here, would you?"

I was only close with a few people at the church, and Barbara was one of them.

"No, it's okay," I said, wiping my face with a tissue Sister Gladys had given me.

Barbara entered and took one look at me.

"Whatever the situation, Angelique, remember God can fix it," she said, hugging me.

Between sobs, I explained to them what Ricardo did. Sister Gladys was always calm and collected, but Barbara was emotional.

"Angelique, no! He didn't do that to that poor child. This is outrageous!" Barbara said, pacing the carpeted floor. "So, what you plan doing?"

"That's the thing. I really don't know what to do besides move out with the children."

"Angelique, it is 'for better or for worse' and I really don't think you should leave your husband," the assistant pastor said. "You can arrange some counseling sessions for him. He needs counseling."

"Well Angelique, I won't advise you on what to do regarding your marriage, but I suggest you allow Kianna to stay with me at my home until this situation is sorted out," Barbara said.

"Will you keep her?" I asked.

"Yes, I will get her this afternoon," Barbara said.

Leaving Sister Gladys' home, I felt no better than when I first arrived. I picked up Romaine from school and went home. I told Kianna I was sending her to stay with Barbara for a while.

"Okay, Mommy," she responded.

When it was approaching the time for Ricardo to come home, I asked Junior to take Romaine to the nearby pasture, so she could ride her tricycle.

He was hardly in the doorway when I addressed him:

"I had my suspicions but I tried ignoring them. I know all the while you molested that woman back then, but you not going to do that to my daughter and get away with it. You will die tonight, or I'll get you lock' up.

Ricardo stopped abruptly, looked at me, a smirk appearing on his face, and then he proceeded to the kitchen.

"What is that you talking 'bout now, nah?" he asked casually over his shoulders.

"Is this a joke? Do you see a smile on my face? Why the hell did you molest my child? You know what you playing with? Prison!" I screamed.

I followed him to the kitchen. He washed his hands and took a plate to take out his food. I grabbed the plate and tossed it hard into the sink. It shattered into pieces.

"Look, Angie, I don't know what you talking 'bout. That girl lie! I ain't do she nothing!" he shouted.

"My child has no reason to lie on you and I know she won't make up such a tale!" Why did you do it, Ricardo? Ain't there enough whores on the streets since I'm unable to satisfy you? Why did you do it? Why did you do it?"

I shouted, pounding my hand hard on the cupboard top. Then I couldn't say any more as my body heaved from sobs.

"Alright Angie, alright, I sorry. Stop crying, now," he said, approaching me with outstretched arms. "Don't – you – ever – touch – me – again!" I spat at him, the same time heading for the sink and retrieving the largest piece of the broken plate.

He retraced his steps and heavily sat down in the chair.

"I didn't mean to do that. I really sorry, Angie, and I would never do that again."

"I have no guarantee I can trust you. I believe now you indeed put your hand under the woman's skirt. You are sick and I will take my children and leave here. I cannot continue to have them at your mercy. Heaven knows what you will try next!"

Ricardo bent his head on the table and began crying. His shoulders wracking from sobs. The assistant pastor's words turned over in my mind.

"It is for better or worse, you can't leave your husband. You should get counseling for him."

I looked at him long and hard. "Will you go to counseling?"

"Yes, Angie," he said, raising his teary face, looking at me. "I will do anything to keep you and the children. I am really sorry."

I heard Junior and Romaine in the yard.

"Then hear me and hear me good. I will arrange some counseling for you, but if you ever touch any of my children again, this marriage will be over and I will lock you away in prison!"

"It is for better or worse, you can't leave your husband. You should get counseling for him."

Every advice is not good advice.

Subsequently, anytime that incident crossed my mind, shame washed over me. I knew I needed to take the children and go far away, but I couldn't do it.

Subsequently, anytime that incident crossed my mind, shame washed over me. I knew I needed to take the children and go far away, but I just didn't do it.

In moments like these victims should reach out to someone they trust. . . don't suffer alone.

The next day I called a counselor the assistant pastor recommended. The first appointment for Ricardo was fixed for three weeks later and the counselor advised me to attend the sessions with him.

Kianna stayed with Barbara for about three days, then she said she wanted to come home. After that incident, I never left the children alone with Ricardo. Kianna seemed happy to be home although I noticed her keeping her distance from Ricardo. I eyed his every move. I tried talking with Kianna to find out how much that Ricardo incident bothered her.

"I'm fine, Mommy" she would reply.

"Are you awake in the nights thinking about it, or do you get bad dreams?"

"Mom, I said I'm fine."

I knew she wasn't fine, and a call from her teacher confirmed my suspicions.

"Mrs. Coppin?" The voice asked when I answered the telephone.

"Yes, it is."

"This is Mrs. Brathwaite, Kianna's math teacher. I am concerned about Kianna. For a while now, I noticed she is lagging behind in her assignments, doesn't participate in class, and her mind seems to be preoccupied. I was glad this call came while I was at home. I explained the situation to the teacher and asked her to be patient with Kianna. After talking for a while, Mrs. Brathwaite said goodbye. The next day, Kianna's guidance counselor called me.

"Mrs. Coppin," she said, "We need your permission to call in the childcare board in this matter with Kianna and her step-father."

"How would that help? What would be the result?" I asked.

"A court case—and he may be locked up," the guidance counselor bluntly said.

"Ma'am, I really don't want to do that. I am trying to find an apartment so we can leave here. Ricardo may not be Kianna's father, but he is Romaine's dad. I really don't want to have him locked up. I prefer you leave it alone."

I came to regret those words a little later. The guidance counselor called me twice more, then backed off.

On the day of the first appointment, Ricardo said he had to work and refused to go. There I was, trying to help him, and he acted as if he was doing me a favor. That day I made my decision. My children and I weren't going to remain at his mercy. I began apartment hunting.

Our marriage had ended. We had numerous quarrels because I refused to sleep in the same bed with him. I couldn't stand the thought of him ever touching me again. One night, I tried sleeping with the girls and Ricardo ventured into the children's room to molest me for sex. I didn't want to wake them, so I hurried out of their room. There were nights when Ricardo wrestled with me nearly all night for sex.

Many times, at work a few of my coworkers remarked, "Angelique you look tired." Or, "Angelique you look like you had no sleep last night."

There were times when to get some much-needed sleep, or not to awake my children, I submitted myself to his abuse. Then I began having nightmares of beatings I received from William. But when I compared these two situations, the abuse from Ricardo was worse. I would have preferred to go through anything myself than for my children to endure what they had. I prayed an apartment would become available, so we'd be free of him. I began inquiring about a place to rent. I asked church members, co-workers, friends, almost everyone with whom I could have a conversation. Finding a place to live seemed to be taking longer than I expected. Staying with anyone was not an option I was willing to consider because there were four of us.

It was a Friday afternoon while I was apartment hunting when I stopped to visit Susan.

"I'm looking for an apartment for my children and me. Your brother and I are finished," I said. She was eating a sandwich and watching a re-run of the soap, *The Bold and the Beautiful.*

"What?" Susan asked. Her head jerked briskly in my direction and the sandwich was suspended in her hand halfway to her mouth.

"Yep," I said, nodding my head. "He wants to have sex with mother and daughter, and before I kill him and end up in prison, I will leave. I tried getting counsel for him and he refused. I give up. I cannot trust an animal like him around my daughters."

"This is disgraceful! You telling me Ricardo interfere' with Kianna?" Susan asked, tossing her sandwich to the plate, bounding out of the chair and pacing the unpolished hardwood floor of the dining room.

"Exactly!"

"No, no, no! Tell me no, Angelique! Susan screamed. This is disgusting! You good, girl, if that was me, he would be paralyzed by now or dead. Angelique, I am Ricardo's sister and I telling you this afternoon--You right! Leave his sorry tail!" she shouted.

There were times when I was bathing I used to see him peeping through cracks in the bathroom. We were much younger, though. Now he is a grown man, I thought he would be done away with those kinda' things.

Before committing to a relationship, it is best to find out about that individual, their childhood, hobbies, cravings, family background – everything. Truthfinder.com gives some interesting insights.

https://www.fionaharewood.com/resources

Susan sat down again. "Ricardo was always different to all of us. There were times when I was bathing, I used to see him peeping through cracks in the bathroom. We were much younger, though. Now he is a grown man, I thought he would be done away with those kinda' things."

"I also now have no doubt he did put his hand under that woman's skirt all those years ago. I'm so stupid. I should have left him since then."

"Of all the things, I never expect' hearing this," Susan said. "So, you looking for a house to rent?"

"Yes."

"Well le' me tell you," she said, shaking her forefinger, "while he still around, try and watch he with the other children too, especially Romaine. Don't mind she is his child, you neve' know what somebody like he would do. He makes me sick," Susan finished, sighing, shaking her head.

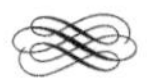

During that same month, the church held its harvest service, and the children and I went. Ricardo was not at home all that Sunday and when we returned, he still wasn't home. We went to bed and shortly after falling asleep, I was awakened by a banging on the door. I opened the door and Ricardo was standing there. He had forgotten his keys. I let him in and went back to sleep on the sofa. The next morning, Kianna shouted for me.

I walked in her room and found her sitting up in bed.

"Mommy, I was sleeping last night when I feel somebody spreading my legs. When I open' my eyes, I see Uncle Ricardo walking out the bedroom . . ."

I believe I became insane that moment! Not wanting to know anything else, I ran to the kitchen, charging at Ricardo, lashing out at him—punching, kicking, biting, butting. He grabbed my neck and tightened his grasp. Lifting my right leg, I drove my knee to his crotch. His grip loosened. He doubled over, clutching his private part. Stumbling back, everything my hands found, I hurled at him—plates, glasses, silverware, pots, everything! Eventually, he ran into the bedroom and locked the door. All the while the children were screaming and there was a mess to clean afterwards, but I didn't care.

Taking some deep breaths, I hushed the children then took them to their room.

"Okay, okay, y'all stop crying. It will be fine. Mommy will not let anything happen to y'all."

Soon the house was quiet, and I realized Ricardo had sneaked out.

Oh, how I wished there was someone I could talk with. I thought about calling Barbara, but she was at work. There was no energy to get the children ready for school and then go to work, so, I called out and kept the children home.

I still didn't want to move to anyone's home with my children, but then the idea of shelters came to my mind. I searched the telephone directory but was unsuccessful since in Barbados, shelters were mostly available during times of hurricane or other disasters.

That afternoon, a sister from the church called me.

"Angelique, I heard you looking for some place to rent," Carlotta said.

"Yes, I am. You know of any?"

"Yes, I rented this three-bedroom house in Christ Church and it is too big for me. You want share it?"

I paused.

Carlotta was only an acquaintance and could be unfriendly. She was two years my junior. Her offer was certainly not the best, but given my circumstances, it was *any coat for a storm*. The children and I had to get away from Ricardo and fast. "Are you sure you can live in a house with three children?" I asked.

"Come on, Angelique--I know your children. They're not bad kids."

"Okay, what's the rent and how soon may I move in?"

"It's $700. How much can you afford? You will have two bedrooms and one bathroom. I'm in the self-contained room," she said.

"Is it okay if I pay four hundred dollars?"

"You sure you can manage that?" Carlotta asked.

Although I knew it would be hard to start paying my own rent, I wanted to be professional and I didn't expect her to share the rent equally since we outnumbered her.

"Yes, I can. How soon may I move in?"

"Tonight, if you want."

That's risky.

"I'll move in tomorrow."

I felt relieved, discussing my moving plans with Carlotta.

Ricardo didn't come home at his usual time, so later that evening I gathered some courage and called my mother. She listened in complete silence while I retold the events.

"Gosh Angie, I don't understand why all this happenin' to you. I don't understand," she cried.

"Mom stop crying. It'll be okay once we get out of here."

"He might look to worry you on the road or at yo' job," she said.

"The police will take care of that. I have to go. I'll call you later in the week."

"Angie?"

"Yes, Mom."

"You is a good mother. Them children goin' love you fo' doin' that fo' them.

"Thanks, Mom. Bye, now." Those words made me feel a tad better.

My next call was to arrange a truck for the move. I decided to call Lloyd. He was a brother from our church who loved my children. It was difficult, telling Lloyd my reason for leaving Ricardo. Yet, I couldn't sweep it under the carpet anymore. The first time Ricardo molested my daughter, besides telling the assistant pastor and Barbara, I kept it to myself. I couldn't do this any longer. Embarrassment washed over me, filling Lloyd in on the situation and asking his help with a mover.

"Angelique, you blurted out all that in one breath. How you holding up? How is Kianna? This must be real hard for you. I agree you should leave."

"Under the circumstances, we aren't doing too bad. Anyway, Ricardo may soon be home. You know anyone with a truck?"

"Yes, but I will have to call him and get back to you," Lloyd said.

"Don't call me back, Lloyd, I will call you first thing in the morning. Thanks a lot," I said, before hanging up.

Ricardo came home about half an hour after my last call. He said nothing. Romaine was all over him as he ate.

That night, I lay on the sofa and the entire scenario of the end of my first marriage flashed before me like scenes from a horrifying movie. Those scenes were about to be replayed. I wished I would awake and find it was all a horrible nightmare. *Weren't some people made to be happy?* The pain I felt when I knew my marriage to William ended was different to what I felt then. The pain William caused wrenched at my heart's strings and left me empty. Now, deep down in my soul there was another pain—a pain I was unable to describe. But I do know the hurt Ricardo inflicted filled me with shame and drove me to choose my children over him.

While lying on the sofa the following morning, Ricardo came to me.

"Angie," he began, touching my arm.

"Don't push yo' luck. Don't touch me," I snapped, springing to my feet.

"I wan' tell you I will go for counseling. We can't continue living like this."

"Of course, we can't continue living like this, and you may go to whatever counseling you want to. I don't care anymore."

Ricardo sighed and headed to the bathroom.

"I wan' tell you I will go for counseling. We can't continue living like this."

Abusers behave this way.. . . They promise to change but hardly do – insincerely repentant

https://www.fionaharewood.com/resources

By 7 AM he was on his way to work. As soon as he left, I dialed Lloyd's number.

"I spoke to the gentleman last night and told him you will call him this morning and let him know the time. Write down his name and number."

"Thanks, Lloyd."

Junior and Kianna helped with the packing. They both seemed nervous, and kept glancing out the window at every opportunity.

"Mommy what if Uncle Ricardo come back and catch us?" Junior asked.

"By the time he gets back, we will be long gone."

"My daddy coming with we?" Romaine, then five, asked.

"No Ro, daddy's not coming."

"Why?"

"Your daddy doesn't have manners. When he learns some manners, he will come with us," I said. Romaine repeated those words a couple of times afterwards when people asked her about her father.

Only Kianna didn't ask any questions. She packed her things with urgency.

By 9 o'clock the trucker arrived with a helper and immediately started loading our stuff. I didn't take anything Ricardo purchased. I planned to buy a bunk bed and a television. Carlotta told me we could share her refrigerator and stove.

"If you wouldn't be offended, le' me guess—you movin' and leavin' your husband," Mr. Jackson said.

"You got that right," I muttered under my breath without looking up. I wished he wouldn't start a conversation.

"I know you'll say it's none of my business," Mr. Jackson continued on a more serious note, packing some utensils into a washing pan. "But I hope you considered this decision. After all, you have three children."

"Okay," I said, straightening up from the box over which I was leaning. I quickly glanced around for the children. They were in the patio. "If you should know, yes, I considered long, and I considered hard. But the worst part—I shouldn't have considered at all. Who wants a husband who would sleep with both his wife and her daughter?" I asked, eyeing him purposely.

Mr. Jackson looked away, then concentrated on lifting the wash pan to his shoulder.

"I—I—I'm sorry Madam, I'm so sorry," he said on his way out, shooting me a remorseful look.

Within 90 minutes we were on our way. Junior rode in the back of the truck with the helper while Kianna, Romaine, and I rode in the front with Mr. Jackson.

"It's probably really hard for you, but you did the right thing," Mr. Jackson said, driving along the narrow Sugar Hill road. I allowed his comment to slide, then he finally changed conversations to the sunny and warm weather.

After we arrived at our destination and were finished unpacking, Mr. Jackson handed me a business card.

"Take this," he said. "In case you need help with anything or even if you need someone to talk to, feel free—give me a call."

THIRTY TWO

Persistent Past

Our new home was a spacious one-flat cream concrete bungalow. The fenced yard provided a decent play area for the children.

"Mummy, we love it! We love it!" Junior shouted, after they finished inspecting their new surroundings.

"So, you're speaking for everybody?" I asked, enjoying the care-free attitude he displayed.

"Everybody loves it. Kianna!" he called, turning to her. "You like it?"

"Yes, it's nice," Kianna said, looking around, smiling.

"Ro," he called. She came running from the back. "You like here?" he asked, smiling broadly, gesturing around him with his hands.

"Yes," Romaine replied.

I was happy they were happy.

I cannot function in disarray, so, immediately Carlotta, the children, and I worked tirelessly unpacking and packing, re-arranging and arranging. Within a few hours, we were done.

Since Ricardo was no longer a part of our household, we had to make adjustments. We decided Kianna and Junior would go to school together and I would take Romaine. In the afternoons, I would send them home on a bus then go back to work. I anticipated a hectic schedule.

My first day back to work, after leaving Ricardo, I instructed the guards not to allow him into the building. I made arrangements for a co-worker to give me a ride to work, trying to avoid any clashes with Ricardo. On that first morning, when I called him, he backed out of his promise. Others backed out too.

I made arrangements for a co-worker to give me a ride to work, trying to avoid any clashes with Ricardo. On that first morning, when I called him, he backed out of his promise. Others backed out too.

When faced with these situations, sometimes the people closest to you who can help, turn away from you. Don't let it bother you. Pray, gather strength, and keep pressing on. Somebody else will help.

The morning moved along smoothly, but I was tense. Every time I answered the telephone, I expected to hear Ricardo at the other end. At about 10:15 AM, the unwanted, but expected call came.

"So, after you get what you want, you decide to go your way, huh? Time does always tell. I know you had a man all along."

"Ricardo, listen to me and listen well," I said. "You call this number again and I will call the police. It's not something I want to do, but you push me and I'll do it." I hung up the telephone. But that was only the beginning. In the evening, after work, I found Ricardo waiting across from my job. When I saw him, I called a taxi to get home. The following morning, I found Ricardo waiting at Romaine's school. He followed me all the way to work, verbally abusing me the entire journey. That afternoon, he showed up at Junior's school and asked Junior to tell him or show him where we lived. Junior ignored him. We were forced to take a taxi home again while he waited across the road from my job.

Ricardo's stalking frustrated me. All week there were confrontations between us. On Friday morning, he waited at the bus terminal, in the same dirty sky-blue polo shirt from the previous day. He tucked it untidily into his jeans and carried his worn haversack thrown over his shoulder. As if invited, he walked with us all the way to the school, cursing and threatening. After dropping off the children, I headed down Whitepark Road and walked into the police station. Ricardo followed me as if he had no regard for the law.

Criminals in handcuffs were impatiently waiting their journey to court, while family members buzzed around in the spacious, but due to the crowd, undersized police station. A few officers were shouting at some of the troublemakers. Waiting my turn, I wished Ricardo would go his way, but he appeared more patient than I was.

"Are the two of you together?" an officer finally asked, raising his voice above the noisy crowd. I stepped forward and explained my situation.

"Wait, you mean to tell me you are offensive to this woman and think it is okay to walk in here with her?" The officer asked, angrily eyeing Ricardo. "You don't have a job to go to? Let me tell you this," he continued, shaking an index finger at Ricardo, "You better desist from this type of behavior because if this woman comes back in here, we will deal with you harshly. Leave here and go your way now," the officer instructed him, gesturing with his arm. Ricardo walked out of the station, head bent, and shoulders sagged.

"Madam," the officer turned to me, "I advise you to go to the court on Monday and file a restraining order."

"Okay. Thank you, sir."

On my way out of the station, I breathed a sigh of relief--Ricardo had disappeared. But I hadn't gone 50 yards up the road when he emerged from a side street.

"I want you know I ain't frighten no police. You's my wife and in spite of what they say, I got all rights to you. And the next time you complain to any police for me, you goin' know."

Ricardo became boisterous and obnoxious. I ignored him. There were throngs of people on Broad Street, hurrying on their way to and from work and heads turned in our direction due to the fuss he made. That evening, after work, I found him waiting again.

"I want you know I ain't frighten no police. You's my wife and in spite of what they say, I got all rights to you. And the next time you complain to any police for me, you goin' know."

These are threatening and fighting words; words that cause victims to go missing or be killed. Don't play with your life. Find help.

https://www.fionaharewood.com/resources

At last it was Saturday. After a stressful week, it felt good being at home and I cleaned while Carlotta cooked. Later we enjoyed television and two videos. It was a while since I had some spare time. Retrieving my three notebooks, I scanned through them. For the five years I spent with Ricardo, I scarcely did any writing. There wasn't enough time and I was busy at work, so I shelved my writing. That evening, I added a chapter.

On Sunday we all went to church. It was a long distance from our new home and required two bus fares each. After church, the children and I went home while Carlotta spent the evening with her family.

Later that evening, we were enjoying a comedy when someone knocked at the door. Brows knitted, we looked at each other. It couldn't be Carlotta. She never knocked. She had her keys. I wasn't aware anyone else knew where we lived.

"Who's there?" I asked.

"Open and you'll see," a male's voice, sounding vaguely familiar answered. Cautiously, I opened the top half of the wooden louver. For a moment, I didn't recognize him, but then the beer bellied gentleman smiled. It was Mr. Jackson, the trucker, who had moved us to the house. He wore a long-sleeved navy linen suit with matching leather shoes. This time he was free of the dingy cap he wore on the day of our move, revealing salt and pepper curly hair. A thick gold chain hung from his neck and he had three gold rings on his fingers. From his neatly groomed moustache and the creases around his eyes when he smiled, I presumed him to be in his late forties. The man appeared completely different from the person I met a few days prior.

"Hi, what brought you by?" I asked, opening the door.

"I had a business transaction with a friend a few blocks away, so I pass to see how you settle' in, and if there's anything I can do to help," Mr. Jackson replied, peering over my shoulders into the house. "But I probably wasted my time because this place looks as if you all been living here for a while."

"It started looking like this a couple hours after we moved in," I replied.

"Good for you."

Continuing to chit chat, I finally invited him in.

Mr. Jackson joined us, watching *The Simpsons*, chatting during commercials, mainly about the likes and demands of our jobs, hobbies, and church. More than half an hour later, he had not made any attempt to leave.

"Don't think me rude," I said, standing up, proceeding to the door and opening it, "but I have to be heading to the kitchen to prepare dinner. Nice of you to stop by."

"That's cool. I am leaving anyway," he said. He got up, said goodbye to the children, extended a firm handshake to me, and left. Once he left, I sat down and continued watching TV. Carlotta came home about five minutes later.

"You missed our visitor."

"Visitor?" She echoed me. "Who was that?"

"Mr. Jackson, the gentleman who moved us here." A frown covered her face.

"Oh really! What he wants?"

"Said he was on some business in the area and stopped by."

A knock at the door intruded the moment. Carlotta looked through the louver.

"May I help you?" I heard her ask.

"Hello Carlotta. I was here a while ago. I only just realize' I forgot my glasses." I quickly looked around and there they were on the center table next to the vase. I retrieved the spectacles, opened the door, and handed them to him.

"I believe I understand all you're goin' through, but you don't have to operate as if you're an iron woman carrying a '*no entry*' sign. Please, allow me to be your friend—I would never hurt you." He said it in such a beseeching tone, I was sickened.

"Here we go again. Same old lines! Ain't you all say that? I've heard that one time too many. Bye." I gently closed the door, then made my way to the kitchen. Carlotta followed after me.

"I bet he did that on purpose," she said, irritation creeping into her voice.

"I believe so too. Some men think they have the most brains," I responded, opening the refrigerator and retrieving the lemonade.

"You shouldn't be interested in men anymore anyway. You had enough of them already," Carlotta said.

Ouch! What does she really mean? Hmmm.

"I'll pass on that." I poured my lemonade and left the kitchen.

The next morning, I followed the police officer's instructions and went to the courthouse to file a restraining order against Ricardo. The date was set for a month later. Meanwhile, I had to endure Ricardo's verbal abuse on the road. At times, he made me so angry we quarreled in public. He didn't care what he said and spoke dirty in the children's presence.

Finally, it was the day of the inquiry. At the court's hearing, hurt turned to frustration, and then to anger. Neither of us had a lawyer. The magistrate asked me to state my side of the issue. I outlined the facts, relating the truth.

Then Ricardo told his side.

"Your Honor," he started sadly, wiping tears from his cheeks. "I had only known this woman for one week before we marry. I meet her on the beach, and she beg me to marry her because when she came to Barbados for the first time, the authorities gave her only eleven days to remain in the country and she didn't want to return home." Ricardo paused, buried his face in his hands and sobbed loudly, putting on a show.

The magistrate sat back in his chair with folded arms and a somber expression on his face. Sitting numb in my seat, hurt, more than humiliation, enveloped me. Ricardo pulled a handkerchief from his pocket, dried his face, and continued,

"Your Honor, I liked her from the first time I meet her and felt sorry for her, so I decide to help her out by marrying her" he said, his voice echoing drearily throughout the silent courtroom. Before we get married, she promised me she would stay with me as my wife. Next thing I know, sir, as soon as I fixed her papers, she find a good job, and started *horning* me. She use' to leave for work at 6:30 in the mornings and don't ever get back home 'til nearly 10 o'clock in the nights—every night, sir," Ricardo stopped and wiped his eyes again. "Your Honor," he continued, "that sexual molestation she talking 'bout never happen'. She wants an excuse to go her way like what all the Guyanese women normally do to the Bajan men. But sir, I don't mind if she go her way. All I want is the right to be able to see my daughter at any time. I am really distressed I can't see her, sir," he finished.

Ricardo buried his face in his handkerchief, his shoulders heaving from faked sobs.

Soft murmurs rose among the spectators. The magistrate pounded his gavel.

"Quiet in my court, please!" he shouted.

A hush fell over the courtroom.

"Sir, may I say something please?" I asked, with an upraised arm.

"Madam, you already had your turn," the Magistrate sternly responded.

In horror, I watched and listened. The entire case turned at Ricardo's testimony. I regretted not having consulted an attorney, but I never thought I would need one for as trivial a case as a restraining order. The Magistrate wanted to give Ricardo visitation rights to my home, every week, so he could see his daughter, Romaine.

But it is said that even the devil has a friend. At that moment, the court clerk intervened. She left her desk and approached the magistrate's side. I don't know what she told him, but after speaking with her, the magistrate granted my restraining order for three months. Then he issued instructions to a probation officer to look into our case before he made a final decision regarding visitation rights for Ricardo. In the meantime, the court ordered that Romaine be taken to the park every Saturday for two hours between 1 and 5 PM so she could be with her father.

On my way back to work after the court's hearing, I thought about Kianna's guidance counselor who told me to report Ricardo to the childcare board and Mrs. Red, the immigration officer, who wanted to deny us the marriage license. *Why didn't I listen to the guidance counselor? I should've gone to the childcare board and assisted them in turning Ricardo over to the police. But it is too late now. Mrs. Red was interested in shielding Ricardo from a Guyanese woman, whom she thought wanted to marry him to get status in Barbados. Was she going to protect my daughter from a man who wanted to have both her mother and her?*

The lies Ricardo told the court left me depressed and with no urge to work. Suddenly, my intercom buzzed. An agent announced I had a call on the general line. The few people who called me at work used my direct line. *Who could that be*?

"Thank you, Melanie. Send the call, please," I said, slowly going through a pile of mail on my desk. I planned to work late that evening having been away for half of the day. Pam and Kevin were already at my desk, reminding me of their sales report.

"Good afternoon, area manager's office. How may I help you?"

"Would you really assist if you had the chance to do so?" A crisp voice asked at the other end of the line.

"Pardon me?" I answered, thinking I recognized the voice.

"Angelique, it's George. How are you doing?"

I knew it was him. His voice had an attractive and distinct ring.

"Well, this is a surprise. I'm fine. What about you?" I asked.

"Under the circumstances, I'm doing the best I can."

"What circumstances?"

"Life does not always go how you want it you know. Anyway, I am calling to find out if you will accept a dinner invitation for tonight."

"Are you celebrating something?"

"Not somethin'. Someone special. You're special you know," Mr. Jackson replied, a smile in his voice.

Tapping my pen on my desk, several thoughts raced through my mind. *After such a hectic morning, a relaxing afternoon would surely be fine. But Angie, you don't know a thing about this man. What if he's married? Is he honest or just a player? No. I'm not even out of deep dirt with Ricardo yet. What if he's another Ricardo?*

"Angelique, you there?"

"I have lots to do at work. I can't make it."

"Come onnn," he began. "I'm sure you won't be workin' later than 5 o'clock. I will see you get to your children by 9. That daughter of yours seems very responsible."

"She is, and thanks. But," I paused, "I cannot make it. And, this is the reservations line. I shouldn't be tying it up this long. Thanks for calling."

Replacing the receiver, I thought about George and the time he visited my home, uninvited. "*You don't have to operate as if you're an iron woman carrying a 'no entry' sign.*

Please, allow me to be your friend--I would never hurt you." I smiled.

"Girlfriend, I ain't see a smile on your face for a while. Like everything went well in court today," Jackie, my co-worker, said. Taking a few deliberate steps away from my desk, she looked at me intently.

I laughed.

"On the contrary, court sucked today. Sometimes, even in the courts one cannot find justice," I replied.

"I see," she said. "But before you continue on that court thing, tell me what or who is responsible for the warm expression on your face just now. I'm only curious because I haven't seen you look like that in a long time. And, I think I like that part of you."

"Jackie, it's nothing," I said, smiling. Turning away, I concentrated on some urgent work.

"I will find out," she warned, then hurried down the corridor at the sound of the V.P.'s voice.

Eventually Saturday, that dreaded day came when I started the court-ordered visits for Romaine and her dad. Ricardo clearly was not interested in spending time with Romaine, although she yearned for his attention. He spent those two hours every Saturday, using the dirtiest of terms, trying to find out if another man was in his place, saying how much he missed me and begged me to go back home.

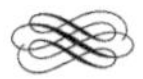

The restraining order didn't prevent Ricardo from being a nuisance. His frustrating behavior continued throughout the three months we waited to re-appear in court. During that time, the probation officer visited our home, twice. She received reports on Ricardo about the sexual assault case he had five years prior. One would think that would've changed the court's opinion, but it didn't. Ricardo told the probation officer he had spoken to Romaine, who told him a man usually visits our home. Whoever the man, she said, he used to be in the bedroom with her mother, then he and her mother would go to the bathroom.

"Children don't lie. Your husband is hurt," the probation officer said. She probably never once stopped to consider that Ricardo may have made up that entire scenario. Furthermore, he could have grilled the five-year-old, placing those thoughts in her head. The probation officer angered me, but I remained composed, stifling the urge to throw her out of my home.

During the three months wait to return to court, I realized the best course of action would be to file my divorce from Ricardo. That way, he may realize regardless of how much he begged and annoyed me, I wasn't going back with him. After the papers were served, I knew beyond a shadow of any doubt that Ricardo would contest the divorce. As sure as dawn, he did.

The magistrate court's hearing came up before the divorce in the high court. It was probably my lucky day, or the judge forgot all about Ricardo's outburst during the first hearing. The magistrate asked me to tell the court how things were coming along between Ricardo and me.

"In spite of the order, sir, the situation has only gotten worse." The magistrate sat forward, listening.

"What did he do?" he asked. I told him how Ricardo would meet me on the road every day and abuse and threaten me with obscenities. I told the court he followed me to my home one day and stood with his head through the window for more than two hours.

"Orderly," the magistrate shouted, pounding the desk with his gavel, "get me some documentation. I'm sending this man straight to prison." He turned to Ricardo, "Stand up!" I gave you an order and you disobeyed it? You're going to jail!"

Immediately, the probation officer stood up. She was the same officer who visited my home.

"Your Honor," she said, "I have a probation report on this family." She handed the magistrate a file and he started flipping through the pages.

"Sit down, both of you," the magistrate said. "This matter will be called at 11:30 this morning. Next case!" It was then 9:15.

At 11:30 the case called, and the magistrate appeared in yet another mood. He seemed to have forgotten he planned to send Ricardo to prison. Instead, he quickly dealt with the case. It was ordered that Ricardo continue seeing his daughter in the park until further notice from the courts. Nothing was said about the restraining order. On our way out of the court, the probation officer eyed me with disdain, shaking her head.

The threats from the magistrate did one good. Ricardo never came near me again. I even turned up with Romaine in the park a few times and Ricardo didn't show up, so I stopped going.

In contrast to my first divorce which was called up on a grim, rainy Friday morning in Georgetown, Guyana, this divorce was held on a sunny Tuesday afternoon in Barbados. Unlike the lower court, where Ricardo gained sympathy, when the high court judge read the reason I walked out of the marriage, he became visibly annoyed.

"Cases like these disgust me. I'm really sorry I cannot have my own way in matters like these," the judge remarked, eyeing Ricardo with contempt. The divorce was granted to me as well as custody of the child of the marriage. Ricardo was ordered to pay alimony.

"I can only afford $40 a week, sir," Ricardo said.

"In these times, you believe $40 is enough to maintain a child?" the judge asked.

"That's all I can afford, sir."

Alimony was set at $40 per week.

My attorney raised the issue of division of property and the judge granted an order which stated either party could retain the property and pay the other for his or her portion. Or, he said, the property could be sold, and the proceeds be divided equally among us. Ricardo opted to do the latter after we met with our lawyers.

Time passed, and Ricardo pretended to forget about the court's order, and sometimes he gave no money for Romaine's upkeep. Three years went by, and Ricardo claimed that the house was still unsold, and subsequently, he moved back into it. I bore my loss even though I was still repaying the loan on the house. I could have gone back to the courts, but I didn't care for another legal battle. I am grateful to my parents, who taught me to do what is right in this life because as they said, there will one day be a *payday*.

PART THREE

Penchant For Bad Choices

THIRTY THREE

Love Comes Calling

Life for my children and I became more challenging financially, but we were happy. At times, I smiled at the sound of their cheerful screams, senseless laughter, and off-key singing. It dawned on me then that they didn't laugh and play much while we lived with Ricardo. Back then, the children, mainly Kianna and Junior, were usually tense and spent the majority of their spare time in their bedroom.

Additionally, living with Carlotta became problematic. Among other things, she complained about the children, expecting them to be seen and not heard. And she would never eat when I cooked but expected us to eat when she did. It was time to end that partnership.

With summer approaching, the children kept reminding me it would soon be time for their holiday in Guyana. I wished they would forget. I couldn't go with them and I knew I would be lonely without them. But it was a great treat for Kianna and Junior since this was the only time they spent with their father, grandparents, aunts, and uncles.

The day for their departure to Guyana came quickly. I stood at the airport, waving goodbye, watching them disappear through the waiting lounge, unaccompanied minors, in the care of an air hostess. Gazing after them, tears settled in my eyes, and my heart melted.

On the journey home, I thought about the best way to spend my spare time. Sometimes it seemed as if Carlotta was never home. When I was around, she spent most of her time in her room or with her family. Sometimes I would call out to her and she would answer without opening the door. "I'm fine, what about you?" My parents used to say that it is better to eat salt and rice and live on your own as opposed to sharing a home with some people.

Eventually, I came up with a plan. I decided to spend longer hours at work and use my spare time to find an apartment. There was much to do at the office, and I could work as many hours as I liked. When I got home, there would be time enough to grab a bite to eat, have a shower, and retire to bed. Saturdays would be my cleaning day. I would cook if I felt like it and watch movies. On Sundays, I would spend a few hours at church and continue my writing. Before I knew it, one week would be over, then another and another and eventually summer! Sounded like a plan.

After two weeks of my planned schedule I became bored and longed for my children. It was still another six weeks before their return, but a terrible loneliness enveloped me. I wished I could talk with someone. Friends make a difference in one's life and it was only then I realized how few friends I had. Several church members used to call me at home, but Ricardo was annoyed when I used the phone. Eventually, my world revolved around my children, my husband, and my job. I realized then, that I should have made some more time for friends.

My mother used to say, "In order to have friends, you first have to show yourself friendly." I later learned it was part of a bible verse. I lacked in that regard. Since I had moved further away from Grace, we stayed in touch mostly by telephone. After the disgusting issue with Ricardo, I kept mostly to myself because it embarrassed me when his name came up. Simone had eventually taken her two children and moved back to Guyana. It became extremely difficult for her since she wasn't working, and Alex had completely neglected his duties as a husband and father. My two co-workers, Sandra and Jackie, visited me sometimes, but they didn't have children and enjoyed life their way.

Ricardo was annoyed when I was on the phone. Eventually, my world revolved around my children, my husband, and my job. I realized then, that I should have made some more time for friends.

An abuser is unhappy to see his or her spouse or partner surrounded by friends. This may stem from control, jealousy, insecurity etc. Try curbing those actions as soon as you are aware. If unable, seek help.

https://www.fionaharewood.com/resources

One Sunday evening, with absolutely nothing to do, I retrieved my journal from the filing cabinet and proceeded to fill about ten pages. Eventually my fingers became tired and I found myself gazing into space. I laid the notebook on the center table, got up, stretched, and then rummaged through the refrigerator and cupboard. Finally, I settled for some strawberry ice cream and potato chips. I returned to the sitting room, inserted one of Sylvester Stallone's movies into the VCR, and sat down. It was action-packed from beginning to end. My spirits lifted. After 11 PM when the last of three rental movies ended, I concluded the evening hadn't turned out badly after all.

The chiming of the alarm clock woke me up at 5:30 AM. I smiled, realizing it was Monday. I gave thanks to God for his mercies which allowed me to see the dawning of yet another day, then I stretched and rolled over. Ricardo came to my mind. The thought of him sickened me even after nine months after our separation and divorce.

Once at work, time flew, even though I wanted it to linger. I broke for lunch at 1 PM and on my return, Pam, from the sales department, gave me a message on a pink while-you-were-out leaf.

I smiled, reading the name: George Jackson. I hadn't heard from him after I turned down his dinner invitation.

"Ah ha!" Pam said, nodding her head, trying not to smile. I burst into laughter.

"Who is that gentleman? Pretending he is speaking in this nice voice and asking me all these questions about you. Like, if you'll be back. If I know what time. Look, tell him I don't like people questioning me, okay," she finished, laughing.

I turned my attention to the pile of paperwork, lying on my desk. The phone rang.

"Thank you for calling BWIA; This is Angelique."

"And, Angelique, would you want to try guessing who this is?"

"And, Mr. Jackson, how may I help you, today?"

There was laughter at the other end of the line.

"I remembered a friend and decided to call to find out how she's doing."

"Oh? Then that's nice of you. I'm fine."

"I'm extending that same dinner invitation, yet again. Promise, I won't keep you away from your children for too long. Please, don't say no. Please say yes," George said. I didn't bother to enlighten him about the children being on vacation.

"What time?" I asked, without hesitation.

"Be ready by 7 PM. Thank you so much for accepting, Angelique."

"Thank you too," I responded.

After replacing the telephone receiver, I smiled. *Did I really accept a dinner date from Mr. Jackson? Of course, I did! One couldn't hurt anyway.*

For the first time since starting my job, 5 PM, our official dismissal time, couldn't come quick enough. It were as if the clock had suddenly stopped. That was one evening nothing could keep me in the office after hours. I began going through my wardrobe in my mind. By 5:10, I knocked on my boss's door, hoping she wouldn't become curious.

"Come in."

"I'm leaving. See you tomorrow," I said, swinging my bag to my shoulder.

Mrs. Bishop lifted her head from the paperwork she was perusing, and peered at me over her spectacles.

"You're not ill, are you?

"No, I'm fine." I smiled.

As if studying me, Mrs. Bishop remarked, "You do look mysteriously happy this evening. Got a date or something?"

I laughed, waved, and closed the door.

"Whatever you do, have a great evening," she shouted after me.

Once at home, I rushed to the wardrobe and started going through the few evening wears I had. I eventually selected a forest-green sleeveless dress with silver threadwork border. It fit snug and stopped about two inches above the knees. It was ideal with a pair of silver high heeled toeless shoes and silver accessories. *It's been a long time since I went on a real date.*

I drank a glass of sorrel, showered, and began dressing. Carlotta wasn't at home. At 7 PM sharp the toot of a car horn alerted me. I looked out and saw Mr. Jackson alighting from his vehicle. Opening the door, I invited him in.

"Thank you for accepting my invitation, and if I may add, you do look fabulous!" He said, smiling. The fragrance, Red, which I remembered from his first visit to our home, filled the air.

"Thank you," I replied. "You look great yourself."

"Boy, it's absolutely quiet around here. Where are the children?"

"They're on vacation."

"Oh really? Where?"

"Guyana."

"Good for them. I didn't know you were here by yourself."

"Not by myself, Carlotta's here," I interrupted, walking past him to the door. He followed me.

"Is she home?"

"No."

"You probably miss the children."

"Of course, I do," I replied, my thoughts wandering to my babies.

"Are we ready then?"

"Sure Mr. Jackson," I replied.

"Not so quickly." He held my shoulders and gently turned me around.

"It will be so nice if you would stop this *Mr. Jackson* thing and call me George," he said, his eyes connecting mine.

"Noted! *George*." We laughed and were on our way.

Now, I cannot remember where we dined. It was an unfamiliar restaurant in St. James, gorgeous ambience and casual conversation flowed between us.

"I like this side of you," George said.

"So, you know another side of me? Enlighten me about that other side."

"Work, work, work, and then it's all about your kids with whatever time remains."

"Hmmm—didn't realize I was monitored."

I couldn't remember being that relaxed in a long time. We spoke freely and then the discussion switched to ourselves. I found myself sharing many personal things such as issues with both William and Ricardo. I thought George was Barbadian, but learned he was St. Lucian. His parents also were St. Lucians who migrated to Barbados at age six. George said his marriage was over, but he still shared the matrimonial home due to his two children whom he loved dearly. He then added that he was searching for another home to purchase, since both he and his wife had agreed to go their separate ways. Hearing that piece of information, I warned myself—*be careful Angie! Is he one of those players Grace and Simone used to warn me about? Those who wanted to have their cake and eat it too?*

Nearly three hours later, it felt as if we had just arrived, but we both knew we had to be on our way. Half an hour later, George escorted me to my door and said good night. The silence in the house enveloped me like a thick, dark cloud. I quickly turned on the radio. A few minutes later, I drifted off to sleep, hoping George would ask me out again, although I had no real reason to expect he would.

The telephone woke me up before six o'clock the following morning.

"I wanted to hear your voice and wish you a pleasant day before going my way," George said.

"Wow! You're a poet now," I remarked. He laughed.

I didn't want to admit it, but that call made my day. Before the day was through, George called me at work. From that night on, I wasn't lonely anymore because almost every time the phone rang, George was at the other end. I found it was easy talking with him and he knew the right things to say. Sometimes Carlotta answered the phone, and whenever she did, I saw displeasure in her face, but I didn't allow her countenance to worry me.

Before realizing it, George and I became closer. The sound of his voice on the other end of the line sent my heart into somersaults. I even compared what I felt for George with how I felt when I first began speaking with William. I hadn't felt that way since William. Not even for Ricardo. But from the inception, I knew this was not the best place to be with George. While my heart said go for it, my head warned against any relationship with George.

Angelique, you gotta watch it! You don't know if what he's telling you is true. He has a wife. Angelique, be careful! I didn't listen to that inner-voice.

For the most part, that inner voice does not lead us down the wrong path. If we would listen more, we would save ourselves heartaches.

Angelique, you gotta watch it! You don't know if what he's telling you is true. He has a wife. Angelique, be careful! I didn't listen to that inner-voice. After all, it had been for more than eight years since I really experienced that sweet sensation that real love brings. I had actually forgotten what it felt like to be in love. I knew Ricardo had loved me at one time, but I never loved him in that way, even though I tried. My love for Ricardo was more a brother-sister love, and until George, I never realized how much I had short-changed myself.

I was on cloud nine with George, but something kept gnawing away at my conscience—he shared a house with his wife. I knew I was wrong to continue, but I couldn't—or rather—wouldn't stop myself. I shared my feelings for George with my co-worker, Sandra.

"I knew it had to be something with you," Sandra stated. She laughed and pulled her chair closer to my desk. "I can't remember seeing you this happy, and I'm glad for you, Angelique. But you still got to be careful until he moves away from his wife. Some of these men tell us women a set of sweet nothings, and when they get us where they want us, that's it," she said, snapping her fingers.

"I know," I responded, nodding. After speaking with Sandra, I was sorry I felt so strongly for George. Time and again, I would admire career women who had one or two children, but absolutely no man in their lives. I wondered how they did it. Frankly, that was not me. I enjoy basking in affection, love to be loved, and cherish that feeling of loving someone when that someone loves me back. Without that somebody to love, I felt lost, lonely, and empty.

Things continued moving quickly between us. I fell in love with George, forgetting all the relationship rules which I had laid down for myself. We started seeing each other frequently. George was extravagant, and many times he showed up at my job, took me to lunch or presented me with gifts. We enjoyed the movies, went driving, and went picnicking. Then our relationship moved to a different level when we became intimate. George used to tell me how much he loved me, and I begged him to never leave me.

George used to tell me how much he loved me, and I begged him to never leave me.

Victims of abuse are often insecure and lack self-esteem which tightens their hold on their abusive partner. This is not a healthy place to be.

https://www.fionaharewood.com/resources

After George and I became intimate, I stopped going to church again. Guilt consumed me and I couldn't sit through a sermon. Instead of choosing the Man whom I knew would never let me down, I chose George over my Savior.

I became comfortable in the relationship, even though George still shared a home with his wife. I never thought I would ever be that happy again. Our relationship moved along blissfully. However, sin is only sweet for so long. The adversary sets us up and then allows us to come crashing down.

One evening, I received a telephone call from Lloyd, my favorite church brother. I hadn't spoken with him in a while.

"Angelique, I hearing things about you and that fella who assist you to move. Is it true?"

"If what is true? What did you hear?"

"I believe you know only too well, don't you, Angelique?" Lloyd asked. The remorse I heard in his voice sent an odd feeling through me. "Angelique, I telling you, that fella is no good and if I'd only know it would lead to this, I wouldn't have sent him to move you."

"Hey, you have no way of seeing into the future. Don't bother though. He's cool, man," I replied.

"Angelique, I believe you went through enough already. I'm scared for you."

"I'm a big girl, Lloyd. Remember?"

Lloyd sighed.

Very soon summer ended, and the children returned home.

"Mr. George, I remember you," Junior said, responding with a broad smile and a high five to George's upraised palm. The air hostess accompanied them to us at the Grantley Adams International Airport.

"Why he come here for us? "Kianna asked, folding her arms across her chest and stopping abruptly when she saw George.

George looked down at her and smiled

After the children returned, George and I didn't go out often, although he came by sometimes and we spoke on the phone. Whenever George visited, Kianna disappeared to her room, sulking. That bothered me and I tried talking to her, but it didn't help. *Given time, she'll come around,* I thought. Later on, I realized my selfishness in subjecting her to be around George after her experience with Ricardo.

Meanwhile, George helped me look for another apartment. One afternoon, after work he took me to view a small two-bedroom, one-bathroom cottage, undergoing repairs. It wasn't in the best of neighborhoods, but it was close to my job and Romaine and Junior's school. By this time, they both attended the same primary school.

"I will pay the $400 for one month's security deposit," George said. "And you can pay the first month's rent when the repairs are completed." I thanked him and then told Carlotta I would be leaving within a month. One week later, I returned home to find Carlotta had vanished. She moved back home with her parents.

THIRTY FOUR

Unethical, Immoral, Unlawful

It was great between George and me for about four months until I received that call.

"Angelique," George said somberly at the other end of the line. "I have to see you. Let's go somewhere to talk briefly after you leave work."

"Is something wrong?" I asked. Instinctively, my heart began racing.

"I'll see you at 5:30," he said without responding to my question. Then the line went dead. It was 11:15 AM.

Anxiety engulfed me the remainder of the day. My sixth sense told me something was dreadfully wrong. Finally, my watch said 5:20. I tidied my desk, grabbed my bag, and headed downstairs.

"Hi, good afternoon," I said, smiling, climbing into the front seat of the car.

"Good afternoon," he responded without looking at me.

Silence followed. Having to think about something to say felt strange because we always had something to joke or talk about.

"So, how're you?" I asked.

"I don't really know," George answered after a long, uncomfortable pause.

We didn't speak again until he pulled into the parking area of Brandon's Beach, fifteen minutes later. On another afternoon, under different circumstances, I would be admiring the tall palm trees leaning dangerously over the blue waters, heads bobbing in the sea, and bikinied women strolling the seashore.

"Angelique, I don't know how to say this to you," he began in a soft, unsteady tone. "But I have to say it. I know it will hurt you, but I believe it will be best for both of us." He leaned his head against the driver's window and half turned his body facing me. I had no idea what to expect, but I knew it wasn't good. My head began pounding, and I felt sick.

"Just say it," I replied.

"My wife and I went to see a marriage counselor today."

It were as if a dagger went through my heart. My entire body felt numb.

"We had a pretty long heart-to-heart session," George continued. "When it almost ended, the counselor ask' her if she wanted the marriage." He paused. "She said yes. Then he ask' me if I wanted the marriage."

Please God, don't let him say what I think he will say.

"Somehow, before then, I didn't think I wanted to remain married to her, but when the counselor ask' that question, I realize' how much I really needed my marriage." George paused again, looked at me, then continued. "I too, answer' yes."

I felt limp. Suddenly, it were as if I choked, but I sat there, numb. I stared blindly ahead of me, not even flinching. I heard nothing else until George reached over and firmly shook my shoulders.

"Did you hear me? Are you okay?"

"Ye-yes," I managed.

"The counselor then told us we both need to break off our extra marital relationships. He gave us a six-week appointment and said during that time we must do nothing immoral, unethical, or unlawful which will hinder the healing process of our marriage. We both agreed. Angelique because of that, I have to break off our relationship. You know I love you, but I have to put my marriage first. Anyway, if at any time you ever need anything, call my cell phone and I will get whatever you want, but we cannot continue seeing each other."

A long, agonizing silence ensued.

"Okay, I understand. Perfectly. I need to go home now," I finally said.

A deafening silence, besides the soft buzzing of the car engine, replaced the once happy chatter while driving home with George. *This fairy tale relationship was too good to be true.* Those were the only words occupying my mind. It became difficult to even breathe. Eventually, he brought the car to a stop at my house. I slowly got out and made it to my door at a snail's pace. George's words had drained all the energy from my body.

My children ran to me as soon as I unlocked the door.

"How you guys doing?" I asked, forcing a smile, and bending to share kisses. "Everybody had something to eat and showered?"

"Yes, Mummy," they chorused.

"What about homework?"

"I am revising math for a test tomorrow," Kianna said.

"I finish' mine, Mommy," Junior answered.

"Okay, I'm not feeling well. I'll go to my bed early. Kianna, please watch them for me until bedtime."

I then heard George's car drive away from my home for the last time.

I entered my room and tiredness seemed to explode within me. My nerves remained tense, even after I had a hot shower and crawled into bed. Sleep escaped me. George's final words kept flashing across my mind.

I felt as if life had finally stopped. I couldn't eat. Sleep became a stranger, and I lost weight rapidly. Usually, to ease pain I would bury myself in my job, but this time around it didn't work. Most of my time alone I spent crying and often, I sent the children off to school and remained at home. Many times, when I eventually made it to work, I couldn't stay for the entire day. Every time the phone rang at my desk or at home, I hoped it was George. He never called—not even to find out about me. I couldn't believe right in the midst of a blissful relationship, someone could treat me as if I never existed. My hurt that time around felt worse than the one inflicted by William—when I thought I would never love another man, I went head over heels in love with someone, who basically cared nothing about me.

"Mommy, how come Mr. George ain't come by in a while? I beat him at dominoes the last time he came and he promise' to pay me," Junior said after about two weeks of George's absence.

"Well, since he owes you, he may show up one day."

"Mommy, you not even watching TV with us anymore. You always say you tired," Kianna said one evening. "

"Okay, give me a little break this afternoon and tomorrow I will watch with you," I said, trying to appease her.

I had to pull myself together. If not for me, for my children. I made a desperate effort to try. Using my credit card, I paid a visit to the hair stylist. After a sophisticated cut, I went shopping. That did something. Despite considerable weight loss and the fact that George's rejection hurt like hell, I was pleased at my appearance. Everybody at the office wanted to know why the impulsive change. I tried living one day at a time and whenever George crossed my mind, bitter thoughts accompanied him. *Men are sweet nothings! They're not worth it!*

During the fifth week of our break up, a co-worker and I spent our lunch hour downtown. When I returned, Sandra told me George had called.

"Angelique, he didn't sound normal," she said. "He sounded rushed and breathless, sort of."

"Oh really! Thanks." I replied.

When Sandra left, I thought about what she said. It bothered me. *How dare he call at this time when I'm now beginning to get over him—how dare him!*

I decided against returning the call and hoped he would not be at the other end of the line when I answered the phone that afternoon. *After all, I came a long way without him, and I will continue without him. He can stick to his wife for all I care.*

I remember the following morning oh so well—a bright, sunny Thursday in May of 1996. I took my time getting to work but was still earlier than usual. Over the last week, my spirit lifted slightly. Habitually, most of the junior staff congregated in the lunch room when they were early.

Sometimes, I did too, but there were other times when I went to my desk and started working, whether or not it was 8 AM. That particular morning, I stopped in the lunch room, meaning to chit chat with the others. From the moment I opened the door, four pairs of anxious and unhappy eyes stared at me. Besides Sandra who leaned against the cupboard, they were all sitting on one side of the long dining table.

"Angelique, you hear wha' happen?" Sandra asked in an excited, but gloomy tone.

"No, what?" I asked, stopping short, and still holding on to the doorknob. My eyes darted from one to the other. Nobody spoke besides Sandra. The others looked at me glumly.

"You didn't hear what happen with Jackson?" Sandra asked again. At the sound of George's name, the energy drained from my body.

"No, I didn't hear. If you have something to tell me, then tell me," I almost screamed.

"Angelique, it's all over the news. How come you didn't hear?"

The others left the lunch room. I walked towards Sandra. "Sandra, I wish you would cut the crap! Tell me what happened! I didn't listen to the news!"

"Jackson shoot his wife!" She blurted out, then flopped herself in the chair nearest to me.

"What?" I pulled a chair and slumped into it. My bag thumped to the floor. I felt as if the bullets from George's gun were piercing through my body, also.

"When did this happen? Where is she? Did she make it?" I wanted to know everything at the same time. "Where is he?"

"She's in the hospital. Critical. The news said she took one shot to her head. There were a total of three shots. He's in custody. This may have something to do with the call he placed to you yesterday," Sandra finished.

"Oh my god!" I exclaimed. Then I prayed silently. *Please God, don't let her die.*

At 10 AM I turned on the transistor radio at my desk and heard the news. The only addition—George had shot himself too, and was also hospitalized, but in police custody.

It appeared one of the longest days of my life. I wished it would end, but it only dragged on, embarrassment continuously washed over me. Nobody said anything to me besides Sandra, but occasionally I saw gossipy little groups and received peculiar stares.

I didn't know what I felt, but for George's sake I prayed his wife would live. If she didn't, his children would lose their mother and father because he would be imprisoned. That night, I determined to keep the children from the television, but Junior heard the news on the radio in his room.

"Mummy, Mummy, listen!" he shouted, turning up the radio and hurrying to me in the kitchen. "You heard? Is that Mr. Jackson we know?"

I sighed. "Yes Junior."

"But why did he shoot his wife? Why?"

By that time, Kianna stood at the doorway, her eyes wide.

"Junior, I really don't know.

The next day's newspapers circulated in the office with George's photograph and details of the incident appearing on the front page. I looked forward to the weekend to get away from it all, but I couldn't get George out of my mind. I needed to see him. I asked Sandra to go with me to the hospital. We went on Saturday evening. A police officer greeted us at the door of his room at The Queen Elizabeth Hospital.

"What's your business here, ladies?" The officer asked.

"We're here to see Mr. George Jackson," I said.

A puzzled expression crossed the officer's face before handing us a small notebook and requested that we sign in. We did.

Upon entering the room, we saw another uniformed policeman standing to the far left of the room. George sat cuffed to the bed. We approached him slowly. He looked sorrowful--clad in blue hospital pajamas, uncombed hair, and his face badly in need of shaving. Seeing me, his face lit up slightly and he smiled ruefully. We greeted him while he continuously shook his head.

"I'm so sorry. I am so, so sorry," he kept saying.

Neither Sandra nor I knew what to say to make him feel better.

"When did you hear of the incident?" He eventually asked.

"Sandra told me the following morning when I went to work. How is your wife doing?" I asked.

"She's still in intensive care. You probably think I'm the worst person on earth, don't you?"

"No, I don't, but I wondered why."

"I thought I'd never see you again, but I'm really glad you came," George said, stretching out his free hand to take mine.

"You could have chosen a different path. There had to be a way out, George. Why didn't you walk?" Tears drowned my words.

"Ladies, Mr. Jackson is not allowed long visits, so wrap it up now," the officer said.

"Bye, George," I said, watching him sitting at the edge of the hospital bed, shaking his head.

Although I tried hard to go on with my life after George walked out on me, I still loved him, but I couldn't see a thread of hope for the two of us. Further, shame washed over me, and I reminded myself our relationship ceased even before that fateful incident. It would remain that way.

THIRTY FIVE

Losing My Identity

Time dragged on. A few days after I visited George, the media covered him leaving the hospital. Being released into police custody they interrogated him for two days before his court appearance. Among other charges, George pleaded not guilty to attempted murder and unlawful possession of a firearm. Bail was denied until the doctors could confirm Mrs. Jackson passed the critical stage.

The day after his court appearance, George appeared on the front of the *Barbados Natio*n—a full, colored photograph. It showed him handcuffed and being escorted out of the courthouse by a police officer, on his way back to prison. George became the *talk of the town* although his name was never mentioned above a whisper in the office.

Sister Barbara from my church telephoned me the day after the newspaper story ran. "What is this I hearing, Angelique? That you is the cause of that man shooting he wife?" Sister Barbara shouted the question without any greeting. I froze, pressing the telephone receiver hard against my ear, staring into nothingness.

"Angelique, you there?" she asked.

"Yes," I replied, hardly above a whisper. "Where'd you get that from?"

"Carlotta. She spreading that around the church."

The saying goes—*Boat gone ah fall, it can't come back*, meaning, the damage was already done. It was pointless defending myself. Besides Sandra, my co-worker, no one else knew George and I had finished prior to his incident.

"Barbara, I have no control over what people think or say. I cannot speak now. Let me get back to you," I replied, then hung up.

With such rumors spreading like dry-bush fire, embarrassment enveloped me. Ashamed of the entire situation, I hardly wanted to leave the sanctuary of my home. I stayed at work until dark and left home early in the mornings. Despair engulfed me like a dark, thick cloud. I eventually turned to the same God I had forsaken. I got down on my knees ever so often, begging Him to help me walk the road and hold my head high, despite what people thought or were saying. Prayers always help.

I got down on my knees ever so often, begging Him to help me walk the road and hold my head high, despite what people thought or were saying. Prayers always help.

Sometimes, pray is all we can do.

One week later, I received another telephone call while at work.

"Hi Angelique, it's George," the cheery voice said. "How are you? I'm free again, and you're my first call."

Removing the telephone from my ears I stared at it, hardly believing what I heard.

". . . . you there?" He asked.

"What you mean I'm your first call? Where're you?"

Excitement rose in his voice for a brief moment. "After being lock' up for so long, I'm really glad to breathe freedom's air again."

"Good for you. So, I guess your wife has passed the worst?"

"Yes. She's not out of hospital. They moved her from ICU to a room. Angelique, it may sound weird, but even though I'm glad to be free, I wish I were dead. My troubles now start, and it will be really hard for me to face what is ahead. In three months, I have to return to court," George said. "In the meantime, the magistrate has ordered me to go to our home with police presence to collect only my clothes. The magistrate said after that, I'm not to be seen less than 500 yards away from the property."

"So where will you be staying?"

"With my niece. She lives alone."

My intercom buzzed.

"George, I have to go."

"Okay. Bye," George said.

"Mrs. Bishop, I'll be with you in a few minutes."

With my elbows on my desk, I propped my face with my hand, lost in thought.

"Wow, girlfriend! You look beat. What happen? Still worried?" Jackie asked.

"Life sucks! It seems like only yesterday whenever George called, he lit up my world but now...." I stared ahead.

"And now?" Jackie asked, staring at me.

"They released him from prison. Said he called me first. I finished speaking with him a minute ago, but you know the truth? I wish he didn't call me."

Jackie eyed me. "I really don't know what to say, Angelique. I cannot even say I understand because one has to wear that person's shoes to say that."

"The thing about it is," I continued, "I don't hate him, but I would've preferred to be as far away as possible from him and this mess he has gotten himself into. I feel now, he never loved me. He loved his wife. Don't get me wrong, he had all right to do so. But why get involved with me, stating his marriage was over? If he had ever loved me, when he realized he and his wife couldn't make it, he would've moved on. Instead, he tried to kill her and himself. Look how much trouble he has created. Is there a solution now? Do you think he expects me to be there for him now?"

Jackie hesitated.

"I understand what you're saying, and I agree, but put yourself in his place for a moment. Wouldn't you want a friend to be at your side at a time as this? You may be the easiest person for him to turn to. Be his friend."

"I can't promise that, Jackie. I really can't," I said, getting up and making my way to Mrs. Bishop's office.

After work, arriving in close proximity to my home, I saw George's truck parked at my gate. Anger swept over me, and I became upset at the fact that he showed up at my home, knowing I was at work and only the children were there. *Why would he show up here without warning?* In the house, I found him playing chess with Junior. The girls were in their room.

"Hi," I said.

"Hi, Angie," he replied, smiling. "I decided to come by and play a game with your son."

George had lost about twenty pounds and his left arm hung in a cast. After some small talk I retired to the kitchen, prepared dinner, and we all sat down to a simple meal.

George's presence made me uncomfortable, but I couldn't bring myself to ask him to leave. The children retired to bed and George and I sat up late into the night. He explained what had sparked the shooting.

"Everything was well that morning when I drop' Verne off at work," he started. "About 1 PM, I was having lunch at Cave Shepherd, when my cell phone rang. It was Mark—you know him. I did tell him about my situation and one time I even show' him the man my wife was seeing. In an accusing tone, Mark said to me, 'You saying you want give your marriage another try? It takes two to make a marriage work, George, not one.' I asked him what he was talking about. 'Come out here,' he said, 'Right in Queen's Park. She with the same man she said she done with. I don't understand some women.' I ask' him if he was serious. He said yes and prompted me to drive out to Queen's Park. I was about five minutes away."

"Angelique," George continued, "I felt nervous and weak all at the same time. I didn't want to believe Mark, but I couldn't dismiss him either. That was when I call for you and heard you were out. I really wanted to talk with someone. When I didn't get you, I decided to drive to the park. I stopped a ways off and stroll around the park, and then I saw her car. It was park' in a shaded area under some trees. At first, I didn't see anyone in it. I look' around and neither of them was in sight. I approach' the car quietly from the back. The two front seats were recline' and the driver's side window was half-way down. She had her head in his lap and he was stroking her face while they talk'. I stood there for a few moments, many things rushing through my mind. Then something told me walk away and not do anything stupid. I walk' away, but then turn' back because I knew Ingrid would deny it when I confront her. I tap on the driver's side window and she quickly sat up. You should see the terror on their faces when they saw me. Calmly I said, 'Just know—I have tried. I have tried.' Then I turn' and walk' away. The man got out of the car and started calling my name. I paid no attention to him. Instead, I hurry to my car and drove home. Angelique, I'm telling you, I was really mad, but most of all, I was hurt. I mean—"

He stopped and let out an audible sigh. "We had a plan, and things were going well. She told me she was finished with the man. And I dumped you! The next week was suppose' to be our meeting with the marriage counselor, and she had to mess things up."

George sighed again. Getting up, he paced my sitting room before sitting down again. "She came home about an hour later. I said nothing but she start apologizing. I told her I didn't want to hear anything. She continue' and we start' arguing. I became angry and lost control. I really don't want to replay what happen next."

"You should have left the house, George. Why didn't you?"

"I guess I was too angry. Anyhow," he continued, "I went to the bedroom and she follow me, still arguing. I couldn't take it anymore, so I took out my gun from a chest in the bedroom. As soon as she saw the revolver, she tried to get it from me. Angelique, I could see hatred in that woman's eyes, and I knew if she did get the revolver from me, she would've killed me. We started struggling and the gun went off three times. At the third shot, she fell to the floor. I didn't know what to do, so I got into my car and drove away. Then I reach' this bushy area. I got out and I hold the gun to my head, but no matter how I try, I couldn't pull the trigger. Eventually, I shot myself in the arm, then I drive to the police station and gave up myself," George finished, sighing deeply.

I lived that incident while George spoke. Fear enveloped me. *Suppose he does the same thing to me? Oh my God! What have I gotten myself into?* However, it is said, a story has three sides—my side, your side, and the truth. I heard only George's side, so there were two missing pieces from the puzzle. After listening to George's explanation, I still felt he had a way out. He could have chosen to walk away. He didn't. There was no excuse for what he did.

Before I dressed the following morning, George showed up at my home to take me to work. That afternoon he picked me up at my job to take me home. It embarrassed me to be seen in his company, and so quickly after his incident, yet, I couldn't say no to him. I knew it was time for me to shake him off, but couldn't bring myself to stop him, fearing he would hurt me too. Over the next couple of months, George began sticking to me like a leech.

It embarrassed me to be seen in his company, and so quickly after his incident, yet, I couldn't say no to him.

When you feel as if you are the victim in a situation and cannot say no, find help immediately. Talk to someone.

Time passed and George became more and more depressed. He lay around my house sulking. He hardly worked and started losing most of his clients, causing me to see more and more of him. I tried my best to be there for him without showing the disgust I felt. A day didn't go by without him visiting my home or showing up to take me to and from work.

"I really do not like you just showing up always like this, George," I said one morning after climbing into his truck.

"Why? You shame of me now?"

"No," I lied, "but with all this stuff with you and your wife…"

"I don't have a wife. She is dead to me." His icy tone ceased the conversation. Then, I couldn't help but notice George acted as if he was determined for the world to know he had another woman. Sometimes while taking me home from work he would make stops and if he ran into friends, he would introduce me as his newfound love. I hated it and felt trapped.

Being well-known before the incident, he gained even more notoriety after the episode. Heads turned and some people even hurled remarks when we were together, "Be careful, he may shoot you next."

"She seems a decent lady, don't shoot her like you did your wife."

On a few occasions when we went out, I met a couple of my friends. George expected me to introduce him as my boyfriend, but I didn't. He often became upset and accused me of being ashamed of him, but he always had a means of getting over. When he didn't get his way, he would either kiss me in public, or make some other intimate gesture indicating our relationship went beyond friendship. His actions disturbed me, mostly because I knew what he intended to do, yet I couldn't stop him.

His actions disturbed me, mostly because I knew what he intended to do, yet I couldn't stop him.

When uncomfortable with the controlling abuser, find help.

https://www.fionaharewood.com/resources

Then his court date came. Unexpectedly, Mrs. Jackson decided she wouldn't give evidence against her husband. In return, her lawyer asked that George sign over his share of the property, its contents, the car, and $10,000.00 in cash to his wife. Additionally, her lawyer proposed he pay monthly support for his two children and alimony for his wife. George was stunned. He couldn't believe it when his lawyer advised him to grant Mrs. Jackson her request. Providing he agreed to her terms, the case against him would be dismissed.

"It could be worse sitting before a judge and jury. You're facing up to 25 years in prison for attempted murder, not forgetting the charges in relation to the firearm," his lawyer cautioned.

George had already paid over $10,000 to his attorney for consultation and trial. George Jackson left the court a bitter and broke man.

For more than six months, George couldn't bring himself to accept what had happened to him financially. He never took into consideration the fact that his actions caused the unwelcomed outcome. During that time, George leaned heavily on me for support—emotional, moral, and sometimes financial. I made sure he ate well and was kept clean. Anytime he needed a shoulder to cry on, I was there.

"If it wasn't for you, Angelique, I would've prefer to pay somebody to complete the job on her," George said one day, wallowing in self-pity.

"You gotta' be kidding. Why would you say such a thing?" I asked.

"No joke, she's lucky. She should thank you." Those words worried me for a long time because I realized George's thoughts were murderous and vengeful.

It seemed to take forever, but eventually the shooting incident became stale news while more important stories made headlines. But there were people who still avoided George. It didn't bother me as much anymore. By then, I loved George despite his circumstances. Slowly, our lives began to take shape, and I became comfortable with our relationship. George started working little by little again.

"Angelique, I can never repay you for being so good to me," George would say from time to time. "As soon as my legal problems are over, we will make a fresh start and move on with our lives." At that time, the firearm cases were still pending, and he talked of filing his divorce.

Early the next year, George's lawyer got him off with only a meager fine on the firearm charges. George then seemed to forget his plans of filing for his divorce. He began working every day and became enthusiastic about living again. His daughter started visiting him once more, and this made him feel even better. But his son shut him out of his life. George felt awful about that.

Meanwhile, we became like teenagers in love again. Our social lives improved. We did many things together, including making overseas trips. The children were included in most of these outings and they enjoyed them. Even Kianna looked forward to some of the family activities.

Even though we were having fun, little by little, I became uncomfortable with the relationship. For many months, George ate at least two meals a day at my home without any contribution. A

George ate at least two meals a day at my home without any contribution. A woman should not be made to ask her man for financial help.. . . I found myself submitting a budget, month after month, on his request.

Financial abuse and control raise their ugly heads often in relationships.

https://www.fionaharewood.com/resources

---

woman should not be made to ask her man for financial help. I never depended on him for anything and even assisted financially, where necessary. But I noticed when George's situation improved, he never bothered to assist me, although he was extravagant when we first met.

Although George wasn't assisting me financially, presumptuously he questioned me on my finances. Stupidly, I found myself submitting a budget, month after month, on his request. *William made me do the same thing.* Not that he assisted where he found a deficit. Instead, he approached me with a crazy idea.

"Angelique, in order for this relationship to be more binding, we should open a joint account. You should try to save no less than $150 a month and to everything you deposit, I will double yours."

"George," I began, "Every month I'm broke even before I'm paid. My salary is already allocated, and it simply cannot do everything I need to do. Where would I find $150 to save?"

"If you want to do it, you will find a way. You will cut down on some of your spending and do it," George informed me.

Hesitantly, I went along with the plan. I didn't get far. After the first five months, I had only two month's saving in the account with George's amount of $600 doubling mine. He refused to make any deposits when I couldn't. Eventually, he withdrew his portion, claiming I wasn't interested in saving.

George's financial position became stronger, but mine deteriorated. I found myself buried in credit card debts as well as two bank loans. I needed to have a talk with George. He claimed to be my man, saw me going under financially, and refused to help. I swallowed my pride and spoke with him. Of course, George was a listener and he did listen. He addressed me afterwards.

"Angelique, as much as I would like to assist you, I cannot. I have my own financial obligations. I have to give my niece some money for my upkeep. I also have to pay the support for my wife and the children. My daughter needs assistance. Although she is of age, she is still studying. Also, I have a goal to save $500 a week towards a new home, since right now I am living with a family member."

Later I realized George was right to do what he did because I allowed it. I still wonder why I let him treat me that way, but I guess I couldn't bring myself to stop loving him. I found myself hoping he wouldn't leave me—being trapped in a terrible place—giving sex for love to a man who cared nothing about me.

I couldn't bring myself to stop loving him. I found myself hoping he wouldn't leave me – being trapped in a terrible place – giving sex for love to a man who cared nothing about me.

If you find yourself in this place, get counsel immediately.

https://www.fionaharewood.com/resources

THIRTY SIX

A Step of Faith

The months dragged on and my financial situation worsened. I began receiving red notices for my accounts, and I took action. Even though the court ordered Ricardo to maintain Romaine, he did so for a short while, and then stopped. I took him back to court—something I vowed never to do while I worked with the law firm. It disgusted me when men showed up in court telling the magistrate they could not support their own offspring. Ricardo walked the road in only brand-name clothing and boots after we separated, but he turned up in court with an old polo shirt, bad looking jeans, and beat up shoes, informing the court he wasn't working. He got away with that excuse because he was self-employed. When asked, he told the magistrate he still could only afford $40.00 a week. The order remained $40 and I didn't receive the arrears. I told Ricardo if he didn't start paying, I would have a warrant issued for his arrest. He complied.

Next, I penned a letter to William, my ex-husband, who was then in a second marriage and had a son.

"Hello William:

I am writing this letter to let you know I need financial assistance for the children. It may surprise you, but many days while you have a good meal, your two children hardly have anything to eat. It would be great if you would start honoring your obligations, since for most of their lives, I have been their main provider. Hoping to hear from you soon.

Angelique

William did not answer immediately. I had forgotten about the letter I sent to him. Then one Sunday night, I took the children to church. I had only two dollars with which I planned to buy sugar on our way back from church, so they could have tea. Shortly after we arrived at the church, they were ready for offering. I reasoned to myself I only had two dollars for sugar and I could not put that in the offering plate. However, the pastor then said, "Tonight when you give your offering, ask the Lord to multiply it 100 times." The usher then stopped at the bench where we were sitting, and without any hesitation, I placed the two dollars in the offering plate. I then prayed. *Lord please multiply that two dollars 100 times.*

One week later, I received a call from my sister.

"William gave me $100 U.S. to Western Union to you fo' the children. He also said he sent you a letter."

"Oh really? I wrote him, but I didn't even expect a response. Like he has changed."

"Girl, he is a totally different man now. That second wife must be fix he," she laughed. "You was too soft fo' he. And listen--you say you don't go to church now, but I want you know he goes again."

"Well good for him," I replied.

A few days later I received William's mail.

"Hello Angelique,

Glad to hear from you, but the contents of your letter saddened me. I really thought everything was well with you and the children. Anyhow, they are my responsibility. I will send $100 U.S. every month to assist you with them. If at any time you need anything else, please let me know. You can send me your telephone number so I may call and let you know when to go to Western Union.

Love always, William

Not only did the Lord answer the prayer about the two dollars once, but for a few years later, every month, I received that $200. I didn't deserve it, but He heard my prayers and supplied our needs.

Take anything to God in prayer and launch out in faith. He will hear you. He is kind like that!

After reading William's letter, I remembered the two dollars I had given for offering and the prayer I prayed, asking God to multiply it 100 times. The Lord did multiply that two dollars by 100 because one US dollar exchanged for two Barbados dollars. I lifted my heart in praise and thanksgiving to God. Not only did the Lord answer the prayer about the two dollars once, but for a few years later, every month, William sent that $200 for the children's upkeep. I didn't deserve it, but He heard my prayers and supplied our needs.

My mind then drifted back to those old days. I couldn't believe that William had changed. Something drastic took place. If he had changed his attitude toward me, then I should change mine toward him, I reasoned. At that moment I planted the seed of forgiveness. The next time I spoke to my family, I told them to give William my telephone number. He started calling occasionally to find out how the children and I were doing. I knew he sacrificially supported the children because at that time the U.S. currency exchanged for $150 Guyana to one U.S. dollar. In his case he purchased the foreign exchange at a more expensive rate.

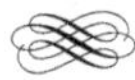

I felt restless. Mostly when that feeling consumed me, I would find some place to go – somewhere out of Barbados. Not having to pay airfares, we traveled quite often. The following Monday was a holiday, so we had a long weekend ahead. I packed Friday morning before going to work and told George the children and I were spending the weekend in Guyana. Later that day, George took us to the airport.

It was great being home. William and I were seeing each other for the first time since my animosity for him subsided. The children were going to his home that Saturday morning, so he collected them. Even though Romaine wasn't his child, whenever he collected Junior and Kianna, he would ask for Romaine to go along. I never sent her, but since we were friends again, I sent them all.

Looking at William, he seemed different and appeared extremely thin.

"What happen' to you?" I asked, looking at him closely. "Are you dieting or something?"

"Not really," he replied, smiling, looking down at himself and patting his stomach. "Doing some exercises. Needed to lose some weight. I don't mind."

"You sure about that?"

"Why you say it like that? You don't believe me?"

"Yes, I believe you, but you seem to have lost a lot of weight quickly. The last time I saw you, I can't remember you being that small. We were here only two months ago."

"Ha, ha, ha!" William laughed. He turned, walked away, then came back. "I want tell you something."

Suspiciously I looked at him. "Go ahead." "Though you wouldn't speak to me for all this time, at least you noticed me. I'm glad," he laughed again. "Ahhh anyway, it's nothing. I'm fine," he finished, dismissing the issue with his hand.

I later spoke with my mother. "Mom, don't you think William is losing weight rapidly?"

"Yes, yo' know. And I ask he, but he say he exercising and watching wha' he eat."

"He said the same thing to me, so I suppose we're worrying unnecessarily."

Time flies when you're having fun. As usual, our weekend in Guyana turned out great and the children and I returned to Barbados.

THIRTY SEVEN

Life is Fragile

At the beginning of October in 1998 William called me at work.

"Hi, Angie, how are you?" he asked.

"Doing good. How about you?"

"Not so good."

"Why? What happen?"

"Going into hospital tomorrow for a minor surgery. Have a hernia. Also, the doctors ran some tests today and found I also have diabetes."

"What! I'm sorry to hear that, man. Hope you be better soon. How long will they keep you in there?"

"Not sure. Maybe a week."

"I'll let the children know. We'll pray for you. Call us as soon as you get out," I said.

"Sure, I will. Anyhow, I sent the children's money. You may collect it at Western Union anytime. Also, I want you to continue taking good care of them. Ensure they eat the right things, especially Junior. He is like me--loves all the sweet things. Let him know bad eating habits got me sick."

"I'm so sorry, William," I said.

"That's all right, Angelique. I'll be fine. Take care now. Goodbye, Angie."

"Goodbye William."

Replacing the receiver, both joy and sadness enveloped me, simultaneously. Happy because I never expected a time would come when William and I could be civilized—friends even; and sad because he was sick.

About five days after I spoke with William, one of our friends, Mike, from Guyana, visited Barbados and I invited him to have lunch with us. We made William the topic of our conversation. We talked about the good times, the bad times—everything.

"Mike, I never expected William and me to be friends again. You'll not believe it if you hear the two of us on the phone now."

"I know Angie. You two use' to scare me when y'all start quarreling. I glad y'all pass that stage now," Mike said.

Around three o'clock that Sunday afternoon, George's truck pulled up in front of my house. He exited the vehicle bareback; his shirt thrown on one shoulder and his boots in his hand. Upon entering the house, he introduced himself to Mike. Mike and I were in the sitting room. The children were in their bedroom.

"Excuse my appearance," George said, turning to Mike. "Angelique told me you know the children's father well," George said.

"Yeah, man." Mike answered. "Angelique and William are a little older than me, but we went to the same church and did stuff together. I remained the good boy though," Mike laughed, patting his chest with both hands. "William was good at first, he strayed a while, but now he back to good."

"Yeah?" George said with raised brows. "Come man," he held Mike by the arm and started leading him towards the kitchen. "I want ask you something. I don't want her to hear though," George cupped a palm to his mouth, but spoke loud enough for me to hear. "I just got this strong feeling she liking William again."

"Stop playing," I said. We all laughed, and they disappeared from my view.

They were silent for too long. I got up and joined them. Entering the kitchen, I saw Mike sitting with his elbow on the table, and his hands propped his face. George stood solemnly, leaning against the stump wall which divided the kitchen from the eating area. Something wasn't right.

"What's with the two of you?" I asked. Looking closer at Mike, I realized he was crying.

"What're you crying for?" I turned to George.

"What'd you do to him?"

George gestured me to keep it down, then said: "The children's father has taken a turn for the worse.

"What? How you know?"

"Eric called me. He said you must be careful how you tell Junior and Kianna."

"Why didn't they call me? How bad is he?" I asked, my head spinning.

"Angelique, you forget the problem with your phone? How would they get through to you?" George asked.

"Oh Yes, that's true." I pulled a chair next to Mike and sat down.

"Tell me, what did they say? How bad is he?"

"Can you make arrangements for the children to go down?" George asked, eyeing me.

"School is still on. Why should they go down? Are they expecting William to die or something?" I panicked.

Mike butted in. "Tell her George, just tell her."

George heaved a sigh, his shoulder rising then falling.

"Tell me what?" A strange sensation I couldn't explain gripped me.

"William passed away this morning."

George's words were like a dagger going through my heart. A violent scream escaped me. The children rushed from their room. Their eyes pierced me with questions. I didn't know what to do or say. I just cried.

I decided not to tell the children everything at once.

"Your father is really, really sick," I said after composing myself. "We can expect anything to happen at any time."

"You mean he may die, Mommy?" Kianna asked. They looked at me searchingly.

"Yes, the doctors seem to think so."

Junior and Kianna started crying. Romaine cried too, although she didn't understand the situation. The following morning, I told Junior and Kianna of their father's death. I believe the suddenness of the situation hurt them most.

We then learned William's surgery appeared successful, but two days later complications set in and he fell into a coma, never regaining consciousness. We traveled to Guyana for the funeral--a journey we all would have preferred not to make. William wasn't a major part of their lives, and they only saw him periodically, but they loved their dad.

Hugging my children close, one at either side of me, we proceeded around the coffin. The solemn crowd, dressed mainly in black, white and purple, pressed close to us. Fragrances from cologne and flowers added queasiness to the air. My heart broke, staring at the body of 38-year-old William Larrier, lying lifeless in his coffin. He looked the picture of perfect peace, a slight smile covering his handsome face. At that moment, I realized William bade me goodbye when he called me before being hospitalized. Junior and Kianna just cried. I didn't know what to say or do to make them feel better. "Junior and K, don't cry. [1]Your daddy has gone to heaven and you'll see him again. All you have to do is live a life that is pleasing in God's sight."

William was well-known. Hundreds of mourners overflowed the church. The occasion was bittersweet. Bitter because a loved one passed unexpectedly. Sweet because in spite of the life William once lived, we believed when his call came, he was ready.

Life is fragile. Knowing not what the next moment holds, we should aim to live every moment as if it is our last.

1 *Many years later, after studying the Bible with the Seventh-day Adventist Church, I realized that like all others who have passed away, William is asleep in his grave, and will awaken when Christ returns the second time. The dead do not go to heaven at the time of death, as I was led to believe. 1 Thes. 4: 16-17; Eccles. 9:5*

THIRTY EIGHT

I Need Some Space

George's selfish attitude worsened. Needing someone in whom to confide, I spoke with Grace.

"Have you ever found yourself in a place where you know what somebody is doing is wrong, but you just can't bring yourself to tell them?"

Needing someone in whom to confide, I spoke with Grace.

You must not tell your business to everyone, but it is good to find at least one person in whom you can confide. That person can be anyone you trust.

"I know what you talking 'bout, girl, but not me. I don't care who it is, I would tell them." Grace said, busying herself in her kitchen. "I sure you talking 'bout that George."

I nodded.

"What he do now? You know from day one, I never like he. He puts on this big-shot air and likes to show off. Then, after he shoot the woman, he put he tail between he legs."

"Girl, through everything I supported him. He still eats at my home and I do his laundry, even iron his clothes, yet he doesn't help me in any way. Food is expensive and laundry detergent costs money. Girl, I'm embarrassed to tell you about this because I know he's using me, but I don't know why I allow him. Whenever we travel, I give him a free ticket, but if we rent a car, I have to pay my half. If we share a hotel, I have to pay my part of the bill."

"What? He ain't shame! You try with that, he didn't getting my tickets," Grace interrupted. "That's why some women does fix them good. He wants one o' them women. And you get to me too, Angelique. Because you act as if you can't find another man. He takes advantage of you and you allow him."

Grace shook her head and sat down at the kitchen table. I got up and started pacing, tears stinging my eyelids.

"Why I'm staying with this man, Grace, I don't know. It's not that I don't realize he is an absolute user and an attempted murderer. I suppose my heart says differently. And you know, whenever we share gifts, I get him the best. When he gets me anything, it turns out to be a stupid ornament with some foolish words like, 'Honey, I don't love you because I need you. I need you because I love you.' He is such a liar and a user! Then every time he opens his mouth, it's *me, my daughter, and I.* He never has any plans for us anymore."

"Angelique, you should tell he directly you need help, financially."

"I told him that once, but he told me he had responsibilities and goals to achieve. I realized he wouldn't help me, so I never asked him for money again."

"Well Angelique, you know me, I would've send he packing ever since. He wouldn't be in my bed. I know you love him, and you ain't goin' do that, so I think you should tell him again. If you can't tell him, write him. You always writing something anyway."

"That's a good idea. I should do that--"

"Not *should--do it*! Like you scared of him or something. He should've had me to deal with."

I left Grace's house feeling a tad better. Talking or writing about my problems always helped me relieve some tension.

I wrote George that same night, but it took a couple of days before I gathered the courage to give him the letter. I even considered mailing it. In the letter, I told George about the things that bothered me in our relationship. The evening, I finally decided to hand him the letter, he appeared to be in a good mood. He was chatting with the children when I delivered it. After they went to get their homework done, George sprawled on the sofa and began reading. I sat across from him. Reading it, his face portrayed no emotion. Finally, he finished, held the letter in his hands for a while, and a frown crossed his face. Then, he coldly addressed me.

"You know something, Angelique, I already told you my position on this issue. I have lots of financial obligations. I cannot assist you. You need to travel less, and you will find your money will go farther."

A low snarl tore free from my throat, and my temper flared. "Is my traveling a problem to you? That's my only form of relaxation! Tickets that are expensive cost me nothing! We don't even go anywhere anymore, and it's not that I travel every month either, and I could do that if I want to. Am I just suppose' to sit around waiting for you?"

George lifted one hand, palm up. His icy glare chilled me to the bone.

"I am saying, you have to put money aside for times like these, when you need," he said, getting up. "Anyhow, I think we both need some space in this relationship. If you don't, I do. I will hear you another time." George left.

I came to regret writing the letter. For more than a month, George didn't come by or call. I did all the calling, and my messages went unanswered. Whenever he answered the telephone, he seemed merry about something or other. He never made time to talk, and excused himself saying he was busy. Still, I hung on.

After about two months, George eventually started visiting my home again and we went out a few times. For some time, his car had mechanical problems, and every place he and I went, he used the big truck. But I noticed when he had any special functions to attend by himself, he hired a taxi and even rented a limo for his daughter.

Another time he invited me to his association's yearly banquet. I remember wearing a burgundy, stretch velvet, spaghetti strap dress, matching shoes, and silver accessories. George bought the dress during his more generous times. To my embarrassment, he showed up in the big truck. Both of us were well-dressed, but we rode a big truck to the banquet. I couldn't keep quiet.

"If I only knew you wouldn't pay a taxi for us to get there, I would've stayed home," I said, heaving myself up and climbing in.

"What's with you? What happen to the truck? I don't see a problem."

"If it was your daughter, you would've arranged limo service, but for stupid old Angelique, anything goes."

We were silent for the remainder of the journey. I contemplated asking him to either take me back home, or to stop and allow me to get off. I did neither—just remained miserable. At the end of the banquet, George stood around chatting with friends.

"I'm cold," I said, realizing he wasn't ready to leave. May I have the keys so I can wait in the truck until you're done?"

Looking at me coldly, he handed me the keys. He said nothing on our way home until he dropped me off.

"Look, I need some space."

Those were becoming his favorite words. It made no sense to argue.

For the first couple of days, I tried forgetting about him, but then his absence started getting to me. I called and tried talking with him many times, but for the most part only I talked. Finally, one evening I called him, and he talked on and on.

"I really don't know how to please you," he said. "It seems as if you only want me around for convenience—things like takin' you to and from the airport and being there to give you and your friends a ride when you need one. Besides that, what are you contributing to this relationship?

Arguing with him made no sense—I could never win. Yet, I couldn't bring myself to allow this man to go his way and move on with my life.

Another six weeks passed before George started showing up at my house again. After he returned, no conversation took place in which he didn't question my contribution to the relationship. Whenever he asked that, I felt guilty, so I started going over to his house once a week, cleaning and washing for him. By this time, he had his own apartment. I knew this was ridiculous, so I didn't let anyone know. Not even Grace.

"It seems as if you only want me around for convenience . . . . Besides that, what are you contributing to this relationship?"

If you find yourself here, knowing you are not the wrong party but your partner is making you believe you are, do not accept blame . . seek help. Get counsel to help you through it or out of it.

Two months after George moved into his new

home, his wife served him the divorce papers. He became visibly upset, and the murderous threats re-surfaced. George then consulted an attorney who told him, among other things, he could help him win the case. From my knowledge of working with lawyers, I explained to George there was no truth in what the lawyer told him. But greedy George turned a deaf ear to my advice and listened to the lawyer, paying five thousand dollars for representation.

On the day of the divorce hearing, according to George, the proceedings went on as if he were absent. His wife received her divorce and his portion of the property. For a second time, George walked away from the courthouse a discontented and unhappy man. As if it were I who did him all the wrong, that night, he spoke to me briefly.

"Angelique, I need some space. I prefer you don't call or come to see me."

He resumed his absence.

PART FOUR

The Decision & Getting It Right

THIRTY NINE

Breaking Bad

Besides going to work, I confined myself to the four corners of my room. I couldn't eat or sleep and frequently cried in my pillow. Although I tried acting normal around the children, I believe Junior and Kianna realized my struggles. They mostly allowed me my space and helped with Romaine.

"Mommy, *Days of Our Lives,* your favorite show, is on," Kianna would sometimes announce, knocking on my bedroom door a few times.

"Be there soon," I would answer, pulling myself together and eventually joining them. Other times, I ignored her.

I realized George didn't care anymore for our relationship and gladly used any reason to request his space. Although he was only a companion and more a liability than an asset, I missed him. I called his cell phone and his beeper many times a day and left countless messages, but George seldom returned my calls. Whenever he did, he complained of being busy and had no time to spare.

Those were days when I wished the world would stop and allow me to jump off. Night after night, I cried incessantly and wished my life would come to a standstill rather than have to face the pain of another tomorrow. I couldn't concentrate at work. I wished every telephone call coming through to my desk was from George. It was everybody *but* him. I kept up my outward appearance, but deep within, it were as if an electric knife was unceasingly at work.

I realized George didn't care anymore for our relationship and was glad for any reason to request his space. Although he was only a companion and more a liability than an asset, I missed him.

If you are there, get up and take action. Don't let your abuser put you through this. It will not be easy, but finding help will equip you to move on.

Then, my birthday came.

"*Happy birthday to you, happy birthday to you.*" I rolled over in bed and my children were standing there, singing, broad smiles on their faces.

"I made this card for you, Mommy," Romaine said, climbing in the bed.

"No, I made it!" Junior shouted, attempting to snatch the card from Romaine.

"Both o' them lying. I made the card," Kianna said in her simple, but no-nonsense tone.

"Okay, okay," I said, pulling myself up and bracing my back against the headboard. "Let me read it:

"You are the best mother in the whole wide world.

Happy Birthday, Mommy.

From: Kianna, Junior and Romaine."

"Niceeee! Thank you! So, it is from everybody. Lemme get my birthday hugs and kisses."

I made my way to work. Hardly likely anyone at the job would remember my special day besides Sandra and Jackie, and I begged them not to tell anyone. I wasn't in a celebrating mood. They honored my request., Sandra and Jackie wished me happy birthday in the break room and gave me a lovely birthday card. No other co-worker gave birthday greetings. After lunch, I received a few phone calls from family back home in Guyana. I knew my family would remember.

At 6:30 I wrapped up and began preparing for home. Sadly, I realized that George never called. I told myself, *if George doesn't call to wish me a happy birthday, I'll know beyond the shadow of a doubt, our relationship is over.*

I began walking home, frequently wiping away warm, silent tears. Endless thoughts crowded my mind, yet deep within, I felt a slim sense of victory--February 22, 1999--the first day in the four years of my relationship with George that I didn't pick up the telephone to call any of his three numbers.

I felt a slim sense of victory. February 22, 1999 was the first day in the four years of my relationship with George that I didn't pick up the telephone to call any of his three numbers.

I took a long while, but I got there. My hope is that you will see the signs of an abusive relationship and find the strength, faith, and courage it takes to seek help or walk away.

Life became a daily challenge. George's rejection tore me apart. I felt I couldn't go on living, but despite how I felt, every day I determined not to call him. At the end of every day, I felt a sad sense of accomplishment. But my heart literally ached for that man and even though I tried, I couldn't get him out of my thoughts. I felt worse seeing couples hugging, kissing, chatting, and lovingly cuddling each other. Ultimately, I contemplated dating again. I hoped this would help me overcome my hurt. There were quite a few clients who showed more than a casual interest in me, and finally I accepted two dates. On both occasions, I longed for the comfort of my home.

FORTY

Moving On

Six months later, I still hadn't moved on. It only took the sight of George's truck or a few fond memories for my heart to feel raw, as if fresh wounds were bleeding.

Angelique, you gotta stop crying. You gotta pull yourself together! That man is going on with his life. You need to move on with yours. Talking to myself still didn't immediately help.

Grace showed up at my house one day while the children were at school.

"Why were you crying?" she asked.

"No reason. I'm fine."

"No, you're not. I hope you not crying over that loser!"

"Girl, it is easy for you to say, but it is hard," I responded, tears blinding my eyes again.

"Angie, you got your children. If you don't stop, you will die and leave them. Do you want someone else to take care of them? You have a darn good job. You don't need him. Do I need to remind you of some of the crap you suffered at the hands of a man who claimed he love' you?

How many months pass' by and he has not even contacted you? You need to move on.

"When will you get some sense, girl? You should be glad he gone his way. When you not cooking and cleaning for him you're giving him free airline tickets, satisfying his thirst to see the world. The sick part is that you had to pay your own expense on those trips. When it's not that, you trying to please him, even hurting yourself in the process. You remember how mad I was when you told me you paid his truck note that month? When it is not that, you saving what you don't have in the name of contributing to a relationship. What kind of relationship is that? It takes two, girl!

"This man wouldn't help you buy food for your kids when you are broke. Instead he would rent limo service for his daughter. Wouldn't do anything decent for you and you claim you love him! What is there to love about him? Girl, you're a trip! Stop being so stupid! Get over that loser! He is a liability! You can do without him, girl! Do I have to remind you some more of what and who he is?"

Reflecting on some of the things Grace said made me question myself.

Why would I give my love to someone so selfish, undeserving, and mean? I had no answer. *What Grace is saying makes sense. I will just have to try.*

One Saturday evening the children went to their friend's birthday party and I sat staring into nothingness, thinking about George. The radio was playing but I wasn't listening to it. But suddenly I heard a question that caught my attention. **Are you in denial about your situation?** *What?...* Denial gets you nowhere. You have to face reality, accept how you have contributed to the situation in which you find yourself and take steps to make it better.

I felt as if the radio host was addressing me. He made quite a few points before I decided to grab a pen and jot down some of what he was saying. I felt as if my life was flashing before my eyes. The host asked questions and gave helpful tips.

- **Do you have friends with whom you can share?** You need to find someone with whom you are comfortable sharing. You do not have to share everything, but you need to talk about some of what is tearing you apart. Healing comes from sharing and you cannot keep everything bottled up inside. Keeping everything within will only cause you to harbor bitterness and resentment.
- **Do you think this man or woman deserves you?** Do you think he or she is worthy of your tears, and all the stress you are experiencing? If you know he or she does not deserve you, why would you want to settle for less than the best? See the beauty in yourself, see your children, your family, your career, and know that a relationship is not all there is to life. Sometimes, these interactions cause more heartache than anything else.
- **Do you laugh often?** Laughter is good medicine. Sometimes you have to enjoy a good comedy or play, or even join in games with your children and family. Just laugh!
- **Are you ashamed of yourself?** That is one of the biggest problems people face. Some of you may find yourselves wondering what people would think of you. What people would say. You need to give up your personal history. If you don't have a story,

you don't have to live up to it. We sometimes bind ourselves to the wounds of our past. It's not the best thing to do. I went through a great deal and many people did also, but we all have to go through something to get where we are. I suggest you embrace your past, then toss it. Forgive yourself.

- **Where do you see yourself two years from now?** I've learned that wisdom is avoiding all thoughts which weaken you. Whenever a negative thought comes to mind, shift to one that empowers. What you expect, that is what you get. Don't die with your music still in you. There is a purpose for your life. You're not here by accident. Treat yourself as if you are already what you're hoping to become."

By the time the program finished, tears were rolling down my cheeks and I wished I could live my life over again. In my quest for love, I went from one man to another. The results—three children with two different men and—and now? Another man. What an example I set for my children? Aiming to satisfy my own selfish desires, I placed my children in danger. *Angelique, you are crazy! And you know something? You cannot even blame anybody because your friends tried talking sense into your thick head, but you wouldn't listen. Mom used to say, 'You make your bed hard, you goin' lie on it hard!' Huh? Oh no! I gotta get up and make this bed over! I gotta get up!*

"Lord, help me get up," I cried.

I only considered myself. *I was wrong when I disobeyed and rejected my parents' advice and started seeing William. I was also wrong to marry my second husband when I only liked him. Grabbing onto him because he loved me, I thought not reciprocating his love would prevent me from being hurt again. I was selfish, and my egotistical attitude exposed my daughter to sexual abuse. The loneliness and heartache of starting all over again for the third time was overwhelming until I thought I found real love with George, who proved to be nothing but a selfish passerby and a user. It was my fault. I followed my heart and it caused me hurt and pain.*

Foolishly, I neglected the opportunity to break free of George, but when he showed up out of prison, silly me let the loser back in.

I tried getting a grip on myself, but one name kept echoing in my head—George, George, and more George. His name seemed to suffocate me. I couldn't bear the thought of him anymore. Tears flooded my eyes and I cried for the girl full of hope and love who naively thought William was her knight in shining armor. I reflected on William and immediately my mind took me to when he took Roxanne to our home in our bed, and all the unhappiness associated with that incident. Then another name crossed my mind—Ricardo. Uggh! That pervert. I couldn't even bear to think about him.

Lying there on my bed with the names and faces of all these men plaguing my mind, something hit me. Was I obsessed? It was as if I were living my life through these men. Cooking for them, cleaning for them, taking care of their needs, and trying the best I knew how to keep a relationship together. But what did I do for my children and for me? Absolutely nothing.

It was all around me—evidence of a life wasted. I lived for these men and spent time blaming myself when things didn't work out. Starting over, I willed myself to try harder. In every instance, I went overboard—giving them my all, even spending my last dollar on them. With my face buried in my pillow, my body heaving from sobs, I cried to the God I knew, asking Him to heal me; to make me whole again. I had made a hard bed, but I couldn't continue lying in it. I had to do things differently. The thought of starting over yet again scared me. Then I realized it would be even harder without the Creator I had walked with so faithfully during my teenage and young adult years. The time had come to return to my Savior. What better way to start afresh? At that moment, I was glad I knew how to pray. And pray I did.

> *"My Father and my God,"* I began, getting on my knees, tears streaming down my face, "*I know you are a loving God and you truly love me and care for me despite what I've done.*
>
> *I pray you forgive me of my sins and help me to go forward from here without ever turning back.*
>
> *Although I've messed up time and time and again, I thank you for loving me, forgiving me, and caring about me. I thank you because you promised me in your Word that as far as the east is from the west, so far have you separated my transgressions from me.*
>
> *I also thank you for casting them into the sea of forgetfulness, promising you will remember them no more.*
>
> *Lord, please give me the strength, faith, and the courage I need to go on from here.*
>
> *Also, re-direct the paths of every person who may be heading down the road I've trod. And those who may be able to identify with my issues, deliver them, dry their tears, mend their broken hearts, and help them to move on.*
>
> *Lord, I pray even for abusers; sometimes they cannot help themselves, but let them know that they can call on you and find help; redirect their paths and turn their lives around for your glory!*
>
> *I thank you Father for hearing and answering my prayers in Jesus' Name,*
>
> *Amen."*

I felt drained, but immediate inner peace flooded my soul. I got up and looked through the window. Glancing up at the dark but starry sky, words of a song I loved drifted through my mind.

"I'm moving on, things can only get better
I'm moving on to a better way of life."

Then I spoke to myself. It wasn't too late. I was only thirty-eight. Yes, maybe half of my life was over, but I had another half to live. My mother's words from way back flashed across my mind—Life is like a *river—never smoot*h—neither is it rough all the time—and I decided I would get the second half of my life right. Starting from this day, and more importantly, I would care more about me. I would do this for me. I would do this for my children and everyone who believes in me.

The End.

Epilogue

Wow! Many years have since gone by! Things didn't immediately fall into place. It wasn't easy, but after praying that prayer, I stayed close to God, and He equipped me with the strength I needed day by day. Two years later, I met Paul. It was love at first sight for him, but I took my time. We have now been married for sixteen years. No, it was not a fairy tale or bed of roses marriage. In fact, after about six years into our marriage, things started going downhill in our relationship. I felt as if some of the things I had experienced in my other relationships were repeating itself. I felt I had been plagued with the saying—*we attract the same people all the time.*

Then one day, I spoke to myself. *Tomorrow. I will be 54; I've had two previous marriages, and none worked. Why would this one work? Why am I wasting my life and time with someone who cares nothing about me? My kids are grown and on their own; I don't have to put up with this. While I have time, I'm going to get out of this marriage.* I was determined not to live another day of my life in a marriage that simply wasn't working. I deserved better. And yes, I was tired of praying for Paul.

The next day, Monday, February 22nd, was my birthday. It was not unusual that my husband didn't remember my special day. It was not in his nature to remember special days. At one point in time, I used to get upset about it, but not anymore. I now enjoy and giggle at the guilty reaction that would cloud his face when he would eventually realize he has missed an important milestone and try really hard to make it up.

Later that day, Paul left for work. I packed whatever clothes and personal belongings that could fit in my car and moved to a friend's home, hoping to find an apartment soon.

That night before I went to bed, I called Paul.

"When you get home, I will not be there, and I will not be coming back. Ever." There was a long pause at the other end of the line. When he finally answered, his voice had lost some momentum.

"What are you saying? I don't understand," he said.

"I'm saying I've tried hard and long to keep this marriage together, but it is not working. I turned 54 years old today and I am not going to spend the remainder of my life miserable and unhappy. I've had enough. Goodnight." Powering off my phone, I retired to bed.

Although I was tired, sleep was a stranger. Tossing and turning, I tried praying, but just couldn't find the words to say to God. Eventually, I decided to be honest with the Lord. He knew how I felt anyway, but even though God knows everything, He still requires we talk with Him because He likes communicating with us and hearing from us.

Lord, you know this is not what I want. I do not want to be at my friend's house. Paul and I have our own home. Lord, I want to be at our home, in our own bed, and I need my husband. I want us to get along; I want us to start over; I want our marriage to work. Please God, fix this.

At some point, I fell asleep.

Tuesday and Wednesday of that week were uneventful. I knew Paul could be very stubborn, so I wasn't expecting to hear from him. I inquired about an apartment and made plans to move from my friend's home. I started praying again for Paul and our marriage but didn't say much to God those days. The most I said sometimes was, *Lord, please fix this*. Many times, when I am weighed down by heavy situations, I hardly find the words to pray. When I do pray, it is usually one sentence: *Lord, you gotta fix this!*

Around 9 AM Thursday, February 25th, I was at work when my phone lit up, displaying Paul's name. Watching the ring signal for a few moments, I finally swiped it.

"Hello."

"Angie, it's not the same without you here." Paul sounded defeated and sad. I didn't respond. "With you not being here, I had a lot of time to think." I still didn't respond.

"I keep thinking of you, crying a lot, wishing you would come back. I even prayed to God, asking Him to let you come back. After I prayed, words my mother used to say to me when I was a boy came right back to me. She used to say, "*Don't let me have to search heaven in vain for you.*" I have not remembered those words in years, but worrying about us, her words came right back to me and they are still with me—Are you still there?"

"Yes."

"I would like to speak with your pastor. Can you make an appointment for me to see him?"

"No. If you want to see him make the appointment yourself."

"But I do not have his number."

"Here it is," I said, speaking the number slowly so he could write it down. After receiving the number, he thanked me and then hung up the telephone.

Ten minutes later, my phone rang again.

"Can you meet with me and the pastor at the house this Sunday at 10?"

"No. Any meeting with you, I will attend away from the house. Call back the pastor and ask for the meeting to take place at the church," I said.

"Okay," he said. Within five minutes he was on the phone again, confirming that the meeting would not take place at our home, but at the church.

Something about this conversation and how it was going was weird because I hardly ever got my husband to carry out my wishes without a fuss. Sometimes, he simply refused to do what I asked. I didn't even know he prayed.

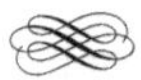

On the morning of Sunday February 28, 2016, the Lord woke me up and I heard, "Pack your things."

Rolling over and sitting up, I rubbed my eyes. Looking around, I remembered my surroundings, which were now almost familiar. *Pack your things.* I audibly heard those words. I realized it was the Holy Spirit speaking to me. I reasoned against that still small voice, but I eventually allowed the Holy Spirit to have His way. I started packing my clothes. While stuffing items into bags, I made a mental note to park my car away from the church so that Paul couldn't see its contents if he happened to pass by. I didn't want him to prematurely discover my instructions from the Holy Spirit.

Waiting in my car on Unity Street in the Frankford, Philadelphia area, I saw the pastor pulling into the parking lot. I hurried to meet him. Paul arrived at the church prior to the pastor and I, and was leaning against a fence, adjacent to the church. I slowed my pace, allowing him to catch up.

"Hi, how are you?" I asked.

"I'm not even sure," he replied.

"You alright?" he asked after a pause.

"I'm okay."

We reached the pastor's study. After inviting us to sit, the pastor prayed, then looked across his desk at my husband.

"Paul, you requested this meeting with your wife and me. What's on your mind?"

"Pastor," my husband began, "I may not be able to say it in the best of words, but I hope you understand. I need forgiveness, healing and salvation."

I cannot now remember our first response, but I do recall the pastor and myself staring at Paul, both of us at a loss for words.

"So, what does this mean and where is all of this coming from so suddenly?" I eventually asked.

What followed was a conversation lasting three plus hours, consisting mainly of my husband pouring his heart out to my pastor and me. At the end of that discussion, with tears streaming down his face, he hugged and kissed me, then dived into the backpack he was carrying. Pulling out a gift bag, he handed it to me.

"Happy birthday. You can start writing," he said.

I was taken aback at his words, "*You can start writing!*"

"Thank you," I responded. "I am coming home."

"You are coming home? Thank you, thank you," he said, smiling through his tears, hugging me.

Tearing off the *Happy Birthday* wrapper, I found the leather-covered journal at which I am now glancing. On the cover there is the imprint "TRUST" in large letters and below that word, in smaller letters: "Blessed is the man who trusts in the Lord." Unzipping it, I found it contained white lined pages with a scripture verse at the bottom of every page. I started journaling for my *Prayer To The Rescue Series* on February 28, 2016.

My husband never knew I told God I would start my book of testimonies when He saved him. I had not uttered a word of the plan I had with anybody else, so when Paul gave me that journal and said, "Happy birthday. *You can start writing*," I saw that as confirmation from God. After all, He has saved my husband! And given me back my marriage! I am eternally thankful and will shout it from the mountain top!

Today, we serve the Lord together. Although there are still thorns in the roses, life is much better, and many situations are handled differently. There were times when little disagreements would cause us to refrain from speaking to each other for weeks, or snowball into bitter arguments. Mostly I had to be the "big one" so that life would go back to normal. Yet, even though I played the role of the "big one," Paul would still hold his speech. Today, he cannot even stand the sound of a developing quarrel between us. Our disagreements are settled long before they could ever get out of hand.

At one time, it seemed as if we couldn't discuss anything without it becoming a huge dispute. Today, we are able to pray about the most disturbing matters, have a discussion, then pray to seal it and watch God move. If you are praying for your abusive husband, wife, partner or loved one, while keeping it safe, *pray on*! *Level with God*! *God has already answered!*

Bibliography

Dunham, Dave. "Counselling After Adultery." Sept. 19, 2019, https://www.biblicalcounselingcoalition.org/2017/02/22/counseling-after-adultery/

Hughes, Jade A. 11 Common Patterns of Verbal Abuse. Dec 10, 2019, https://www.joinonelove.org/learn/11-common-patterns-verbal-abuse/

Lim, Sunny. "Is Cheating Abusive: What Cheating Looks Like When It Is Used For Control." Oct.13, 2019, https://breakthesilencedv.org/is-cheating-abusive-what-cheating-looks-like-when-its-used-for-control/

Markarian, Taylor. "Sneaky Ways Your Partner's Parents Can Affect Your Relationship." Sept. 13, 2019, https://www.thelist.com/72210/sneaky-ways-partners-parents-can-affect-relationship/

Meyer, Cathy. "The Need For Control And It's Relationship To Abuse:" Sept. 10, 2019 https://www.mydomaine.com/the-need-for-control-and-its-relationship-to-abuse-1102407

Morin, Amy. "The Psychological Effects of Divorce on Children." Sept. 27, 2019, https://www.verywellfamily.com/psychological-effects-of-divorce-on-kids-4140170

Tracy, Natasha. "What is Physical Abuse." Sept. 13, 2019. https://www.healthyplace.com/abuse/adult-physical-abuse/what-is-physical-abuse

Petherbridge, Laura. "12 Traits of an Abuser." CBN. Sept. 16, 2019. https://www1.cbn.com/marriage/12-traits-of-an-abuser

Domestic Abuse Intervention Services. "Help a Loved One or Friend," Sept, 10, 2019, https://abuseintervention.org/help/friend-family/

Bible Gateway. "Exodus 20:12" Sept. 10, 2019, https://www.biblegateway.com/passage/?search=Exodus+20:12&version=NKJV

National Domestic Violence Hotline. "Is Change Possible in an Abuser." Sept. 10, 2019, https://www.thehotline.org/2013/09/05/is-change-possible-in-an-abuser/

DV & Economic Justice. "About Financial Abuse." Sept. 19, 2019, https://nnedv.org/content/about-financial-abuse/

"Forgiveness." Sept. 21, 2019, https://www.thehotline.org/2019/03/01/forgiveness/

NSPCC. "Every Childhood is Worth Fighting For." Sept. 27, 2019, https://www.nspcc.org.uk/what-is-child-abuse/types-of-abuse/domestic-abuse/

Help Guide. "Dating Tips for Finding the Right Person." Sept. 27, 2019, https://www.helpguide.org/articles/relationships-communication/tips-for-finding-lasting-love.htm

HealthTalk.org. "Women's experiences of Domestic Violence and Abuse." Oct. 13, 2019 http://www.healthtalk.org/peoples-experiences/domestic-violence-abuse/womens-experiences-domestic-violence-and-abuse/emotional-psychological-abuse-and-effects-womens-self-esteem

"How to Get Out of an Abusive Relationship." Help Guide. Sept. 16, 2019, https://www.helpguide.org/articles/abuse/getting-out-of-an-abusive-relationship.htm

"11 Facts About Teen Dating Violence." Oct. 24, 2019, https://www.dosomething.org/us/facts/11-facts-about-teen-dating-violence

National Statistics. "11 Reasons Why People in Abusive Relationships Can't "Just Leave."" Oct. 26, 2019 https://www.joinonelove.org/learn/why_leaving_abuse_is_hard/

Statistics. Oct. 13, 2019, https://ncadv.org/statistics.

Anonymous Radio Program with Psychologist in approximately 2007.

Acknowledgments

All glory, honor, and praises to God! I thank Him for this journey on which, oblivious to me, He was perfecting me, shaping, molding and making me into the woman I am. Looking back, I can see that through it all, God had a plan. I now thank Him for choosing me and equipping me through trials so I may help others.

My friends, Yvette Nedd, Kay Smith, Cheryl Carmichael, and Linda Yard – You were there for me at different seasons of my life. *Thank you!*

My writers' group, *Evening Sta*r—Karen E. Quinones Miller, Sharai Rucker, Akanke Washington, Jenice Armstrong, and Theresa Brunson, who, week after week, worked with me scrutinizing word by word, thumbing through page after page—critiquing, restructuring correcting errors, and most of all, offering encouragement all the way. Thank you!

My friend, the late June Reid, for her encouragement and support. I miss you, Sis.

My friend Rhonda Harding for her invaluable support.

My friend Racquel Assaye who edited my first draft around 2007 and kept reminding me that my story is worth telling so I can help others.

My sisters, Deon and Shondel, my harsh critics, and who along with my brothers, Rawle, James Jr., Colin, and Darren, were always supportive. The late Dr. Linden Lord, my heart still bleeds for you, my brother.

Bridgette Bastien, fellow author and my source of support who was always ready to answer my questions and offer invaluable critique.

To Lahai McKinnie and Marvin Wilmes for their keen eyes and insight, critique and suggestions while editing. Thank you.

To my readers, thank you for endorsing my manuscript, sharing my book with your friends and family, providing reviews and in love, coming together to make our society a healthy and safe place.

About The Author

FIONA HAREWOOD is an author, speaker and life coach, empowering the abused, people struggling with their faith, demotivated students and dropouts. Through her writing, speaking and coaching, she shows them how to overcome so they can rise above their circumstances.

Fiona knows what it is to be abused physically, mentally, sexually, financially and emotionally. Having triumphed over abuse, she finds it fulfilling and rewarding, coaching groups and individuals, helping them to find healing so they can live life as God intended.

TAKE YOUR NEXT STEPS
With
River Never Smooth:
Reclaiming Power After Abuse

You Decide!

Take the assessment and know whether you are abused. If you answer *yes* to any of these questions you are being abused and must take action.

1. Does your partner call you names, insults you and/or degrade you? ☐
2. Does your partner prevent you from doing what you want to do? ☐
3. Does your partner stop you from seeing family members or friends? ☐
4. Does your partner act jealous or possessive or constantly accuse you of being unfaithful? ☐
5. Does your partner get angry when drinking alcohol or using drugs? ☐
6. Does your partner threaten you with violence or a weapon? ☐
7. Does your partner hit, kick, shove, slap, choke or otherwise hurt you, your children or your pets? ☐
8. Does your partner force you to have sex or engage in sexual acts against your will? ☐
9. Does your partner blame you for his or her violent behavior or tell you that you deserve it? ☐

If you have checked any of the boxes get help! Do you want to:

- Identify and deal with abuse and know when to move on
- Live a life free of regrets
- Toss your pasts
- Find healing
- Rise above your circumstances, emerging an overcomer

FIND OUT MORE AT

https://www.fionaharewood.com/river-never-smooth

BRING FIONA INTO YOUR HOME, CHURCH BUSINESS, OR ORGANIZATION

Author, Speaker & Life Coach

Fiona knows the importance of choosing the correct speaker. The right one creates success while the wrong one destines disaster. Fiona's authentic approach combined with superb content gained from experience, education, and research positions her as top choice for many schools, businesses, churches, and nonprofits. She customizes each message and training to achieve and exceed the objectives of her clients.

CONTACT FIONA TODAY
BEGIN THE CONVERSATION
Fionaharewood.com

DISCUSSION QUESTIONS

1. River Never Smooth opens with Angelique, the protagonist, receiving a fine beating for her third wedding anniversary gift from her husband. She later went back to the matrimonial home. Stepping into Angelique's shoes for a while, what would you have done differently?

2. When Angelique first met William she told her parents about him.
   a) How should Mr. and Mrs. Castor have handled this situation?
   b) How did Angelique err after receiving her parents' advice?

3. Angelique is caught with William; her parents used extreme measures in dealing with the situation. How would a parent today handle a similar situation, if they deal with it at all?

4. You are a senior sister at Angelique's church. You hear of the issues she is having at home due to her association with William. How would you have advised Angelique and William?

5. Angelique's mother sees William in the movies with a woman. She knew the woman was no ordinary friend as she saw them kissing. What would you have done if you were in Mrs. Castor's place?

6. List some of the signs William exhibited proving he was an abuser.
   a) What help would you have offered him?
   b) How would you have advised Angie?

7. We hear of incest in today's society.
   a) How is the situation handled today in comparison to how Angelique dealt with it when Ricardo molested her daughter?
   b) You being in Angelique's place, what would you have done differently?

8. Stepping into Angelique's shoes for a day, how would you have dealt with Ricardo and the marriage upon learning he was indecently assaulting women on the streets?

9. At William's death, Angelique said, *life is fragile* and mentions that *we should live every moment as if it is our last.*
   a) What does she mean?
   b) If your life were to be snatched away like William's, without warning, how should you be preparing now?

10. List some of the abusive situations Angelique experienced at her partners' hands.
    a) Stepping into her shoes, what would you have done differently?
    b) How could you have been her friend and tell her how and where to find help?

11. Angelique found that even in the courts there was no justice.
    a) How would you have dealt with the probation officer that seemed to have had Ricardo's back and a vendetta for Angelique?

12. Discuss the relationship between Angelique and her children. How was she lacking as a single parent and what should she have done better?

13. On several occasions, Angelique suffered through the abuse in silence because of fear and shame. If Angelique were your family member or friend, and you suspected she was in trouble, how would you help her in a non-judgmental way?

14. Do you think that victims of abuse tend to be attracted to would-be abusers, or do abusers fall for a certain kind of person that they believe will be an easy prey? Discuss. What can you do for someone who finds themselves in these recurring relationships?

Never Too Old To Make it happen.

Even if you didn't do well academically in high school, don't worry, you have a new opportunity to excel. Honors, such as summa cum laude, magna cum laude or even cum laude, are not for the brilliant student, but for the dedicated, hardworking student. The most important thing to remember is that you do not have to outdo anyone. Just be you and do your best.

List of Non Profit Beneficiaries

The following nonprofit organizations will benefit from the sale of **River Never Smooth *Reclaiming Power After Abuse***

Domestic Shelters.org
www.DomesticShelters.org

Women In Transition
www.helpwomen.org

Professional Women's Roundtable
pwroundtable.com

4 Real Women International Inc.
www.4rwi.org

RECLAIM YOUR POWER!

EMBRACE YOUR PAST, THEN TOSS IT!

CPSIA information can be obtained
at www.ICGtesting.com
Printed in the USA
BVHW041645090120
569107BV00010B/92/P